Henry Weinhard's Private Reserve Beer
Founded 1856
Carling Black Label Canadian Style Beer
Founded in 1840 Canada
Product of U.S.A.
Pfeiffer Famous Beer
12 Fluid Ounces
Celebration Ale 1984
Brewed and bottled by Sierra Nevada Brewing Co. Chico, California Net Contents 12 FL. OZ.
Hibernia Brewing Ltd. Eau Claire, WI
Eau Claire All Malt Lager Beer
Brewed according to the Bavarian Beer Purity Law of 1516.
Moosehead Export Ale
Export Bière
12 oz fl 341 ml
5% alc./vol.
Lone Star Beer
Cerveza India
La Cerveza de Puerto Rico
Lucky 50 Extra Light Beer
Gold Peak Beer Bière
Premium Lager
Olympia Premium Lager Beer
Since 1896
Bock Beer
Kessler Beer
Brewed from pure artesian well water
Spoetzl Brewery, Inc.
Shiner Premium Beer
Net Contents 12 FL. OZ.
Andeker
New Amsterdam Amber Beer
Miller High Life The Champagne of Beers.
Anchor Steam Beer
Made in San Francisco since 1896
Lager Beer
The Gem of the High Sierra
Since 1862
Tahoe Beer
Famous as the
Budweiser King of Beers.
Genuine
12 FL. OZ. (355 ml)
Shiner Premium Bock Beer
Rainier
Since 1878
Naturally Brewed
Mountain Fresh Beer
Golden Gate Malt Liquor
Schlitz
A Great American Beer Since 1849
Point Special Beer
Stevens Point Brewery
Stevens Point, Wisconsin
Blitz Weinhard
Since 1856
Sierra Nevada Pale Ale
Purest Ingredients
Brew Masters
Carling's Red Cap Cream Ale
Heileman's Old Style
Pure Genuine
W9-BEZ-925

BEERS
OF
NORTH AMERICA

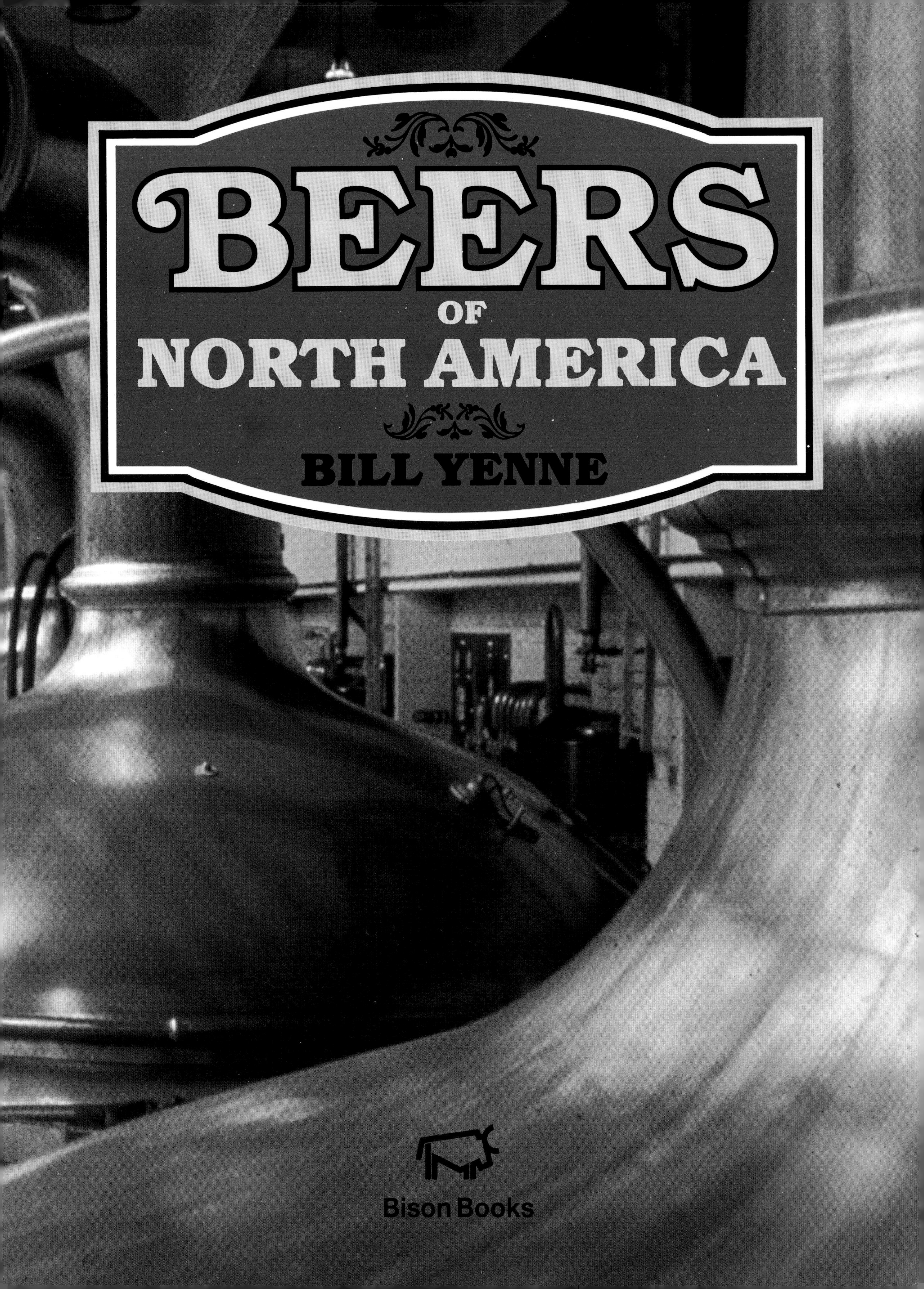

BEERS OF NORTH AMERICA

BILL YENNE

Bison Books

First Published in 1986 by
Bison Books Corp.
17 Sherwood Place
Greenwich, CT 06830

Copyright © 1986 Bison Books Corp.

All rights reserved. No part of this publication may be reproduced, stored in a retrieval system or transmitted in any form by any means, electronic, mechanical, photocopying or otherwise, without first obtaining written permission of the copyright owner.

ISBN 0 86124 266 1

Printed in Hong Kong

Acknowledgments
The author would like to express his special thanks to the following people who helped make this book possible: Jose Paz Aguirre of Cerveceria Moctezuma; Peter Blum of Stroh Brewing; Carl Bolz of Anheuser-Busch; Mark Carpenter of Anchor Brewing; Charles Cooney, Jr, Curator, Milwaukee County Historical Society; Steven Forsyth of Miller Brewing; Hugh Coppen of Molson Breweries; Fritz Maytag of Anchor Brewing; Robert Peyton of Basso & Associates; Pat Samson of Carling-O'Keefe; Don Shook of Adolph Coors and George Westin of Anheuser-Busch.

Edited by Carolyn Soto

Designed by Bill Yenne

Page 1: Adolph Nehls of Milwaukee, a bartender for 24 years before Prohibition, serves up some beer in March 1933 on the eve of repeal.

Page 2-3: An armada of dreadnaughts — Miller Brewing's copper brew kettles at the Milwaukee, Wisconsin plant.

Below: The Milwaukee Brewery at Tenth and Bryant in San Francisco in 1918.

Overleaf: The brewhouses of Christian Moerlin in Cincinnati at the turn of the century when the city's German immigrant population had turned it into one of the highest per capita beer-drinking cities in North America. The sign at the left says Elm Strasse Braueri and at the right it is the Elm Street Brewery of C Moerlin.

CONTENTS

MOERLEIN.
MOERLEIN.
ELM ST. BREWERY
C. MOERLEIN.

PART I
THE HISTORY OF BREWING IN NORTH AMERICA

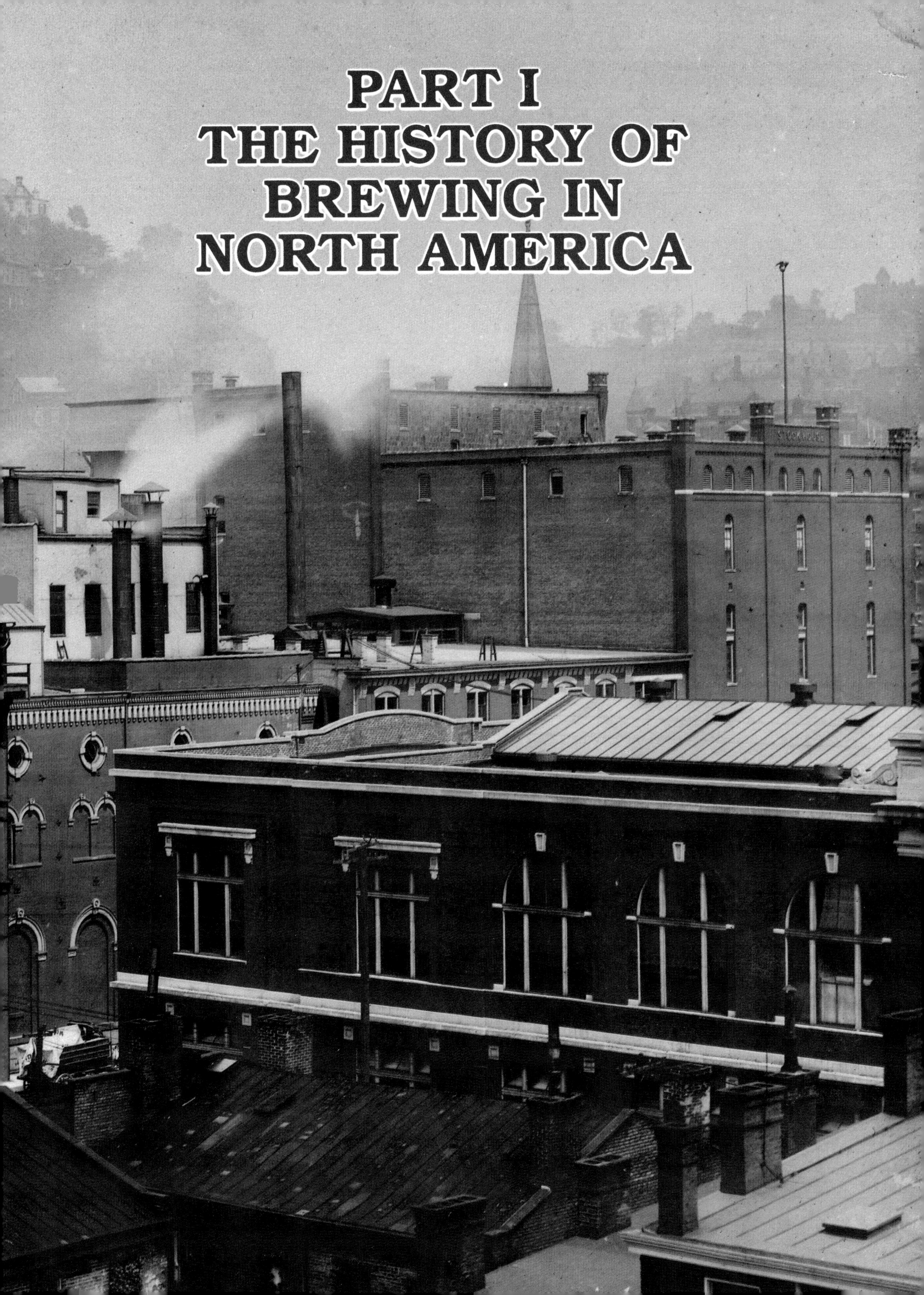

THE HISTORY OF BREWING IN NORTH AMERICA

THE EARLY DAYS

Beer came to America on the *Mayflower* but did not remain with the pilgrims to warm them during their first trying year in the New World. Instead, the crew retained these noteworthy casks to be tapped on their return voyage to England. John Alden, the cooper who had been hired to look after the beer, did stay nonetheless, and became one of Plymouth's more notable citizens.

This colorful story, however, by no means chronicles the first arrival of beer in America. When Captain Christopher Newport arrived at Jamestown on the cold winds of winter 1607 with the 'first supply,' beer (then spelled beere) was prominent on the ship's manifest. Indeed the English were attentive, keeping their Virginia and Caribbean colonies well supplied with this beverage that was considered to be essential to health. It has been suggested that ale was brewed in Virginia as early as 1587, and by 1609 the colony was actively soliciting London brewers to come to the New World. Even before the English arrived in Roanoke and Jamestown, however, Alonso de Herrera had established North America's first commercial brewery in Mexico in 1544.

Also, before the first European beer made landfall in the New World, the brewing art was well established on the Atlantic's western shores. Throughout the Caribbean basin, across Mexico and up into the American Southwest the Indians had been brewing maize (corn) beer —in fact two distinct types—for perhaps centuries. In the Caribbean region the corn was simply chewed to begin fermentation, then placed in a container of water—a practice also common to the early beer-making of South America.

Above: **The first beer in the New World was imported from Europe. *Right:* Peter Stuyvesant was governor of New Amsterdam, the New World's first brewing center, and a city of beer connoisseurs *(far right).***

In northern Mexico and the Southwest, moistened corn was allowed to sprout, then ground and boiled into what is today called a wort. The subsequent fermentation period was relatively short, producing a beer known as *tesguino* with a four to five percent alcohol content within a couple of days. It is not known when this more sophisticated brewing method developed in the present-day United States, but it was still in practice among the Apaches as late as the nineteenth century. For the most part, though, the alcoholic beverages most frequently produced by those Indians first encountered by European settlers were various fruit wines such as the persimmon wine known to have been introduced to John Smith at Jamestown.

The tastes of the European settlers developed in the opposite direction. While in Mexico and the Caribbean demand for wine and distilled spirits, such as rum, exceeded that for beer, in Virginia and the English colonies to the north, beer was the drink of choice. Most of the beer drunk in the English colonies during the early seventeenth century was imported from England, but small attempts at domestic brewing were made almost as soon as the first log cabins were completed. In his history of early Virginia John Smith recorded two breweries established there by 1629. These first European brewers in America, like the Indian brewers before them, used maize rather than barley, and the beer was generally unhopped as had been the earliest beer in England.

NEW AMSTERDAM

The early English breweries in North America usually existed to satisfy a local demand, and their output only supplemented the beer imported from England. Indeed, most breweries in English North America were and continued to be home breweries.

Quite the opposite was true in the Dutch colony of New Netherlands and its capital, New Amsterdam, which became North America's first major commercial brewing center. Beginning in 1632 with the Netherlands West India Company Brewery on Brouwer's Straat (Brewer's Street), a large number of Dutch breweries sprang up, taking advantage of natural wild hops, a resource that the English generally had

ignored. One of these early breweries was that of the Bayard brothers, Nikolas, Balthazar and Peiter, who were nephews of Governor Peter Stuyvesant. Many of the early breweries were associated with individual taverns, while others brewed beer for many taverns. A choice of draft beers was not uncommon in New Amsterdam's watering holes. In 1660 the people of this bustling city welcomed North America's first name-brand beer. It was brewed by the Red Lion Brewery, which was established by Isaac de Foreest on a site just north of present-day Wall Street. The Red Lion Brewery continued in business until it was destroyed by fire in 1675.

NORTH AMERICAN BREWING COMES OF AGE

Even after New Amsterdam was sold to the English in 1664 and renamed New York, the city maintained its prominence as a brewing center. The English even promoted the industry by levying taxes on wine and rum while exempting beer and cider. By this time commercial brewing had begun to flourish in the other English colonies, and the city of Philadelphia was well on its way toward becoming the New World's second major brewing center. Many Philadelphians entered the brewing business in the late seventeenth century following the lead of William Frampton in 1685. Philadelphia beer began to show up as a popular item among the goods the city exported to such places as New Jersey and Maryland where fewer breweries had been established.

William Penn, the founder of the colony of Pennsylvania, like many of his fellow Quakers was fond of beer and featured it prominently in his 1683 treaty with the Indians. At roughly the same time Penn had a 20-by-35-foot brewery built on his own estate and, although his house was later taken by fire, the brewery stood until 1864.

Each of the colonies developed its own perspective on the new industry. New York and Philadelphia brewers affected tastes in their immediate areas but places like Massachusetts and Virginia saw a proliferation of smaller brewers. The first brewery recorded in Massachusetts had been that of a Captain Sedgewick in 1637. It was followed by Sergeant Baulston's in Rhode Island (1639). South of Virginia there was little brewing activity, although a dark beer made with molasses appeared in Georgia in the seventeenth century. In Massachusetts the legislature tried with little success to control its many small brewers, while in New York legislation was passed in 1700 to stimulate the local industry in the face of beers imported from England and from other colonies.

***Above:* William Penn was one of America's first well-known brewers. *Below:* A map of seventeenth-century New Amsterdam, highlighting the Netherlands West India Co Brewery. *Right:* George Washington was both a statesman and a home brewer who was especially fond of porter.**

Technically, the beers brewed the English colonies and imported from the mother country were typical dark English top-fermented ales and stouts rather than the lighter, paler bottom-fermented beers favored on the continent. The typical commercial brewery in the early eighteenth century was roughly 70 by 50 feet in size with a copper brew kettle having about a 23-barrel capacity. Most of the output was indeed sold in barrels. Bottled beer had been imported on rare occasions in the seventeenth century, but it was not until after 1760 that any meaningful quantity of North American beer was bottled. Even then it was not until the next century that the domestic glass industry could support beer bottling on a wide scale.

The original draft beer that came to the colonies was drunk from black leather jugs known as 'black jacks.' By the 1600s in New Amsterdam and elsewhere these were replaced by pewter tankards of the type seen in Dutch genre paintings of the era. It was not until the eighteenth century that it became common for a beer drinker to enjoy his favorite beverage from a glass.

Throughout this period, as the means of brewing, marketing and drinking beer became more sophisticated, the classifications of beer remained roughly intact. Though the beers were all generally in the class of top-fermented brews (today called ales or stouts), they were rated by strength of alcohol content on a four-part scale. Their names give us

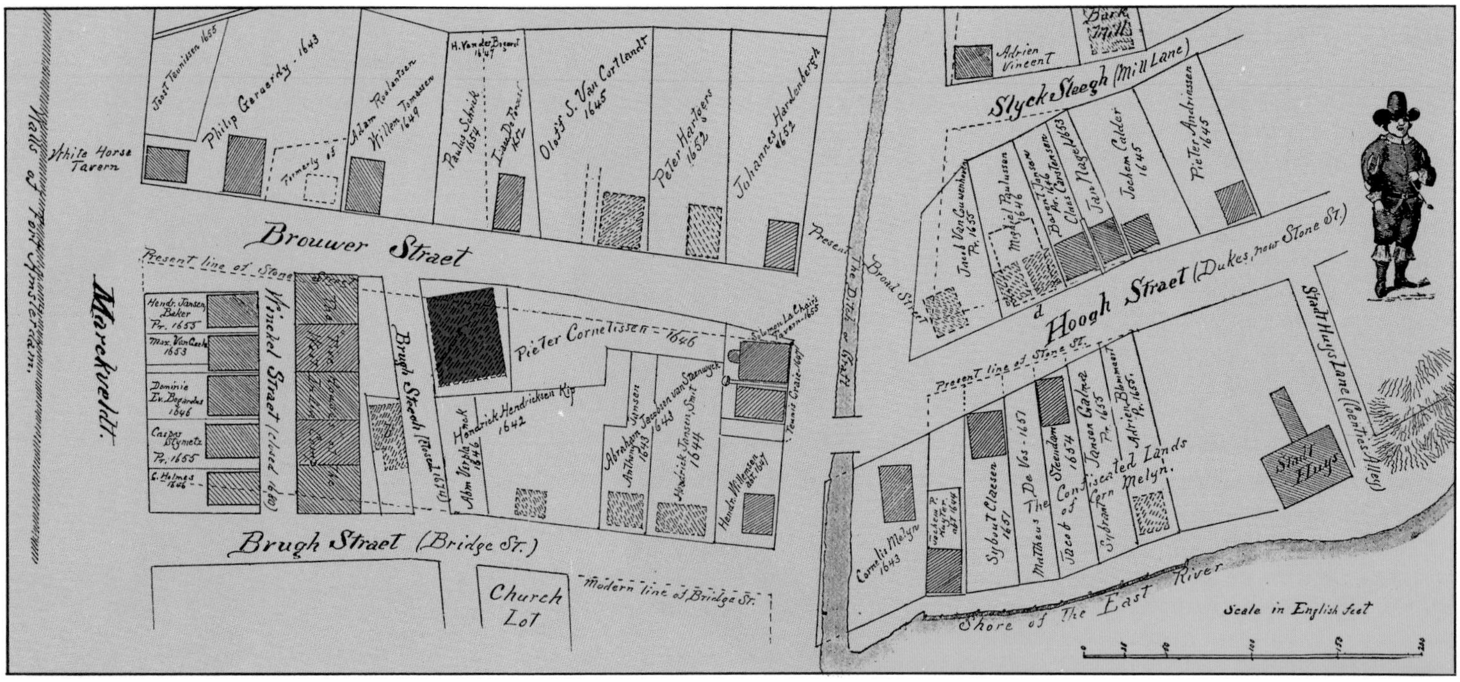

a good idea of how the grades were perceived: (1) small beer, (2) ship's beer, (3) table beer and (4) strong beer.

In 1720 another English top-fermented beer was introduced. Called 'porter' because it was favored by London porters, this new dark sweet beer was made with roasted unmalted barley. Despite its immediate popularity in England porter enjoyed only limited success in the colonies. It is worth mentioning, however, because it came to be the favorite drink of a certain officer in His Majesty's army during the latter third of the eighteenth century.

BEER AND THE AMERICAN REVOLUTION

George Washington was but one of the fathers of the American Revolution who loved beer, but he was himself a brewer, and his recipe for small beer is still preserved in the New York Public Library. He also went out of his way to promote porter. Washington had a particular fondness for the porter brewed by a Mr Robert Hare of Philadelphia. Hare had arrived on the eve of the Revolution in Philadelphia where he began brewing the New World's first porter in 1774.

Above: **In the Revolutionary War US warships confiscated beer from British supply ships.** ***Below:*** **Enjoying a beer before a warm fire in an early American home.**

Above: **During his term as president James Madison considered but rejected Joseph Coppinger's scheme to establish a government-run National Brewery.**

In a July 1788 letter, the first president wrote to Clement Biddle in Philadelphia requesting 'a gross of Mr Hare's best bottled porter if the price is not much enhanced by the copious drafts you took of it!' Apparently Washington was satisfied because he ordered a second gross of porter two weeks later.

In 1790, Washington recommended Hare's porter as the 'best in Philadelphia,' indicating that other breweries were producing the beverage by that time. It is unfortunate to note that 1790 was also the year that Hare's brewery burned. Hare rebuilt immediately and took his son into the business in 1800. The Robert Hare & Son name survived Hare Sr's death in 1810 by seven years. The brewery was taken over by the Philadelphia brewing family of Frederick Gaul in 1824, and in 1869 it passed to John F Betz under whose name it survived (except during Prohibition) until 1939.

George Washington's affection for beer was not unmatched. Both Samuel Adams Jr and Samuel Adams Sr were well-known amateur brewers. The celebrated Boston Tea Party of 1773 was a milestone in the struggle against English taxation, but the affair might very well have happened three years earlier as a Boston Beer Party. In 1770 George Washington had joined with Patrick Henry, Richard Henry Lee and others in recommending a boycott of English beer imports in support of the American brewing industry. It was fortunate for Washington that Robert Hare arrived on the domestic scene a few years later, bringing with him the art of porter.

During the Revolutionary War, the Continental Congress actually specified a one-quart beer ration for the troops. With restrictions placed on other, harder alcoholic beverages during the winter of 1777–78, beer became even more popular. The British army in America contracted with London brewers to produce beer for their personnel, but American raiders intercepted the British supply ships at sea and captured much of this beer before it reached Cornwallis and his thirsty legions.

YEARS OF CHANGE AND THE NATIONAL BREWERY SCHEME

In 1770, America's founding fathers had called for a boycott of British beers. Fifteen years later, there were no more British beers to boycott and the American industry faced a sagging market alone. In 1789 Massachusetts began promoting the healthful qualities of its local beer and three years later New Hampshire, which had seen its first brewery established by Samuel Wentworth in 1670, made its brewers tax exempt. In 1796 James Boyd established a 4000-barrel brewery in Albany, New York that survived in one form or another until 1916.

It was against this backdrop that one of the most interesting characters in the history of early American brewing arrived on the scene. Joseph Coppinger arrived from England in 1802 ablaze with the same sort of entrepreneurial fire that drove so many nineteenth-century schemers and dreamers to the Western Hemisphere's first democracy. Among the baggage Coppinger brought to New York was an invention for processing meat and vegetables for preservation 'without the aid of salt,' the customary method of the day. Shortly after his arrival Coppinger wrote directly to President Thomas Jefferson requesting a patent for his invention. Jefferson replied personally telling him to apply for a patent, but apparently the idea went no farther.

Above: **Thomas Jefferson brewed more beer than any other American president. Had he served for another term, the US might have had a National Brewery.**

Eight years later James Madison was in the White House and another, even grander, scheme was brewing in the fertile mind of Joseph Coppinger who had spent several of the intervening years as a brewmaster at the Point Brewery in Pittsburgh. Coppinger proposed to Madison a National Brewery, a government agency whose purpose would be to brew beer. As he pointed out in his letter, 'The establishment of a brewing company in Washington as a national object, has in my view the greatest importance as it would unquestionably tend to improve the quality of our malt liquors in every point of the Union and serve to counteract one baneful influence of ardent spirits on the health and morals of our fellow citizens . . . .'

He went on to outline a plan for making the National Brewery self sustaining: 'I hesitate not to say that under prudent and good management 100 percent can be securely made on the active capital of $10,000, on all the beer, ale and porter which may be brewed for this company and disposed of in the cask; whilst that which may be sold in bottle will leave 200 percent.'

For a person to administer this new government agency (a secretary of the Brewery), he suggested a man who had 'followed the brewing trade for nearly twenty years in (which) time (having) built two breweries on

Left: **An early American manor house with a home brewery attached at the right.**

Right: **John Molson began brewing in 1786 in Montreal. The Molson Brewery is North America's oldest brewing establishment.**

(his) own account . . . two distinct establishments with success in both.' The man, of course, was Joseph Coppinger himself.

The Madison administration, consumed with other affairs of state, did not take up the idea, but the president shared the proposal with former president Jefferson who became an advocate of the idea. Despite the support of a highly regarded former president, the Coppinger plan was soon overshadowed by national concern for survival when the War of 1812 began. Though Coppinger raised the idea again after the war, it was clear that its time had passed. As for Coppinger himself, he went on to some notoriety as the author of the *American Brewer and Malster.* Published in 1815, it was one of the first major books on brewing published in America. One is left, however, to contemplate what might have been if the idea had been proposed a few years earlier when Jefferson was in the White House. Would amber bottles marked Brewery of the United States line our supermarket shelves today? Would the Brewmaster General hold a cabinet post? Would history have immortalized the first secretary of the Brewery as it had the first secretary of the Treasury: Hamilton on 10-dollar bills and Coppinger on 11-ounce beer bottles?

Thomas Jefferson, Coppinger's advocate, took more than a passing interest in the art of brewing. America's third president was a long-time beer drinker and even operated his own brewery on his estate at Monticello. With the help of Captain Joseph Miller, an English brewer stranded on this side of the Atlantic by the war, Jefferson began brewing in earnest in September 1813. By January 1814 Jefferson and Miller were ordering quart and half-gallon bottles by the gross, so the enterprise was evidently successful. Miller, however, seemed to have a bit of trouble keeping his mind on the project. At one point a cork-buying trip to Norfolk turned into a nine-month absence. Nevertheless, Jefferson seemed to take his friend's inattentiveness with a grain of salt, even once helping him to avoid deportation as a spy. Eventually the city lights got the best of Miller and he settled in Norfolk permanently where he began his own brewery in September 1815.

Meanwhile, farther north in Poughkeepsie, New York another famous name was successfully plying the brewer's trade. Matthew Vassar's father had operated a brewery in this city between 1798 and 1810 when it was destroyed by fire. Young Matthew rebuilt the Eagle Brewery in 1813 (some sources say 1810) and went on to develop a brewing empire that lasted until 1896 and which supplied the bankroll for the founding, in 1860, of the women's college in Poughkeepsie that bears Vassar's name.

Despite these activities, tastes were changing in the United States, and both the consumption and production of English-style beers was in decline. It was not until 1810 that the first official tally was made, but it was generally accepted that the figures represented a drop off since the days before the turn of the century. In 1810 there were recorded to be 132 breweries in the country (48 in Pennsylvania, 42 in New York and 13 in Ohio) but their total annual production of 185,000 barrels was less than some individual breweries in England. The Anchor Brewery in London, for example, brewed 235,100 barrels in 1810.

Between 1810 and 1820, a decade that straddled the War of 1812, American beer production collapsed to barely 10 percent of its earlier level. The drop had as much to do with changing tastes as it did with the war, and signaled an end to the English brewing tradition upon whose ashes a new American tradition would be born.

EARLY CANADIAN BREWERS

As the new United States was beginning to grapple with forming its identity as a nation, life continued as before in that vast tract of land to the north called British North America and which one day would be called Canada. Early home brewing had followed similar patterns in the more sparsely populated north, but the first big name in Canadian brewing was Mr John Molson. From the English county of Lincolnshire, Molson arrived in Montreal in 1782 armed with a copy of John Richardson's *Theoretical Hints on an Improved Practice of Brewing.* The people of Quebec, predominantly French, preferred wine, so there was little brewing tradition in this province. Since imported English beer sold for more than rum in Montreal, the city's beer drinkers welcomed John Molson's first brewery which began brewing in 1786. As Stephen Leacock would later say: 'Molson built his brewery a little

Three great names in nineteenth-century Canadian brewing *(left to right):* John Carling, Eugene O'Keefe and John Labatt.

downstream from the town, close beside the river. Archeologists can easily locate the spot, as the brewery is still there.' In testament to John Molson's choice of sites, the Molson brewery celebrated its 200th anniversary in 1986 at the original location, though by that time there were Molson breweries in eight other Canadian cities from Vancouver to St John's.

During his first season Molson, along with his lady friend and coworker Sarah Insley Vaughan, produced 4000 gallons of beer. Over the course of the next century, production increased 175-fold. The brewery formed the foundation upon which Molson built an empire that included Canada's first railroad (1836) and the Molson Bank (1855) which became part of the huge Bank of Montreal. Molson's brewery went on to share the success of his other ventures and today is one of the three largest brewers in Canada and its beer the second-largest-selling imported brand in the United States (after Holland's Heineken).

The second major Canadian brewer was Irishman Eugene O'Keefe of County Cork. He arrived in Canada in 1832 at age 5 and established himself as a brewer of ale and porter in 1862. O'Keefe was among the first to see a future in Canada for lager brewing and built such a brewery in Toronto in 1879. By the turn of the century, O'Keefe had built his operation into the largest brewery in Canada. O'Keefe eventually merged with the firm established in 1840 by Thomas Carling in Ontario, forming the Carling O'Keefe consortium, Canada's largest brewer, with brewing operations in England and the United States.

The third of Canada's three largest brewing companies was started in 1832 in London, Ontario by John Balkwell and sold to the Labatt & Eccles partnership in 1847. In 1866, upon the death of his father, John Labatt assumed control of the firm that still bears his name. Since then Labatt's breweries have been established in every Canadian province except Prince Edward Island.

NEW BREWING CENTERS IN THE UNITED STATES

When the nineteenth century began, New York and Philadelphia had been America's major brewing centers for over 150 years, but other cities were developing their own traditions, traditions that would help them challenge the primacy of the big eastern brewery towns. George Shiras had started Pittsburgh's first commercial brewery, the Point (that later employed Joseph Coppinger) in 1795, and the Embree brothers began Cincinnati's first in 1805. Jacques Delassus de St Vrain, a relative of the last lieutenant governor of Spanish Louisiana, is said to have established and operated the first commercial brewery in St Louis in 1810, but he may have been preceded by a Mr John Coons who is recorded as having operated a brewery in St Louis between 1809 and 1811. St Louis is important to the history of brewing because it is now home to Anheuser-Busch, the company which became in the latter twentieth century the world's largest brewing empire. St Louis was not, however, the first city in Missouri to host a brewery. This distinction goes instead to the Sainte Genevieve, 50 miles down river, where Francois Colman, probably from Alsace, was brewing prior to 1779.

Farther north, in 1833 William Lill & Company became the first commercial brewery in Chicago, another city destined to become a major brewing center. Until that time Chicago's tavern owners brewed their own stocks. Lill's Company, determined to change the pattern, brewed 600 barrels of ale during the first year and went on to be a major part of Chicago's brewing history for the next 40 years. Even after the lager revolution that swept the Midwest a few years later, Lill and partner Michael Diversey continued to brew ale and porter until an 1871 fire destroyed the brewery.

In 1829 a young German brewer named David Yuengling established a small brewery on North Center Street in Pottsville, Pennsylvania, a town noted for its mountain spring water. The event was notable not because it was the first brewery in Pottsville (many small towns throughout eastern Pennsylvania were getting their first breweries during this period) but because, while the other breweries soon faded from the scene and were replaced by newer breweries who would themselves fade, the Yuengling Brewery continued. It survived the consolidations of the end of the nineteenth century, it survived Prohibition

The brewery premises of Howard and Fuller in Brooklyn. Ale and porter dominated American brewing until 1840.

and it survives today as the oldest brewery in the United States. It is still owned by the Yuengling family. While Canada's (and North America's) oldest brewer, Molson, went on to become one of the continent's largest brewers with national as well as international distribution, Yuengling remained a relatively small, family-owned brewery content with regional distribution.

THE LAGER REVOLUTION

Brewing in North America, the Indian tradition not withstanding, had begun with the arrival of the first settlers and grew steadily until the American Revolution, after which the growth cycle came to an end. Despite the establishment of new breweries over a wider geographical area, production began to decline. Between 1812 and 1840 as tastes changed, the market for English style ales and porters dropped off, and the American brewing industry declined dramatically.

In 1840, however, a Bavarian brewer named Johann Wagner arrived in Philadelphia with the most important innovation since the American brewing industry had begun more than two centuries before. The arrival of Johann Wagner in Philadelphia was to the history of American brewing what the invention of the automobile was to the history of travel.

What Wagner brought with him was a bottom-fermenting yeast that was to soon make Munich, in his native Bavaria, the world's beer capital. The bottom-fermenting yeast not only revived the American brewing industry but made it the biggest in the world.

Lager was the right beer at the right time. It found an immediate popularity with the American public that persists to this day. It has, in fact, become the beer of choice throughout the entire world, with the notable exception of England, where top-fermented beers still hold sway. For the most part lagers are clear and pale, ranging from amber to light gold, whereas ales and stouts are darker, thicker and less transparent. Lager yeast is active at temperatures down to freezing. Lager beers, especially in the United States, are drunk cold, while the English still drink their brews at room temperature, a practice that some Americans find hard to believe. This difference in habit led English humorist John Cleese to parody the American view of English beer as 'nasty warm sticky stuff with odd forms of pond life growing in it.'

In 1840 the golden lagers were just beginning to come into fashion in the area where lager was born, that central European golden triangle whose area encompassed both Bavaria and parts of the Austria-Hungarian Empire, and whose corners lay at Munich, Vienna and Pilsen (now in Czechoslovakia) near Prague. The beers that came forth from this region included the amber Munich beers as well as the especially light and pale Pilsen beers, or Pilseners. Wagner, having little comprehension of the scope of what he

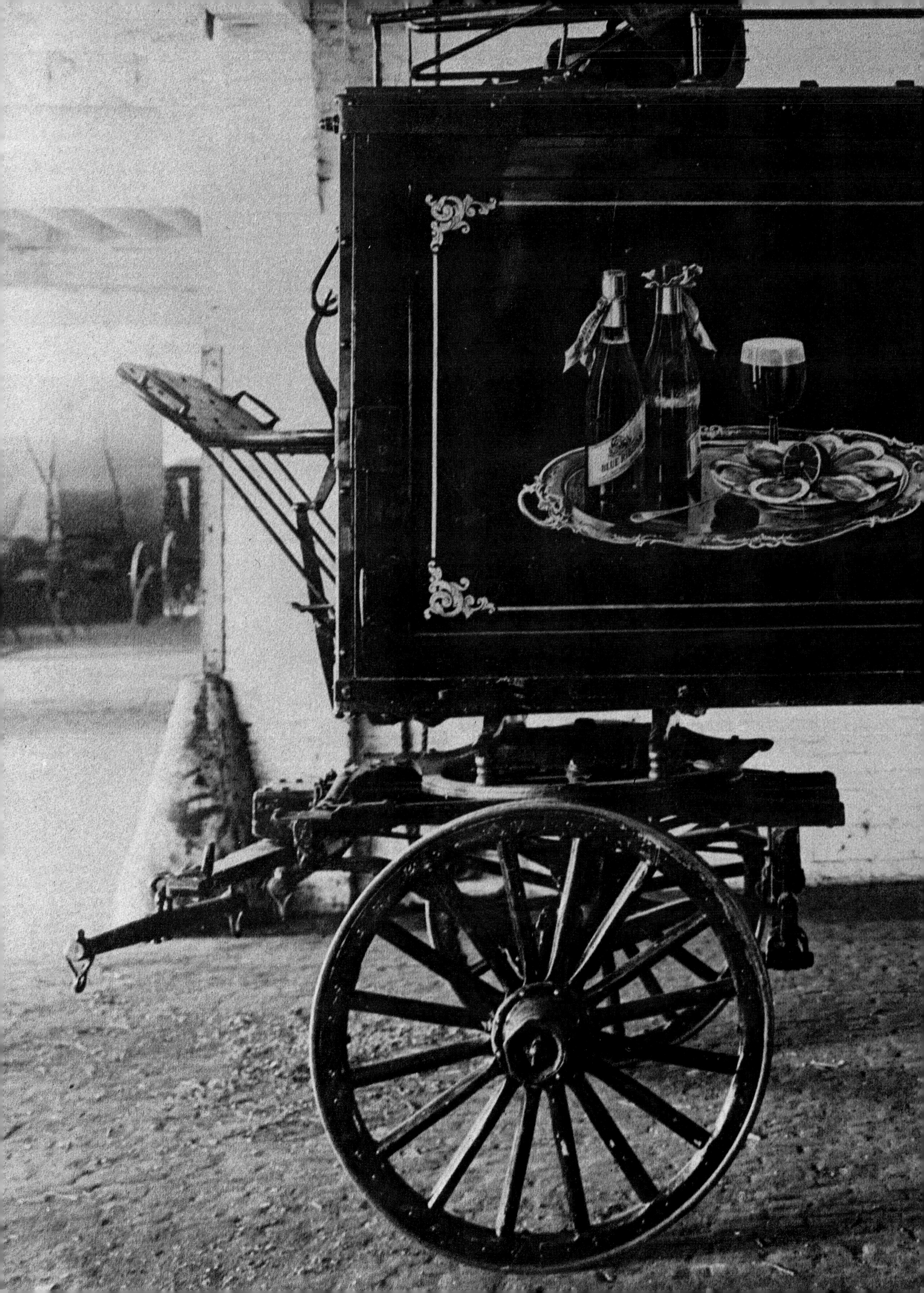

Pabst
Blue Ribbon
The beer of quality.
J. BROWN, Photo,
Milwaukee.

had done, simply brewed small quantities for limited distribution. It took George Manger, who bought some of Wagner's yeast, to set up Philadelphia's (and America's) first commercial lager brewery. By 1844 there were several lager breweries in Philadelphia and lager brewing had spread to other cities. In the years leading up to 1848, the revolution and unrest that swept Germany and much of central Europe resulted in a massive wave of emigration from this region to the United States. Among the emigres were the brewers who would change the face of American brewing and ensure that lager would be its dominant feature.

THE TOWN THAT MADE AMERICAN BREWING FAMOUS

Probably no town is more often identified with the American brewing industry than Milwaukee, Wisconsin. While the beer of the Joseph Schlitz company would be described as 'the beer that made Milwaukee famous,' it was not alone. The fact that so many major breweries evolved there is what probably accounts for Milwaukee's fame. Nearly 75 breweries came and went over the years. There were four giants whose German brewmasters made Milwaukee into America's brewing capital. These included the empire of Joseph Schlitz, of course, but also Valentin Blatz, Frederic Miller and Captain Frederick Pabst as well.

Among those who established the first Milwaukee breweries in 1840 were Richard Owens, William Pawlett and John Davis. Davis's Milwaukee Brewery eventually became

Above, left to right: **Joseph Schlitz, Valentin Blatz and Frederick Pabst.** ***Below and previous page:*** **Early Pabst brewery wagons. The scene below shows the early morning routine in the shipping yards in 1900. Pabst was one of the breweries that put Milwaukee on the map, and at the turn of the century was the nation's largest.**

Powell's Ale and survived until 1880. Other early brewers included Stolz and Krill, whose brewery evolved into the Falk, Jung & Borchert Brewing Company and lasted until 1892, and Herman Reuthlisberger, whose German brewery eventually became the South Side Brewery which closed in 1886. The Eagle Brewery was founded in 1841 and was followed by the brewery of Conrad Muntzenberger in 1842; they survived until 1867 and 1847, respectively.

The first brewery that evolved into one of the big four was the Empire Brewery established on Chestnut Street in 1844 by Jacob Best and his four sons, Charles, Lorenz, Jacob Jr and Phillip. Phillip Best, serving as brewmaster for his father, made the first lager to be brewed in Milwaukee in 1851. Two years later Jacob Best retired, selling his shares to Phillip and Jacob Jr, as Charles and Lorenz had departed from the family firm to start their own brewery in 1850. Phillip Best took over full ownership of the Empire Brewery in 1860. Four years later he took on a new partner, the husband of his daughter Maria, a former Great Lakes steamship captain named Frederick Pabst. Best sold out his interest in the Empire Brewery in 1866 to Captain Pabst and another son-in-law, Emil Schandein, who soon faded from the scene. In 1873 the brewery was incorporated, using the Phillip Best name, and in 1889 it became the Pabst Brewing Company. By that time, the annual output of the brewery was 585,300 barrels.

The second of Milwaukee's big four was begun as the City Brewery by Johann Braun. Five years later Braun died and his widow married a

Above, left to right: Jacob Best, whose Empire Brewery eventually became the Pabst Brewing Co, Philip Best and Frederic Miller. The Plank Road Brewery _(below)_ was built in 1850 by Charles Best, son of Jacob, and bought out by Frederic Miller in 1853 for $8000. Miller's eventually became the world's second-largest brewing company.

This vintage metal tray shows the old Joseph Schlitz brewery in Milwaukee with exquisite and intricate detail.

MALT HOUSE
BREWING CO
600,000 Barrels.
UKEE

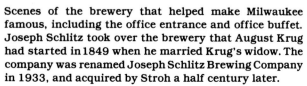

Scenes of the brewery that helped make Milwaukee famous, including the office entrance and office buffet. Joseph Schlitz took over the brewery that August Krug had started in 1849 when he married Krug's widow. The company was renamed Joseph Schlitz Brewing Company in 1933, and acquired by Stroh a half century later.

former employee named Valentin Blatz who took over the brewery. The Valentin Blatz Brewing Company grew into one of Milwaukee's majors and between 1889 and 1911 was affiliated with Michael Brand's United States Brewing Company of Chicago. In 1958, 107 years after Valentin Blatz had gone to the altar with the widow of Johann Braun, the company was purchased by Pabst. The following year, the Blatz name was eliminated and the big four became three.

The third in the order of their founding was Schlitz, perhaps the most famous name of all. In 1856 Joseph Schlitz married the widow of brewer August Krug, the man whom Schlitz had served as bookkeeper. It is an interesting coincidence that the men who built two of America's greatest brewing empires had entered the business by marrying their boss's widows in the same town within the space of five years. The brewery that August Krug had started in 1849 retained his name until 1858 when it became the Joseph Schlitz Brewery. The company was incorporated under Schlitz's name in 1874 and continued as such until 1920 when it was renamed the Joseph Schlitz Beverage Company for the duration of Prohibition. Joseph Schlitz himself was lost at sea in 1875 during a trip back to his native Germany. Reconstituted as the Joseph Schlitz Brewing Company in 1933, the brewery continued to brew the 'beer that made Milwaukee famous' until 1982 when it was purchased by the smaller Stroh Brewing Company of Detroit. Of the original big four there were now two.

The last of the great Milwaukee breweries was started by Charles Best, son of Jacob Best whose original brewery evolved into the Pabst empire. Charles Best started his brewery in Wauwatosa just west of the Milwaukee city limits in 1850. He named it the Plank Road Brewery, presumably a reference to the practice of putting planks or timbers in a muddy roadway to prevent wagon wheels from getting stuck in the mud. In 1852, the Plank Road Brewery was the first Milwaukee brewery to export beer to New York. Charles took his brother Lorenz Best into the firm in 1851, and in 1855 (some sources say 1853) it was sold to a young German brewer named Frederic Miller. Miller's Plank Road Brewery officially became the Menomonee Valley Brewery in 1878, though both names had been used since the days when the Best brothers owned the company. The brewery was incorporated under Frederic Miller's name within Milwaukee's city limits in 1888, although his first name was dropped in 1920, and has remained so until the present. Over the years Miller Brewing became the number two brewer in the United States, second only to Anheuser-Busch. Interestingly, in 1985 Miller began to test market an unpasteurized draft-style beer under the old Plank Road name that had been abandoned, like the muddy streets of Wauwatosa, over a century before.

Below: **A Schlitz beer wagon decked out for a parade, possibly the Fourth of July. The driver is dressed like Uncle Sam, but the man tending the horses wears a strange uniform. The old dray wagons are now a part of Milwaukee folklore.**

Immigrants from central Europe's golden triangle — the region including Munich, Vienna and Pilsen (near Prague) — brought with them the art of lager brewing in the 1850s. Terms like 'Bavarian,' 'Bohemian' and 'Pilsner' came to stand for quality in beer. These immigrants also introduced beer gardens to Americans as a place to sit down with friends to enjoy a stein of one's favorite lager.

Far right: Bernard Stroh came to the United States from Germany in the 1840s to settle in Detroit, where he established the Stroh Brewery Company in 1850. *Far right below:* Like other immigrant brewers from Europe, he began producing a beer that was lighter than the ales being brewed up to then and known as Bohemian beer. To distinguish his brand, he adapted the ancient crest of Bohemia, a gold lion on a red background. In 1893 Stroh's Bohemian beer won a blue ribbon at the Columbian exposition and became a regional favorite.

THE LAGER REVOLUTION SPREADS

Lager brewing in America began in Philadelphia and made Milwaukee famous, but it spread throughout the rest of the continent as well. Lager came to New York City, America's original brewing capital, in 1842 upon the arrival of Maximillian and Frederick Schaefer. They had that year acquired the brewery of Sebastian Sommers on Broadway near West Eighteenth Street. In 1849 after a brief four-year stint on Manhattan's West Side, the Schaefers moved the brewery uptown to Fourth Avenue (later Park Avenue) near East Fiftieth Street, where it remained until 1916. During this period the Schaefer Brewery was to become one of the largest and most important breweries in the eastern United States.

Meanwhile, John Huck and John Schneider started Chicago's first lager brewery in 1847, and the windy city was on its way to becoming Milwaukee's major rival in the Midwest.

By the end of the 1850s German immigrants made up a large part of the population in many of America's major cities. Lager breweries and German-style beer gardens both proliferated. The beer gardens, with their bands, dancing, food and garden-like atmosphere, became major entertainment centers for German-Americans of all ages. A Sunday afternoon at the beer garden was a popular form of family entertainment throughout the balance of the nineteenth century and the first decade of the twentieth.

German immigration was by no means limited to New York and the cities of the north and east. San Antonio, Texas had a large enough German population to support several German-language newspapers and several lager breweries. The first of these was William Menger's Western Brewery in 1855, but it also included those of William Esser (1874), J B Behloradsky (1881), Felix Bachrach (1890) and Lorenz Ochs and George Aschbacher (1890).

Between 1857 and1860 the sales of lager beer in the United States

Above: **Bernard Stroh and *(right)* Stroh bottles over the years. This Bohemian-style beer is still brewed over a direct fire.**

Below: **Frederick Schaefer bought his former employer's brewery in New York and set up F & M Schaefer with his brother Maximillian. They were pioneers of lager beer.**

equaled the sales of all other types of beer. By the Civil War, lager had become America's unsurpassed favorite. In 1850 there had been 431 breweries in the United States producing 23 million gallons of beer annually. By 1860 there were 1269 breweries producing over 30 million gallons—most of them lager.

During the Civil War, the Union troops went into the field without the beer ration that had accompanied their grandfathers in 1776. The beer ration, which became a liquor ration after 1893, was eliminated by Secretary of War Lewis Cass in 1832 in deference to the growing temperance movement. Nevertheless, the German brewers, who were located

BREWED ONLY FROM CHOICEST
INDUSTRIAL EXPOSITION ANTWERP 1911 AND
STROH'S Bohemian STYLE BEER.
REG. U.S. PAT. OFF.
CONTENTS 12 FL. OZ.
INTERNAL REVENUE TAX PAID
SERVED WHEREVER QUALITY COUNTS
BREWED AND BOTTLED BY
THE STROH BREWERY CO.
DETROIT 26,
MICHIGAN
Bohemian Style Beer.
STROH'S Bohemian STYLE BEER.
REG. U.S. PAT. OFF.
CONTENTS
12 FL. OZ.
SERVED WHEREVER QUALITY COUNTS
BREWED AND BOTTLED BY
THE STROH BREWERY CO.
DETROIT 26,
MICHIGAN
200
YEARS
"FIRE-BREWING" PROCESS USED EXCLUSIVELY BY US IN THE UNITED STATES
Stroh's
BOHEMIAN STYLE
BEER
AMERICA'S ONLY FIRE-BREWED BEER
BREWED AND BOTTLED BY
THE STROH BREWERY CO.
DETROIT, MICH. 48226
12 FL. OZ.

1892

primarily in the North, were generally pro-Union. In 1861 the Internal Revenue System was established to finance the war, and the following year a one-dollar tax was levied on each barrel of beer produced in the United States. In response to government taxation and the temperance movement, 37 breweries in New York City came together in 1862 to form the industry's first trade organization, which became known as the United States Brewer's Association in 1864.

ANHEUSER-BUSCH

As a major brewing center, St Louis, Missouri was certainly eclipsed in importance by Milwaukee, Philadelphia, New York, Chicago and even San Francisco. However, the huge brewery that developed from the little firm originally started on Carondelet Avenue in 1852 by Georg Schneider has forever earned St Louis a place in the pages of American brewing history. In 1857, Schneider, like so many small brewers throughout history, realized that he could not compete. He sold his little Bavarian Brewery to Adam and Philip Carl Hammer who were underwritten by a loan from a wealthy St Louis soap-maker named Eberhard Anheuser. By 1860 when the brewery once again verged on collapse, Anheuser realized he needed to take direct control of operations in order to protect his investment. The firm became known as Eberhard Anheuser's Bavarian Brewery. Within a year after Anheuser entered the brewing business, his daughter Lily Anheuser married a 22-year-old brewery supply salesman named Adolphus Busch. In 1864 Busch joined his father-in-law's firm as a salesman. In 1875 the Bavarian Brewery name was dropped and the brewery became Eberhard Anheuser & Company's Brewing Association. In 1879 it became the Anheuser-Busch Brewing Association when Adolphus Busch became a full partner.

Busch was brewing's first marketing genius. He was not the first to

Left: **The Anheuser-Busch brewery in St Louis, once the largest single brewhouse in North America.** ***Right:*** **An early advertising sign for the Anheuser-Busch 'Brewing Association' featuring the A & Eagle trademark adopted in 1872.**

Adolphus Busch *(above)* and his empire. An early view *(below)* of the St Louis brewhouse and delivery wagons. Iced 'beer cars' *(far right)* being loaded for long-distance shipment. Busch started Manufacturers Railway Co in 1877 using refrigerator cars to expand his market. Brewmasters *(far right below)* pose proudly.

dream of an American national beer, but he was the first to realize it. Until Busch's time the American brewing scene was composed only of regional brewers. A large brewer might have customers in a neighboring state, but for the most part local demand was satisfied by a local brewer. Cities with large beer-consuming populations such as Milwaukee or Chicago could and did support several sizable breweries.

St Louis was a mid-sized town with a fairly good market for beer, but nothing compared to the above-mentioned cities or Philadelphia or New York. Some men could have been content to be the part owner of a successful medium-sized brewery in such a town but not Adolphus Busch. Even prior to his partnership, he launched a vigorous advertising campaign and formed a wide distribution network. He established a network of railside ice houses to keep long-distance shipments of beer cool and fresh. In 1877 he was the first brewer to ship his brew in refrigerated rail cars, and later he helped pioneer the pasteurization of beer.

Busch dreamed of a national beer, a brew specially designed to appeal to people of all walks of life throughout the United States. Along with his friend Carl Conrad, Busch created such a beer (a lager, of course) which was introduced in 1876, the centennial of United States independence.

Busch and Conrad considered the recipe and the name of their 'people's beer' carefully. The most popular brews of the day were those brewed in the manner of the lagers of central Europe's golden triangle (Munich-Vienna-Pilsen). Many breweries produced brand names that alluded to that region. Indeed, the Anheuser-Busch Brewery had begun as Georg Schneider's 'Bavarian' Brewery. Of the golden lagers, the

1888
FREIGHT DEPOT.
ANHEUSER-BUSCH BREWING
MANUFACTURERS RAILWAY COMPANY
ANHEUSER-BUSCH'S
Malt-Nutrine
Greatest of Malt Tonics
ANHEUSER-BUSCH
BEER CAR

pale ones from the Pilsen corner of the triangle, the Pilseners, epitomized for Busch and Conrad the style they wanted. In Bohemia (now part of Czechoslovakia) and specifically the town of Ceske Budejovice they found the beer on which they would model America's first mass-market brew. As part of the German-speaking Austria-Hungarian empire, Ceske Budejovice was known by its German name, Budweis. Busch took the German name for his new beer. In 1876 Adolphus Busch's Budweiser brand was born. Budweiser not only survived as a brand name, it prospered. Today Budweiser is the biggest selling single brand in the United States and in the world—the flagship of Anheuser-Busch, the world's biggest brewer. For Adolphus Busch, the master brewer and master marketeer who dared to dream the big dreams, two dreams came true.

Left: **The big copper kettles in the Anheuser-Busch St Louis Brewery.** ***Right:*** **Employees take a break from shoveling coal into the boilers that kept the brewery humming.** ***Below:*** **A vintage metal tray featuring the A & Eagle and the company brands.**

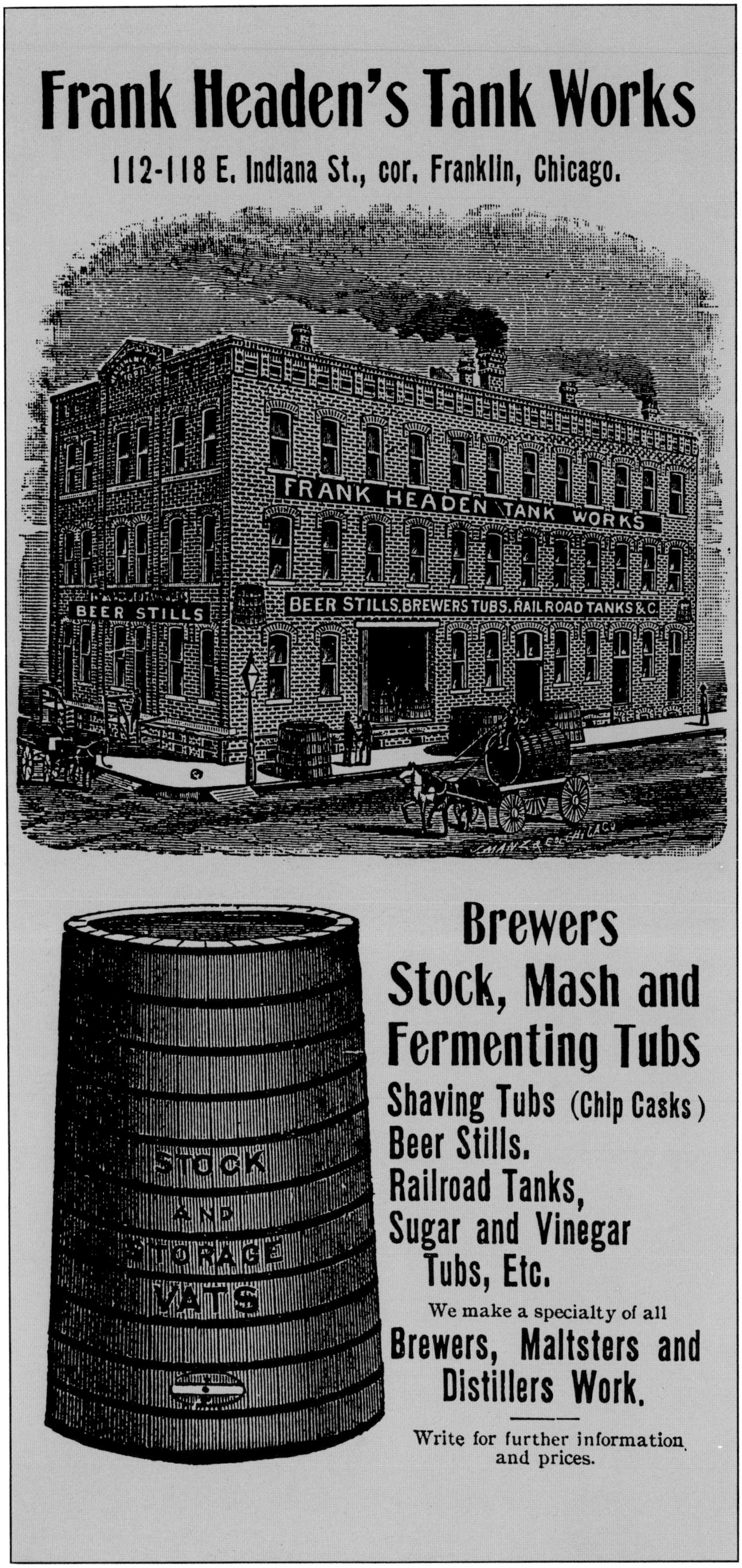
Frank Headen's Tank Works
112-118 E. Indiana St., cor. Franklin, Chicago.
FRANK HEADEN TANK WORKS
BEER STILLS
BEER STILLS, BREWERS TUBS, RAILROAD TANKS &C.
STOCK AND STORAGE VATS
Brewers
Stock, Mash and
Fermenting Tubs
Shaving Tubs (Chip Casks)
Beer Stills.
Railroad Tanks,
Sugar and Vinegar
Tubs, Etc.
We make a specialty of all
Brewers, Maltsters and
Distillers Work.
Write for further information and prices.

BREWING IN CHICAGO

The Windy City has had more local breweries (190) than any city west of Philadelphia, but has never seen the rise of a major national brewery. Perhaps because of Chicago's proximity to Milwaukee or because, like New York, it had such a large number of beer drinkers within its environs, its brewers never thought of a broader market.

In 1833 William Lill had been the first to brew beer commercially, while Huck & Schneider's Eagle Brewery brewed Chicago's first commercial lager in 1847. More than 20 breweries opened their doors in Chicago in the 1850s, and while many did not survive the 1860s, there were at least two new breweries opening for every one that closed. In Chicago, as in the other major cities throughout the United States, the quarter century following the end of the Civil War was a golden age for American brewing.

Among the early Chicago brewers was Valentin Busch, who is sometimes incorrectly mistaken for Valentin Blatz or a relative of Adolphus Busch. Busch started his brewery in 1851 and joined forces with Michael Brand in 1858. Brand is best known for his own brewery which he started in 1878, the year before Busch & Brand Brewing was closed. Brand changed the name of his company to the United States Brewing Company of Chicago in 1889, and in 1890, it became part of Milwaukee & Chicago Breweries Ltd, a British syndicate that owned breweries in both cities, including an interest in the brewery of Valentin Blatz.

Michael Brand's United States Brewing continued to operate with that name, even under British ownership, until Prohibition. In 1932, it re-emerged as United States Brewing and survived until 1955.

Frederick Wacker entered the Chicago brewing world in 1857 as a partner in the former Blattner & Seidenschwanz Brewery. Wacker & Seidenschwanz became Wacker & Company the following year. In 1882, Wacker joined forces with Jacob Birk to form Wacker & Birk Brewing & Malting, a firm that survived until 1918.

One of the more colorful Chicago brewing histories tells of the brewery started by Joseph Jerusalem at the foot of Elm Street in 1868. Twenty years later, ownership was shifted to Ms Ulrike Jerusalem. In 1891, the brewery was owned by Gustav Eberlein who operated it until 1903. In that year the name of Gustav Eberlein was replaced by Ulrike Eberlein, who operated the Eberlein Weiss Beer Brewery until 1908. It appears that Ulrike outlived two husbands in the 40-year history of the brewery.

When Prohibition ended in 1933, 15 breweries reopened in Chicago out of the dozens that had been there during turn of the century heyday. For a quarter century, the number remained relatively constant, but by 1963 consolidations had brought the number of Chicago breweries down to only seven. By the 1970s only the Peter Hand Brewery on North Avenue remained. By 1978, it too was gone. Chicago's last remaining brewery, its last reminder of the great brewing days of the 1890s, had closed after 87 years in business.

BREWING IN THE UPPER MIDWEST

Among the states of the upper plains sitting astride the richest grain-growing region on earth there is a distinct paucity of brewing history. The relatively sparse population and an inclination toward stringent local prohibition allowed Iowa, Kansas, Nebraska and the Dakotas a bare handful of brewers. Even the state of Missouri beyond St Louis boasted only Kansas City as a brewing center, and Kansas City, despite its fun-loving reputation, has hosted just 16 breweries in its history compared to 102 in St Louis.

South Dakota, wracked by prohibitionist fervor from time to time (notably from 1889 to 1896), managed to attract immense talent in the person of Moritz Levinger. Bavarian by birth, Levinger learned the brewing art at Munich's great Spaten brewery and immigrated to the United States in 1869 at age 18. Having worked for both Philip Schaefer and Jacob Ruppert in New York City, he came west to South Dakota where he established the Sioux Falls Brewing and Malting Company. One of only 26 breweries established in South Dakota's history, Sioux Falls Brewing (the 'Malting' was dropped in 1912) survived until Prohibition but an attempt to reopen the establish-

ABE KLEE & SON
DEALERS IN
DRIVING, HEAVY DRAFT, FINE COACH and SADDLE
HORSES
OUR SPECIALTY
BREWERY HORSES
From 150 to 200 Head Constantly on Hand
270-274 NORTH CENTER AVENUE
Long Distance Phone Monroe 1006
CHICAGO, ILL.
Cable Address "KLEESON"
REFERENCES:
Conrad Seipp Brewing Co.
City Brewing Co.
K. G. Schmidt Brewing Co.
Atlas Brewing Co.
West Side Brewing Co.
Gambrinus Brewing Co.
Citizens Brewing Co.
National Brewing Co.
Marshall Field & Co.
Montgomery Ward & Co.
Carson, Pirie, Scott & Co.
Anheuser-Busch Brewing Co.
McAvoy Brewing Co.
P. Schoenhofen Brewing Co.
Star Brewing Co.
Val. Blatz Brewing Co.
Standard Brewing Co.
Fred Miller Brewing Co.
R. H. Graupner Br'y, Harrisburg, Pa.
Altoona Brewery, Altoona, Pa.
United States Express Co.
Swift & Co.
H. W. Hoyt & Co.
Deering Harvester Co.
United States Brewing Co.
Monarch Brewing Co.
Wacker & Birk Brewing Co.
Bartholomae & Roesing Brewing Co.
Pabst Brewing Co.
Chicago Brewing Co.
Seattle Brewing & Malting Co. of Seattle, Wash.
American Express Co.
Libby, McNeil & Libby.
Steele, Wedeles & Co.
New York Biscuit Co.
Sunset Brg. Co., Wallace, Idaho.
John Kazmaier Br'y, Altoona, Pa.
AND MANY OTHERS

Left: Companies like that of Frank Headen supplied the necessary brewing equipment. *Above:* Horses, a necessity in the early days, are now used only in promotions.

ment in 1934 failed. In fact, of five breweries started in South Dakota in 1934, only one survived the first year. Dakota Brewing of Huron (originally established in 1884) survived until 1942. In North Dakota, by comparison, 17 breweries were started between 1874 and 1890, and all of them had gone out of business by the turn of the century. Aside from the East Grand Forks Brewing Company which opened and closed in the town of the same name in 1910, only one brewery operated in the state in the twentieth century. This was Dakota Brewing & Malting which produced its brew in Bismarck from 1961 to 1965.

Among the states of the upper Midwest, Minnesota, with a large German population and ice-cold winters ideal for lager brewing, stands out as the most important to American brewing history. Though overshadowed by neighboring Wisconsin with 542 breweries throughout its history, Minnesota has had 210 compared to a total of 102 for Nebraska and the Dakotas combined. Historically, most of Minnesota's brewing activity took place within a triangle between New Ulm, Rochester and the twin cities of Minneapolis/St Paul. The Twin Cities, however, are the true brewing capital of this section of the United States and have traditionally boasted more breweries than any other city between Milwaukee and Seattle. If Minneapolis/St Paul are the region's premier brewing center, then the establishment started by Theodore Hamm would have to be, along with that of Jacob Schmidt, one of the Twin Cities' premier breweries. Hamm was born in Baden, Germany in 1825 and immigrated to St Paul in 1856. Nine years later he bought the

Above: The premises of the Jacob Schmidt Brewing Company in St Paul Minnesota. Right: The Grain Belt Brewery in Minneapolis, Minnesota as it appeared in 1948, an ideal name for a brewery in the Midwest. The brewery actually started out as John Orth's Brewery in 1850 and went through a series of several name changes over the years. Below: A Stroh Brewing Company wagon photographed at the Detroit brewery in 1885 together with Stroh drivers and their Labrador mascot.

GRAIN-BELT
BEERS
OFFICE

Above: Theodore Hamm created the Theodore Hamm Brewing Co that was eventually bought out by Pabst. *Left:* Hamm's employees c 1910 fill the brew kettle with hops. *Below:* The famous Hamm's bear.

Pittsburgh Brewery of St Paul which had been started by Andrew Keller in 1860. By the turn of the century, the Theodore Hamm Brewing Company was producing a half-million barrels of beer annually. The company survived Prohibition and continued as a major regional brewer in the north plains and mountain states. Its brands Burgie and Buckhorn were important trademarks, but the Hamm's brand and the Hamm's cartoon bear were veritable icons for several generations of beer drinkers. The Hamm's slogan 'from the land of sky blue waters' conjured up images of Minnesota with its

many sparkling lakes. Starting in 1975, however, the Hamm's bear very nearly became extinct as Hamm's sky blue waters transformed in the rapids of a corporate ownership shuffle. In that year, the Theodore Hamm Brewing company was purchased by Olympia Brewing of Tumwater, Washington, which was in turn taken over by Pabst in 1983. First Olympia, then Pabst, chose to retain the Hamm's brand, and the familiar Hamm's bear had a new lease on life.

BREWING IN THE SOUTH

No region of North America has had fewer breweries in its history than the states of the confederacy. Alabama, Georgia and the Carolinas have had a combined total of only 40 breweries throughout their entire histories, and Mississippi stands as the only American state to have never had a commercial brewery. Florida also fitted this mold until after World War II when large-scale brewing began in the state. Kentucky, Tennessee and the Virginias have all had a relatively larger number of breweries than the other southern states, and indeed it was in Virginia that European-style beer was first brewed in North America.

The South's two major brewing cities are located at opposite ends of the region. Louisville, Kentucky is located across the river from Indiana and a short distance from Ohio, which are both states with a large German population. Its opposite, New Orleans, is located deep in the heart of Dixie. New Orleans, with its rich cosmopolitan history, has always been an exception to any rule drawn about the South. There have been 24 breweries in New Orleans compared to just four in the rest of the state of Louisiana, and two of those four were operated for less than a year without permits.

The first brewery in New Orleans and one of the first in the South was started about 1850 by George Merz at Villere and Toulouse streets. This establishment evolved into the New Orleans Brewing Association's Southern Brewery but it finally closed in 1900. Of the seven New Orleans breweries that survived Prohibition, four were gone by 1965. The Jackson brewery, home of the popular Jax Beer, closed its doors in

Below: **An early view showing the old world ambience of the G Heileman office and bottling plant in La Crosse, Wisconsin. Legend has it that Gottlieb Heileman won the brewery in a coin toss with his partner John Gund. As part of the same 1872 transaction, Gund is said to have taken possesion of the bakery that the two had owned.**

OFFICE

H. WEINHARD
BREWERY.
LAGER BEER.

Left: **The staff of the Henry Weinhard Brewery. Cotton was used to simulate foam for the long exposure required for the photograph.** ***Overleaf:*** **The brewery as it appeared early in the early 1900s.**

1974 leaving only the Falstaff Brewery on Gavier Street and the Dixie Brewing Company on Tulane Street. Dixie Beer, the only surviving indigenous Louisiana beer, found increasing popularity as Louisiana's cajun/creole cuisine came into vogue in the 1980s.

BREWING IN THE WEST

Prior to the Civil War the vast majority of the population of the United States was located east of the Mississippi River. With the exception of San Francisco no large cities existed in the West. The major towns such as Denver, Portland, Sacramento and Butte were tiny by eastern standards. Not until the purchase of the Oregon Country from Britain in 1846 and the Mexican cession of California and the Southwest two years later did the present western United States actually became part of the United States.

Founded as a Spanish mission in 1776, San Francisco was populated largely by Americans even before California was given statehood. The gold rush of 1849 turned it into the West's first metropolis as well as the West's major brewing center. Beer may have been brewed in San Francisco as early as 1837, and the city certainly had at least one commercial brewery by 1849.

Outside of San Francisco the first commercial brewery in the West was probably the City Brewery started in 1852 by Henry Saxer in Portland, Oregon Territory. Five years later, a young German brewer named Henry Weinhard arrived in Fort Vancouver, Washington across the Columbia River from Portland where he became involved in the Muench Brewery. In 1859 he became the proprietor of the Muench Brewery, and in 1862 he bought Saxer's City Brewery as well. Two years later he sold his Vancouver interest to Anton Young and moved his entire operation to Portland. Over the years these two breweries would grow to become two of the West's most important brewers. The Vancouver operation grew to become the Lucky Lager Brewery, which became affili-

SODA
FOUNTAIN
SUPPLIE
WASHINC & F

EINHARD'S
BEVERAGES
COLUMBIA
REW
CITY AUTO LAUNDRY
GARAGE
REFINISHING · WASHING · POLISHING
STORAGE
449
UNDRY & GARAGE
SIMONIZING
CITY AUTO LAUNDRY
STORAGE
USED CARS.
USED CARS

Henry Weinhard *(above left)* and Adolph Coors *(above right)* both started major brewing companies in the West that survive today. Henry Weinhard bought into the oldest western brewery outside of San Francisco and made it his own. It became Oregon's major brewery and today produces a private reserve premium beer named for Weinhard *(above)*. The Coors brewery became the largest brewing company in the West and the largest single-site brewery in the world. The first mechanical refrigerating unit *(right)* was installed in the Coor's plant in 1890.

ated with General Brewing in 1964. It in turn became part of the Falstaff brewing empire (under the General name) in 1975. Henry Weinhard's City Brewery became the Henry Weinhard Brewery in 1904 and the Blitz-Weinhard company in 1928. The Blitz-Weinhard Company was purchased by Pabst Brewing in 1979, which in turn was purchased by Heileman Brewing in 1983. The Blitz-Weinhard name, however, continued as a brand name in regional distribution, and Henry Weinhard's name was revived in the late 1970s for a premium beer called Henry Weinhard's Private Reserve which developed a strong following on the West Coast.

The Oregon-Washington area became the West's second major population center. When the Civil War began, for example, only Oregon and California, amid the territories of the far west, had achieved statehood. It was only natural, then, that this area would begin to develop a brewing industry. From the original center in the Portland-Vancouver area the major interest in breweries spread north toward Seattle, although Emil Meyer began his City Brewery in the eastern Washington city of Walla Walla as early as 1855. Both Anton Mueller and Wolf Shafer started breweries in Steilacoom, Washington in 1874, and Martin Schneig, George Cantierri and Stuart Crichton all started breweries in Seattle the same year, although Steilacoom and Seattle may have had their first breweries in 1858 and 1864, respectively.

The year 1874 was important not just in the Seattle area but in the area south of Portland-Vancouver as well. In that year breweries were opened for the first time in an incredibly large number of Oregon cities including Albany, Astoria, Baker, Corvallis, Eugene, Oakland and Salem to name just a few. There were in fact two breweries opened in the state capital of Salem in 1874, as well as three in Portland.

As the discovery of gold in California led to the discovery of mineral wealth elsewhere in the West, mining towns proliferated throughout the Sierra Nevada and soon throughout the Rockies. Colorado evolved as the major territory straddling the spine of the Rockies, and Denver became Colorado's commercial hub and in 1859 the home of its first brewery. This brewery, established by F Z Solomon and Charles Tascher on Seventh Street, was appropriately called the Rocky Mountain Brewery. Acquired by Philip Zang in 1870, it was renamed for Zang 10 years later. The Philip Zang Brewery survived until Prohibition, and was very briefly revived during 1934.

Though bustling Denver was by no means a one-horse town in the 1860s, it did have a One Horse Brewery which was started by Louis Hessner and Henry Graff in 1864 and operated by a succession of owners for eight years. Other early breweries in the area included Moritz Sigl's Colorado Brewery in Denver (1864) and those of Paul Lindstrom in Empire (1862), Conrad Elliot in Chase Gulch (1862), William Lehmkuhl in Central City (1866), Rudolf Koenig in Golden (1868), Henry Weiss in Pueblo (1868), Otto Boche in Silver Plume (1869) and Vincent Albus in Trinidad (1869).

Few of these early breweries started in the 1860s survived the 1870s. Some did not survive the 1860s. In 1873, however, a man arrived who not only survived, but put Colorado permanently on the brewing map of the United States. Adolph Coors was born in 1847 at Barmen, Prussia (now Wuppertal, Germany). At the age of 15 he began his apprenticeship at the brewery of Henry Wenker in Dortmund. In 1868, having worked for three years at breweries in Berlin, Kassel and Velzen, the 21-year-old Coors immigrated to the United States. By the following year he had worked his way to Naperville, Illinois where he got a job as foreman at the Stenger Brewery and where he stayed until the end of 1871. For Coors, as for so many young men of the time, the West represented the promise of a rewarding (or at least adventurous) future, and 1872 found him enroute to Colorado. In Denver, young Adolph invested his savings in a bottling company and within a year he was advertising himself as a dealer in 'bottled beer, ale, porter, cider, imported and domestic wines and seltzer water.'

Below: **The Coors brewery in 1884, eleven years after it was founded. Eventually huge red brick brewery buildings (as shown in the 1900 lithograph on pages 54-55) replaced the early wood and stone ones. The mountain above the Coors plant became part of the company's early trademark *(far right).***

Eager to get out of the bottling business and back into the business of brewing the beer to fill the bottles, Coors decided to start a brewery. He persuaded one of his customers, Jacob Schueler, a Denver ice cream and candy tycoon, to invest $18,000 in the idea, and Coors himself added $2000. They purchased an old tannery by a stream in nearby Golden, Colorado and converted it into a brewery. Before the end of 1873, their Golden Brewery was in business, and within a year it had turned a profit. Seven years later Coors bought Schueler's share of the business, which then became the Adolph Coors Golden Brewery. Between 1880 and 1890, the output of Coors' brewery increased from 3500 barrels annually to 17,600. Ten years later output increased to 48,000 barrels per year. The brewery survived Prohibition, becoming the Adolph Coors Company in 1933, and went on to become the largest single-site brewing company in the world.

Texas, for its size, has had relatively fewer breweries in its history than many other states—fewer than Oregon, Washington, Colorado or even Idaho. California has had four times as many, and even Missouri has had more than twice as many. San Antonio, where William Menger started the first brewery in Texas (the Western Brewery, 1855), became the state's original brewing center mainly because of its large German population. It was in San

The Kessler Brewery *(below)* in Helena, Montana was founded by Charles Beehrer in 1864 and purchased by Nick Kessler in 1866. It eventually became Montana's foremost brewery. The Montana Brewing Co *(right)* in Great Falls was established by Andrew Johnson in 1891 and went out of business in 1950.

Antonio that the Lone Star State's two most important and well known breweries were founded. The first, appropriately named Lone Star Brewing Company, was started by none other than Adolphus Busch in 1884. Busch started the brewery as an early effort in multisite diversification that also led him to invest in breweries in Fort Worth, Texas and Shreveport, Louisiana, all of which produced beer under their own labels rather than Busch's Budweiser label. Otto Koehler, the man hired by Busch to manage Lone Star, later moved to the San Antonio Brewing Association, the brewery originally started by J B Behloradsky in 1881. San Antonio Brewing became Pearl Brewing in 1952; its brand became one of Texas's majors and survives today under the ownership of General Brewing.

Lone Star, which was divested by Busch and went through a succession of other names between 1918 and 1940 before becoming Lone Star again, evolved with an image that was almost synonymous with the lifestyle of the Lone Star State. Still known as the 'National Beer of Texas.' Lone Star was bought by Olympia Brewing in 1976 and then sold to Heileman in 1983.

Few states have had more breweries or more brewing centers for the size of their populations than Montana. Thomas Smith established Montana's first brewery at Virginia City in 1863, the year before Montana became a territory. In 1874 Helena replaced Virginia City as the capital and the commercial hub of the new territory, and in 1883 the Northern Pacific Railroad linked the state's rich mining towns with the rest of the world. By that time, breweries had been established at Bannack, Billings Blackfoot, Bozeman, Butte, Deer Lodge, Fort Benton,

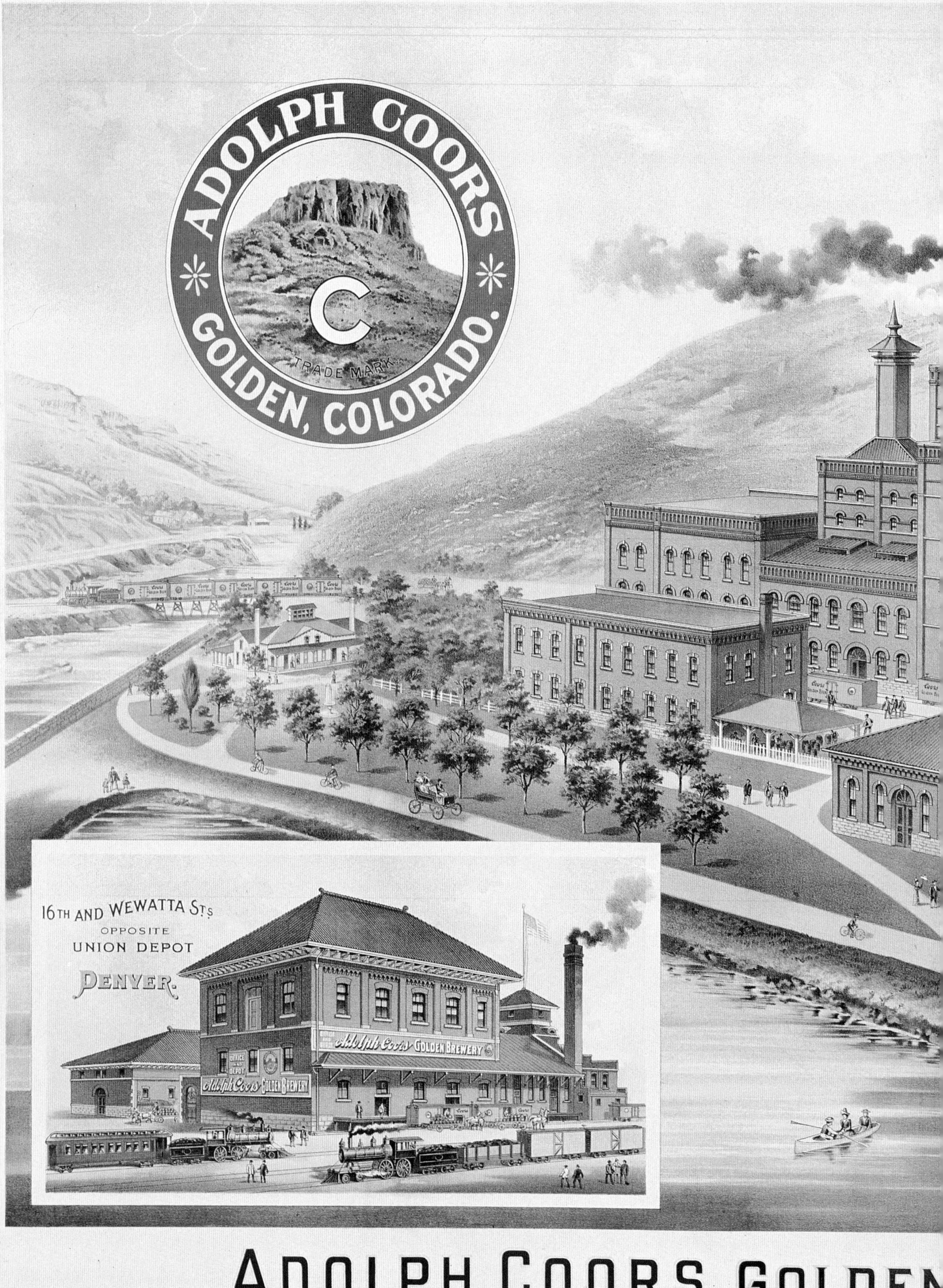

ADOLPH COORS GOLDEN

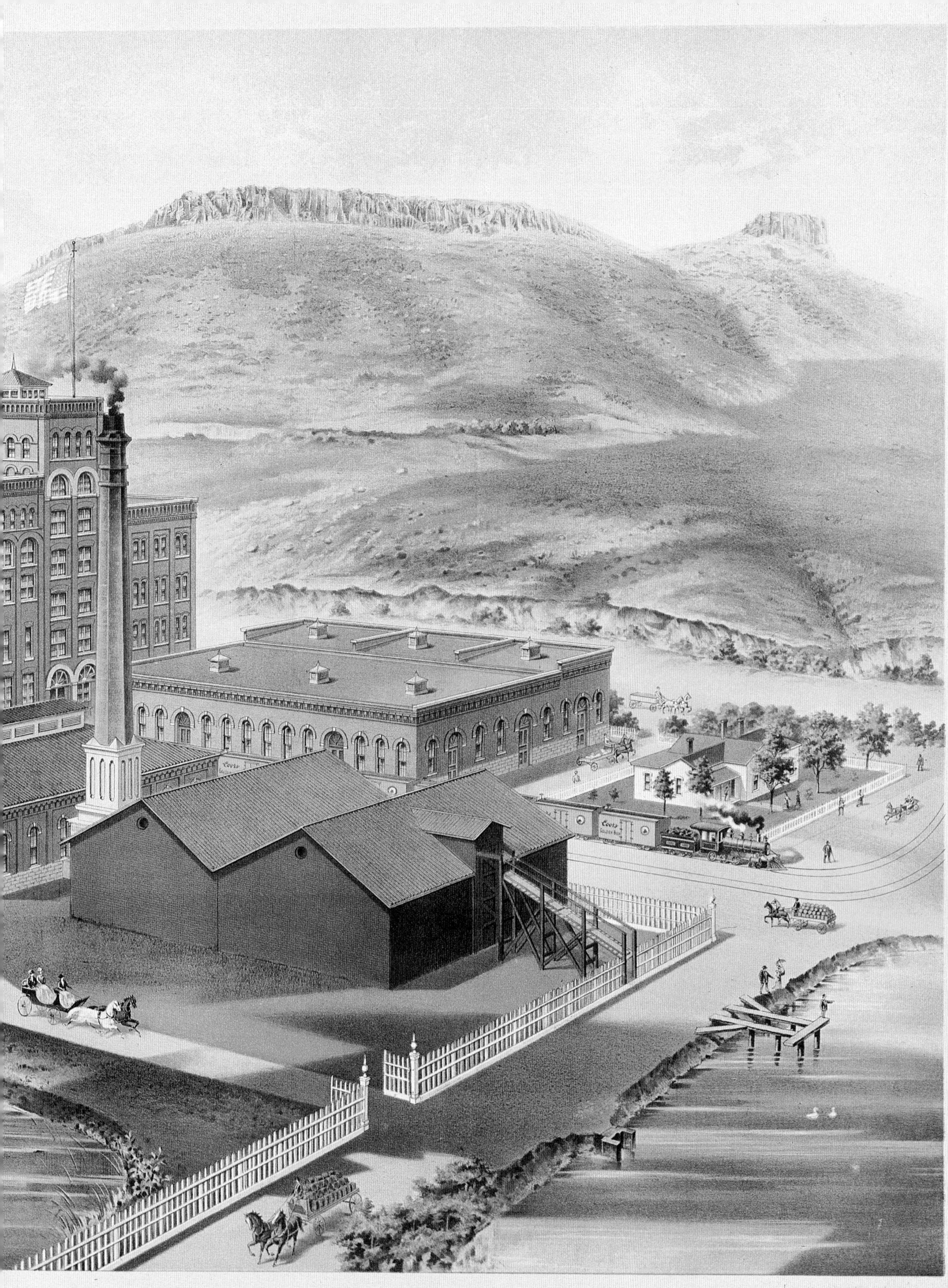

BREWERY, GOLDEN, COLO.

Denver Litho Co. DENVER, COLO.

Nick Kessler *(left)* and his brewery *(below)*. The big fermenting tanks on Norfolk & Western and Seaboard flat cars were brought in from the East Coast as part of Kessler's efforts to remodel and upgrade the plant. He also added the first refrigeration unit to be used in Montana. *Overleaf:* A Kessler brewery wagon around 1927. This single barrel must have been very special.

Glendive, Miles City, Missoula, Philipsburg, Radersburg, Silverbow, Sun River, Townsend and, of course, Helena. It was in Helena that one of Montana's most famous breweries was founded. Started by Charles Beehrer in 1864, it was taken over two years later by an immigrant from Luxemburg named Nicholas Kessler. Nick Kessler turned the enterprise into Montana's finest. In 1886 he built a brand new brewery on the site that included the first refrigeration unit ever used in Montana and the first carbonic acid machine to be installed in any United States brewery. Kessler himself died in 1901, but the brewery survived until 1958.

While Kessler may have been a leading name in nineteenth century Montana brewing, another star shone briefly on the scene in Montana and in Washington. Leopold Schmitt arrived in the Montana boomtown of Butte by way of Deer Lodge, a day's ride to the north, in 1876. Butte, with enormous gold and silver mines in the center of town, was a land of opportunity for anyone who cared to become a purveyor to the thirsty miners, and Schmitt determined that he'd be the first local brewer to cater to the taverns that catered to the tastes of the men who dug the treasure of Butte's self-named 'richest hill on earth.' Schmidt's aptly named Centennial Brewery was Butte's first and a success. Over the next quarter of a century Schmitt also became regionally respected by other brewers. He made a trip to Germany to study brewing technique (something few immigrant brewers did), and re-

KESSLER BREWING CO.
N. & W.
32024
SEABOARD

KESSLER
BR'W'G. CO.

turned to Montana with a new wife at his side.

By the mid-1890s Schmitt's travels took him to Washington where he discovered the natural artesian water of the little town of Tumwater near the state capital of Olympia, south of Seattle. Here, in 1896, he founded the Capital Brewing Company. Schmitt's Centennial Brewery eventually closed its doors in 1918, never to survive Prohibition and Butte's waning mineral wealth, but the Capital Brewery (remained Olympia Brewing Company in 1902) returned after Prohibition to become one of the West's leading lager brewers.

It may or may not be a coincidence that the only Indian tribe in the United States known to have brewed beer before the arrival of the white man was also the last tribe to finally surrender to the white man. Thanks to Geronimo, the Apaches in Arizona were able to maintain their ancient lifestyle past 1890, the year that Congress declared as the 'end of the frontier.' Against this backdrop it is interesting that commercial brewing arrived in Arizona as early as it did. It is also interesting that aboriginal *tesguino* maize beer brewing may have taken place in Arizona at the same time as relatively modern lager brewing. The first commercial brewery in Arizona was Tucson's Pioneer Brewery which was started by Alex Levin in 1866 and operated by him with a succession of partners until 1872 when it was renamed the Park Brewery. The Park Brewery was operated until 1880 by Alex and Zenona Levin when it was sold. Over the next six years the Park Brewery changed hands six times before finally going out of business.

Other early brewing ventures in the Grand Canyon State were Abe Peeples' Magnolia Brewery in Wickenburg (1868–1871) and two Prescott breweries which, like the Pioneer/Park brewery in Tucson, went through an unusual number of ownership changes. These were the Arizona Brewery started by John Littig in 1868 which changed hands eight times through 1885 and the Pacific Brewery in which founder

Right: **The bottlewashing crew at the Kessler Brewing Co in Helena, Montana in the early 1900s, after electric power became available in the state. Note the filled bottles at the lower left.**

NATIONAL BREWERY.
CHAS.

Below: Charles Hansen's National Brewery at the corner of Webster and Fulton streets in San Francisco was built in 1865, ten years after the brewery was established.

John Raible changed partners five times between 1867 and 1890.

The story of brewing in Montana or Arizona during the years between the Civil War and Prohibition was typical of brewing throughout the West as a whole. Most small breweries came and went in the space of less than a decade. Of the hundreds of breweries that each had its brief shining (or tarnished) hour on the stage of American brewing history in the nineteenth century west of Texas, only Olympia, Blitz-Weinhard and Coors became major modern breweries. Of the cities in the West that boasted a group of competing breweries in its nineteenth-century heyday, only one became an important twentieth-century American brewing center, and that one was also the first: San Francisco.

BREWING IN SAN FRANCISCO

The City by the Golden Gate has always been a city of hard-working people who thoroughly enjoy the rewards of their hard work. Unlike any American city since perhaps Jamestown, San Francisco grew to maturity isolated from the rest of the world and thus developed its own traditions and its own economic infrastructure independent of any other center. Its nearest neighboring American city was several months and several thousand miles away by ship. By the time the transcontinental railroad was completed in 1869, San Francisco was a major self-sufficient and self-reliant metropolis.

The first beer came to San Francisco in the holds of ships that had carried it from the East around Cape Horn. This beer, which had en route crossed the equator twice and been subjected to freezing temperatures in between, was hardly fresh, and the means of its delivery were hardly reliable. As with other things, San Franciscans decided that local beer demand required a local supplier. The first to answer this demand may have been William 'Billy the Brewer' McGlore, who is said to have been brewing beer in San Francisco as early as 1837. Though records of this first 'Billy' beer are sketchy, the 1849 gold rush provided the catalyst for Adam Schuppert's brewery at Stockton and Jackson streets which

Above: **The Philadelphia Brewery, founded by John Weiland in 1856, was located at 228-246 Second Street in San Francisco.**

is recorded as being California's, and the West's, first commercial brewery. The choice of this site near Portsmouth Square was ideal because the square was the commercial hub of San Francisco and home to more taverns than existed in some entire western territories. Another brewery which opened its doors in 1849, and perhaps even sooner, was William Bull's Empire Brewery at Mission and Second streets. These were followed in 1850 by John Neep's California Brewery at Powell and Vallejo.

By 1856, when many territories had yet to see the founding of their first brewery, the city of San Francisco had 15 commercial breweries in operation, most of them in the area which today is the site of the city's financial district. Included were those of Ambrose Carner on Sacramento Street and of G F Joseph on California Street. In its history, San Francisco has had roughly 80 breweries, more than most entire states, and more than most American cities including even Milwaukee.

Some of San Francisco's notable early breweries included those started by Charles Wilmot in 1856 on Telegraph Hill and John Wieland's Philadelphia Brewery established on Second Street during the same year. Called simply the John Wieland Brewing Company after 1887, the firm survived until 1920 and the eve of Prohibition, but an attempted revival in 1934 failed. Farther from the center of the city was the intriguing American Railroad Brewery on Valencia Street near 15th which was started in 1858 by Thomas Pfether and which merged with the Union Brewing and Malting Company in 1902. The latter grew out of the brewery started by Albert Koster in 1854 and which was finally disbanded in 1916.

In 1858, a 30-year-old German immigrant and Second Street grocer named Claus Spreckels started the Albany Brewery at 71–75 Everett Street. It was the first major business venture by the man who later went on to control the Hawaiian sugar trade and much of the Pacific shipping trade. By 1877 when the 'Sugar King' sold his Albany Brewery to F Hagemenn, Spreckels was one of the richest men in the West. Hagemann's Albany Brewery went on to survive at 271 Natoma Street and later at 405–415 Eighth Street until 1920.

In the 1860s, two breweries were started in San Francisco which changed hands a number of times, but which because of their size evolved into major city landmarks over the next 100 years. The first of these was the National Brewery established by John Glueck and Charles Hansen at Fulton and Webster streets near San Francisco's city hall. The firm operated under its original name until 1916 and under the California Brewing name until it closed in 1958, except during the Prohibition era (1923–1936) when it was known as the Cereal Products Refining Corporation. The brewery was best known, however, for the brand name Acme, kept alive by Blitz-Weinhard until the late 1970s.

The second of San Francisco's really big breweries was started by O Lurman in 1868 as the Bay Brewery at 612–616 Seventh Street. In deference to the city that was making beer famous, Lurmann in 1880 renamed his company the Milwaukee Brewery, a name that it retained until 1920 and for two years after its post-Prohibition revival. It is curious to note here that whereas midwestern and eastern brewers of the era often named their breweries after places in Germany and central

Vintage nineteenth-century brewhouse equipment from San Francisco's Anchor Brewery. The malt mill *(above)* readied the malt for mashing, and the device *(above right)* capped the filled kegs. The gauge told the pressure in the keg, which would increase as the beer continued to ferment. The sturdy oak kegs *(below)* were banded with iron straps. Empty they could weigh 100 pounds.

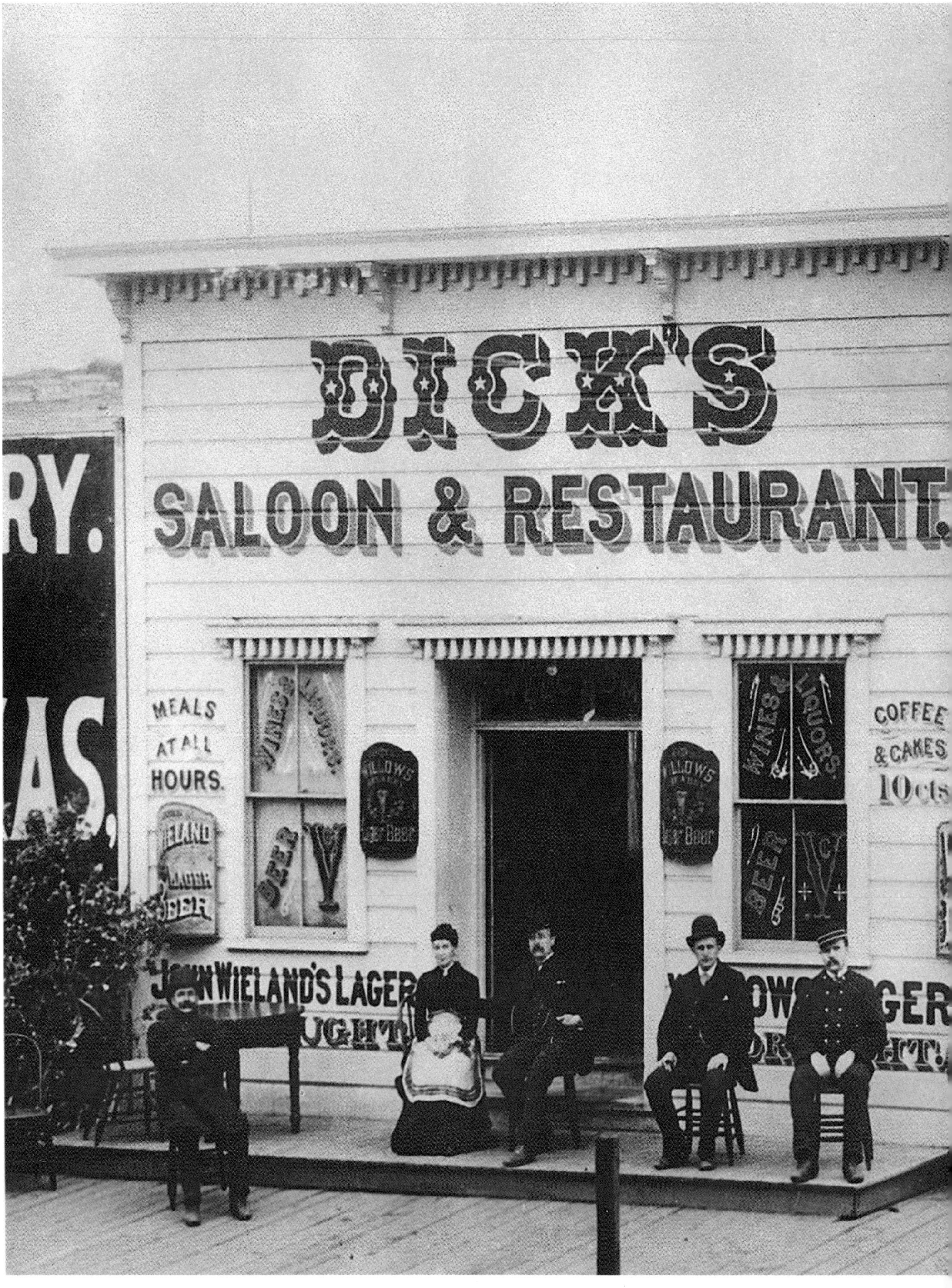
DICK'S
SALOON & RESTAURANT.
MEALS AT ALL HOURS.
WINES & LIQUORS
BEER
COFFEE & CAKES 10cts
Lager Beer
JOHN WIELAND'S LAGER

Dick's, at 43rd and Point Lobos, was one of San Francisco's original 24-hour restaurants and it featured the lager of the Willows and Wieland breweries. The Broadway Brewery's steam beer *(right)* was another San Francisco favorite.

Europe, San Francisco brewers often named their firms after places in the East and Midwest. In addition to Philadelphia, Albany and Milwaukee breweries, nineteenth-century San Francisco boasted breweries named after Chicago, Jackson, New York and St Louis.

In 1935 The Milwaukee Brewery finally adopted the city where it was born and the big white building on Tenth Street where the brewery had moved in 1891 became the San Francisco Brewing Corporation. This name was retained until 1956 when it became the Burgermeister Brewing Corporation, which in turn became a division of first the Joseph Schlitz empire (1961–1969) and then of Meister Brau of Chicago (1969–1971). The building then became a Falstaff brewery until the doors were closed in 1978.

When the forty-niners arrived in San Francisco en route to the gold fields they brought with them the ales, porters and lagers they had enjoyed at home. When the first brewers arrived in San Francisco around 1849 they realized that it would be virtually impossible to brew lager. Lager brewing requires fermentation at temperatures very near freezing. Such temperatures were taken for granted in Milwaukee and Chicago where ice could be harvested in the winter and stored through the summer. In San Francisco it can get very cold. Ironically the summer

WIELANDS
WIELANDS
WIELANDS
John Wieland's
Extra Pale
John Wieland Brewery
BREWERY'S OWN BOTTLING
Wieland's
BREWERY'S OWN BOTTLING

John Wieland *(above)* established the Philadelphia Brewery in 1856 and renamed it the John Wieland Brewery in 1893. The Wieland drivers *(left)* pose for a photo sometime before Prohibition.

months are the coldest because of ocean fog, but the temperature almost never dips below freezing. Practical artificial ice-making would not be commonplace for nearly 20 years and it was almost that long before a railroad linked the city and the ice fields of the high Sierra Nevada. Ice could be brought in by ship from Alaska, but that was very expensive.

San Francisco's early brewmasters solved the problem in a logical way. They began the brewing process the same way as they would have brewed lager. They even used bottom fermenting lager yeast. Once it was brewed, however, the wort was fermented in large shallow pans at San Francisco's year round median temperature of roughly 60 degrees rather than in tanks and fermented at near-freezing temperatures. The resultant product lacked the sparkling carbonation characteristic of a lager because the open fermentation allowed the carbon dioxide to escape. This flat beer was then pumped into kegs where fermentation was allowed to continue. When the kegs were tapped the carbonation that had built up with the kegs escaped in what appeared to be cloud of steam. This is perhaps what led San Franciscans to call this unique creation 'steam beer.' In the 1850s and 1860s steam beer was extremely popular in San Francisco and throughout the West. A thirsty patron ordered beer simply by asking the bartender for 'glass of

Below: Staff and patrons assembled for a group photograph in front of San Francisco's famous '7 Mile House,' notable for its hot steam clams and cold steam beer. *Far right:* An assortment of vintage keg taps from the Anchor Brewing collection.

steam.' By the late 1870s, however, artificial refrigeration was introduced and lager brewing at last became possible in the West. For a time many brewers brewed both lager and steam since the latter was cheaper to produce. Gradually the steam beer brewing art died, disappearing like the cloud of vapor escaping from a newly tapped keg.

No recipe for steam beer is known to exist, but it was certainly more complicated than just a beer brewed with lager yeast and fermented at any median temperature. When Prohibition ended only one brewery reopened making what it called steam beer. The Anchor Brewery, founded in San Francisco in 1896, reopened to a market that had forgotten steam beer. By that time the precise definition of steam beer, if it had ever existed, was forgotten as well. The Anchor Brewery struggled along for another 30 years until 1965, when it was snatched from the brink of bankruptcy by appliance heir Fritz Maytag. The young Maytag reintroduced quality control and the notion of using only pure barley malt to produce the wort. He took what little was known about the idea of steam beer, refined it and made it his own. Over the next two decades he turned the dilapidated Anchor Brewery into a showplace. He took a beer of inconsistent quality and turned it into a highly prized premium product. In so doing he built a landmark small American brewery and molded the elusive legend of steam beer into his own trademark. Whatever 'steam beer' meant in the days of the California gold rush, after Maytag it meant Anchor Steam Beer.

BREWING IN CALIFORNIA

San Francisco quickly became the brewing capital of the West, but it was not California's only brewing city. Sacramento, the state capital, probably had some brewing activity during the 1849 gold rush, and by 1859 Hilbert & Borchers had established what evolved into the City Brewery in 1865 and survived until 1920. Los Angeles didn't really become a brewing town until after Prohibition, but Joseph Leiber, Henry Lemmert, Louis Schwartz and Ed Preuss are all recorded as active brewers briefly during the 1874 to 1879 period.

While many California towns had breweries by the 1870s, several breweries had come even earlier, such as those of Joseph Hartman in San Jose (1851), Frederick Walter in Weaverville (1852), Gottlieb Lieber in Marysville (1854), Bush and Denlacker in Stockton (1855), Samuel and Frank Daiser in Auburn (1855), Gottfried 'Fred' Krahenberg in San Jose (1856), Gottfried Gamble in Yreka (1858) and John Bauman in the Sierra Nevada gold town of Sonora (1866).

BREWING IN ALASKA

As with California, it took a gold rush to spark economic development in Alaska, but unlike California, Alaska's harsh climate prevented any significant economic growth until late in the twentieth century. The gold rush in Alaska and in Canada's neighboring Yukon

Continued on page 77

BREWERY CLOSE-UP

A SMALL AMERICAN BREWER

ANCHOR BREWING COMPANY

Right: The Anchor Brewing Company was born on San Francisco's Potrero Hill in 1896, but it moved to the city's South of Market Street industrial district after Prohibition. The brewery was on Eighth Street and also on the verge of collapse when Fritz Maytag bought it in 1965. In 1979, Maytag moved Anchor into new quarters, a former coffee roasting plant, back on Potrero Hill.

Above: The Anchor hop room, chilled to retain the freshness of the hops. Anchor uses only air-dried hops from Germany, Czechoslovakia and Washington's Yakima Valley.

Below: The elegant copper vessels in the Anchor brewhouse were built by Ziemann in Germany and once graced a small Karlsruhe brewery. The brewhouse has a 110-barrel daily capacity, double that of Anchor's Eighth Street brewhouse. *Left to right,* in order of use, are the mash tun, the lauter tun and the brew kettle.

Above: Breweries traditionally have used copper brewing vessels because they provide even heat. In the mash tun crushed barley malt is mixed with warm water and gradually warmed to 170° as starches in the malt turn to fermentable and unfermentable sugars. Anchor prides itself on being an 'all-malt' brewery. Except for the malted German wheat they import for their wheat beer, Anchor uses only malted two-row barley, grown in Washington and malted in California.

BREWERY CLOSE-UP

Above: After being filtered in the lauter tun, the wort trickles through the grant, a trough with adjustable spigots, where it is aerated and checked for clarity.

Right: The lauter tun serves as a gravity filtration system; the husks from the malted barley form a porous filter bed.

Below: After the lauter tun, the wort is placed in the copper brew kettle where it is boiled for 90 minutes. During this time a blend of fresh hops (in yellow barrels, *left*) will be added. The hops are carefully blended to provide the precise mix of aroma and bitterness required for the distinctive taste of each Anchor product.

Above: After cooling, wort that will become Anchor Steam Beer is placed in the unusual, wide, shallow stainless steel fermenting pans. Bottom-fermenting lager yeast is then 'pitched' into the wort and fermentation begins.

Anchor Steam Beer is fermented at between 60°F and 72°F, the typical year-round San Francisco temperature. If it were to get hotter, the automatic refrigeration system would be used. The large surface area of the pans helps to keep the temperature uniform.

Anchor's ales are fermented in much deeper open stainless steel tanks using top-fermenting ale yeasts.

Above: Anchor's copper brewing vessels are cleaned frequently to keep them sparkling clean inside and out.

Left: The initial fermentation process yields a 'big tub of flat beer,' which is placed into large closed stainless steel tanks where the beer is 'krausened,' or naturally carbonated, by the old German method. A few days after it is placed in the tanks, fresh still-fermenting beer is added to the original batch. For the next several weeks the fermentation continues in an environment of gradually increasing pressure, as the yeast continues to produce carbon dioxide.

The krausening of the beer produces a finer bubble and better bonding between beer and carbon dioxide, which gives Anchor Steam Beer its characteristic rich creaminess and longer-lasting head.

Below: During bottling, Anchor uses special techniques and quick handling to avoid exposing the beer to air.

KOTTE
BUCKEYE BREWERY
CINCINNATI, O

Territory began in the mid-1880s, 35 years after the forty-niners poured into California. Like the forty-niners, the followers of Alaska's gold rush brought a taste for beer, but unlike California's early brewers, the first Alaskan brewers had no trouble finding an adequate supply of ice for lager brewing.

The first brewery in Alaska was established in Juneau by Abraham Cohen about 1870. In 1874, with two partners, he opened a second brewery in Sitka. These two establishments on Alaska's southern panhandle were the territory's only breweries for over a decade, but the gold rush also brought a rush of brewers to the frozen north. Between 1888 and 1906, 32 breweries were started in 15 Alaskan towns, but most were short-lived. Many survived less than a year. By 1919 and the eve of Prohibition, only four Alaskan breweries remained in Fairbanks, Nome, Valdez and Juneau. Both of the original Cohen breweries were gone by 1904.

After Prohibition, none of the earlier breweries reopened, but three new ones started up. The Fairbanks Brewing Association and the Pioneer Brewing company opened their doors in 1934 in Fairbanks and the Pilsener Brewing Company of Alaska began brewing in Ketchikan the following year. Fairbanks Brewing survived for only one year, but the other two continued until 1942 when the shortages of materials that accompanied the Second World War forced them out of business. The only other Alaskan brewery to open since Prohibition was Prinz Brau Alaska, which operated in Anchorage between 1976 and 1979 at the end of the North Slope oil boom.

THE MAKING OF A MAJOR REGIONAL BREWERY

Most of the major brewers who emerged as national powers in the last years of the nineteenth century and went on to dominate American brewing in the twentieth century trace their origins to the era prior to the Civil War. However, a number of breweries started in the late 1800s survived as major regional breweries. A good example is the Hudepohl Brewery in Cincinnati. This city in the fertile Ohio River valley had attracted a large number

Left: **Ludwig Hudepohl at the St Aloysius Orphanage festival c 1900. The tent had a sign that read: 'Alive within the rail, Where the head is, Ought to be the tail.' Festivalgoers paid a dime to enter only to find a horse with his tail at the feed trough. Hudepohl gave everyone a stein of beer to soften the joke.** ***Above:*** **Ludwig Hudepohl's display ad for the Buckeye Brewery, placed between 1885 and 1900 and believed to be the company's earliest.**

of German settlers who by 1850 accounted for 77 percent of the city's population. Their German taste for lager invited German brewers. In 1848, there were 11 brewers in Cincinnati and 12 years later there were 36. During this time, such big names of early Cincinnati brewing as John Hauch, Herman Lackman and Christian Moerlin were just getting started. Moerlin's brewery, in fact, enjoyed a brief national reputation and survived four years after Prohibition as the Old Munich Brewing Company.

Most of Cincinnati's brewers were content to remain regional; because of the area's large German population, they could do so with comfortable success. It was in 1885 that Ludwig Hudepohl and George Kotte acquired the Koehler brothers' Buckeye Brewery (founded in 1852) on Buckeye Street. Their timing was perfect, because by the 1890s the people of Cincinnati were drinking more beer per capita than the people of any other city in the country; when the per capita national average was 16 gallons, the people of Cincinnati were drinking 40. German-style beer gardens abounded and there were over 1800 saloons in town. George Kotte died in 1893, and in 1900 his widow sold his share to Ludwig 'Louis' Hudepohl II, the son of Kotte's former partner. Louis Hudepohl II promptly renamed the brewery the Hudepohl Brewing Company and introduced his Golden Jubilee brand which became popular throughout Kentucky and Indiana as well as Ohio. Before his death in 1902 at the age of 59, the enterprising younger Hudepohl gained a reputation as quite a character. His regional marketing success aside, his notoriety as a practical joker rivaled that of P T Barnum. At the St Aloysius Orphanage Festival in 1900, for example, he set up a tent marked with a sign reading 'Alive within the rail, where the head is, ought to be a tail.' Expecting to see some bizarre freak of nature, many people paid 10 cents to peek into the tent only to find a horse standing with its tail over a feeding trough. Once duped, the embarrassed or irate Cincinnatians were each treated to a cold mug of Hudepohl by the brewery's proprietor.

Like many German-American institutions, the Hudepohl Brewery suffered in the anti-German backlash of the First World War era besides the disaster of Prohibition and the depression. Unlike most of its contemporaries, the Hudepohl firm not only survived but flourished and remains today a major American regional brewer.

BREWING AT THE TURN OF THE CENTURY

The history of American brewing in the nineteenth century can be broken into five 20-year periods. The first two periods (1800–1840) saw the general decline of brewing, followed by a period of very little brewing activity, the establishment of Yuengling in 1829 notwithstanding. The third period (1840–1860) saw the rise of German-style lager brewing and an increase in the number of breweries. The fourth period (1860–1880) saw a tremendous brewing boom from coast to coast, with more new breweries established throughout the United States than at any other period in history. Between 1860 and 1873 the United States went from 1269 to 4131 breweries.

The final two decades of the nineteenth century and the first decade of the twentieth was a period of consolidation and merging. This era saw fewer and fewer breweries producing more and more beer. The record number of 4131 breweries in 1873 produced 9 million barrels of beer. In 1910, 1568 breweries produced 53 million barrels. This meant that the average brewer of 1910 produced 15 times as much beer as his counterpart of 37 years before.

The last decades of the nineteenth century saw both the collapse of many small breweries and for the first time the rise of major national brands. Making this possible were such innovations as salt brine artificial ice-making and a network of railroads that had spread across both the United States and Canada in the years following the American Civil War. Between 1865 and 1890 railroad mileage in the United States increased from 35,085 to 163,597, a fivefold increase in just 25 years. Railroads and ice-making paved the way for the emergence of truly national brewers. Some of the emerging giants even established their own railroads. Joseph Schlitz owned Union Refrigerated Transit Corporation, and Anheuser-Busch set up the Manufacturers Railway Company, a subsidiary which is still going strong 100 years later.

In many other ways, the major brewers became increasingly sophisticated as they discovered the finer points of the art of 'marketing.' Two of the finer points exploited to their fullest potential prior to the last quarter of the nineteenth century were bottling and brand names. Bottling produced a convenient consumer item that permitted a higher retail price than could be asked for an equivalent volume of draft beer. The large-scale adoption of the bottling process was delayed and made difficult for smaller brewers by a federal government law that prohibited brewing and bottling to take place on the same premises. Until the law was repealed in 1890, brewers had to move their product across town to off-site bottling plants, a process that kept many small brewers from competing for the bottled beer market.

While bottling produced a convenient consumer item, brand names helped produce an identity for the item, and an identity helped to generate loyalty to a particular product. Adolphus Busch's Budweiser brand, adopted in 1876, exemplifies a successful brand name. Another is Pabst's Blue Ribbon brand derived from the gold medals won by the brewery at Philadelphia's 1876 Centennial Exposition and the 1893

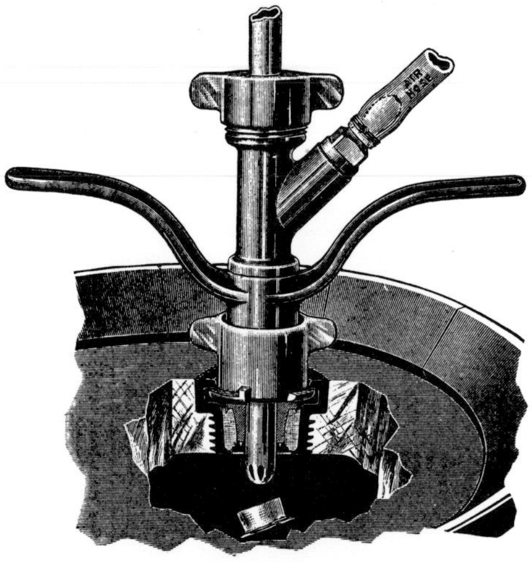

MAGIC BEER TAP IN USE

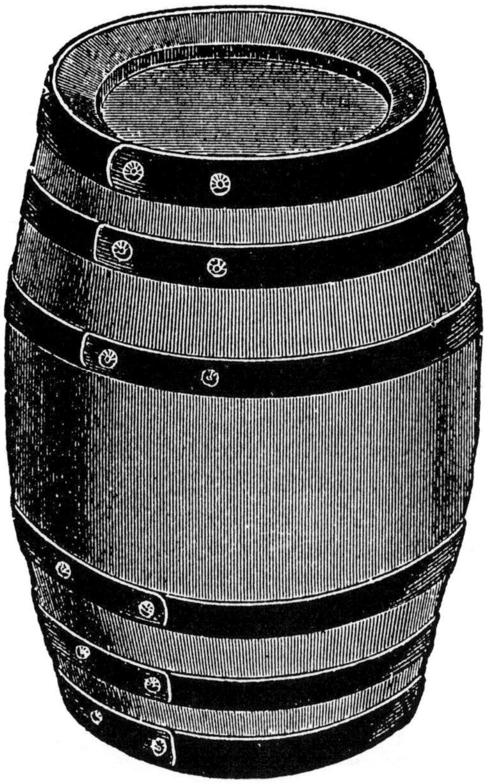

Top, both: **Charles Stolper's cooperage made and repaired wooden casks like the one above. The cutaway drawing shows how the beer tap fits into the keg. Anheuser-Busch's Clydesdale team *(left)* and Pabst's pin-up girl *(right)*. These companies were North America's largest brewers in 1900.**

PABST
MILWAUKEE

Paris World's Fair, as well as its first place showing at Chicago's 1893 Columbian Exposition.

Throughout the American brewing industry, the trend pointed to fewer brewers brewing less beer. Through mergers smaller brewers could pool their resources. In 1889 eighteen St Louis breweries merged in a single firm, and in 1890 six brewers in New Orleans followed suit. In 1901 mergers brought 10 brewers in Boston and 16 in Baltimore into two regional conglomerates. A merger in Pittsburgh is particularly illustrative of the trend: in 1899 and 1905, no fewer than 36 brewers funneled themselves into just two brewing companies—Pittsburgh Brewing and Independent Brewing.

The size of the breweries that survived this era was staggering compared to their predecessors. In 1880, a brewer was considered large if he produced 150,000 barrels annually. By the turn of the century, three brewers (Pabst, Anheuser-Busch and Schlitz) were each brewing a million barrels each year!

By the turn of the century, the United States had surpassed England as the world's second largest brewing nation. Germany was still brewing twice as much beer as the

Continued on page 84

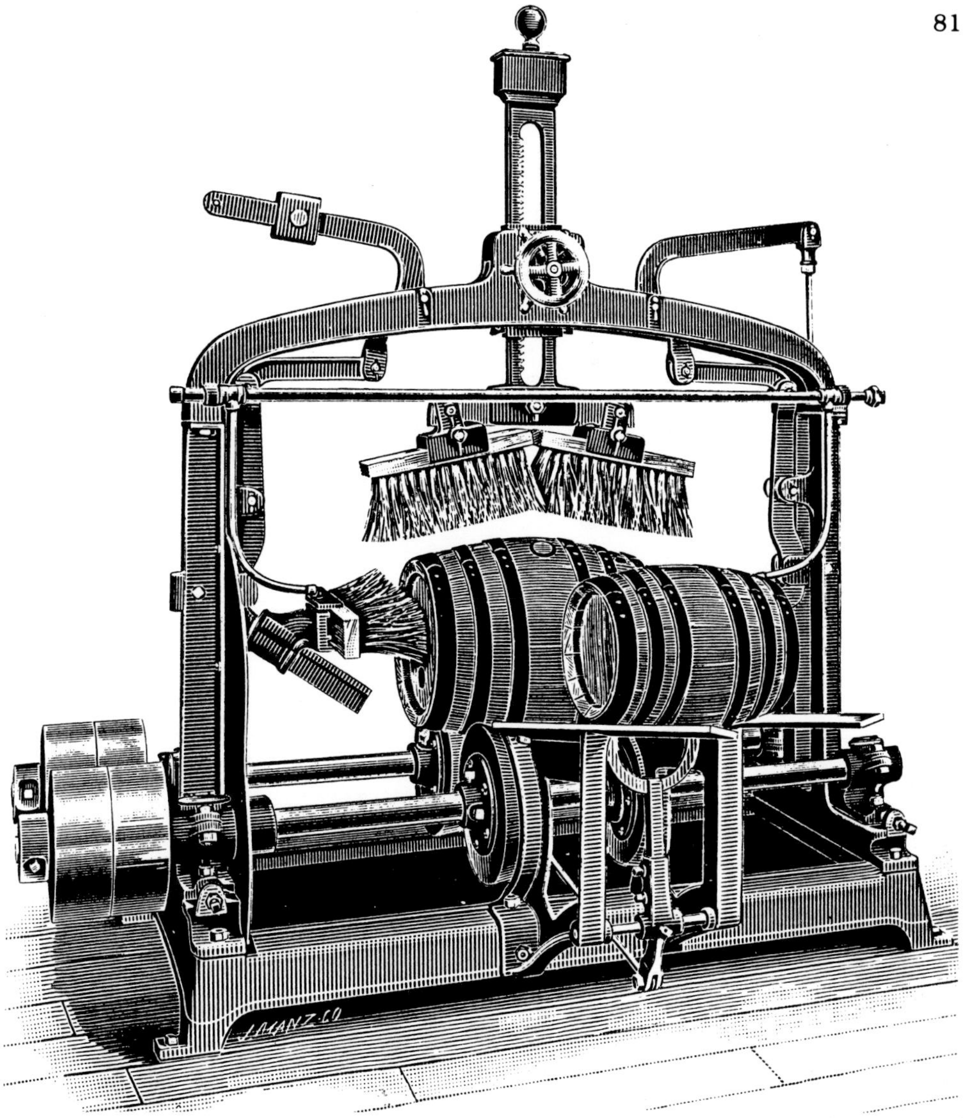

Left: **Pabst was the world's largest brewer by 1900. Its 'dreadnaughts' were brew kettles named after the battleships of the day. The malt extract was boiled in the kettles with the hops. The belt-driven keg scrubber *(above)* cleaned the kegs for reuse.**

Breweries in the United States, 1905

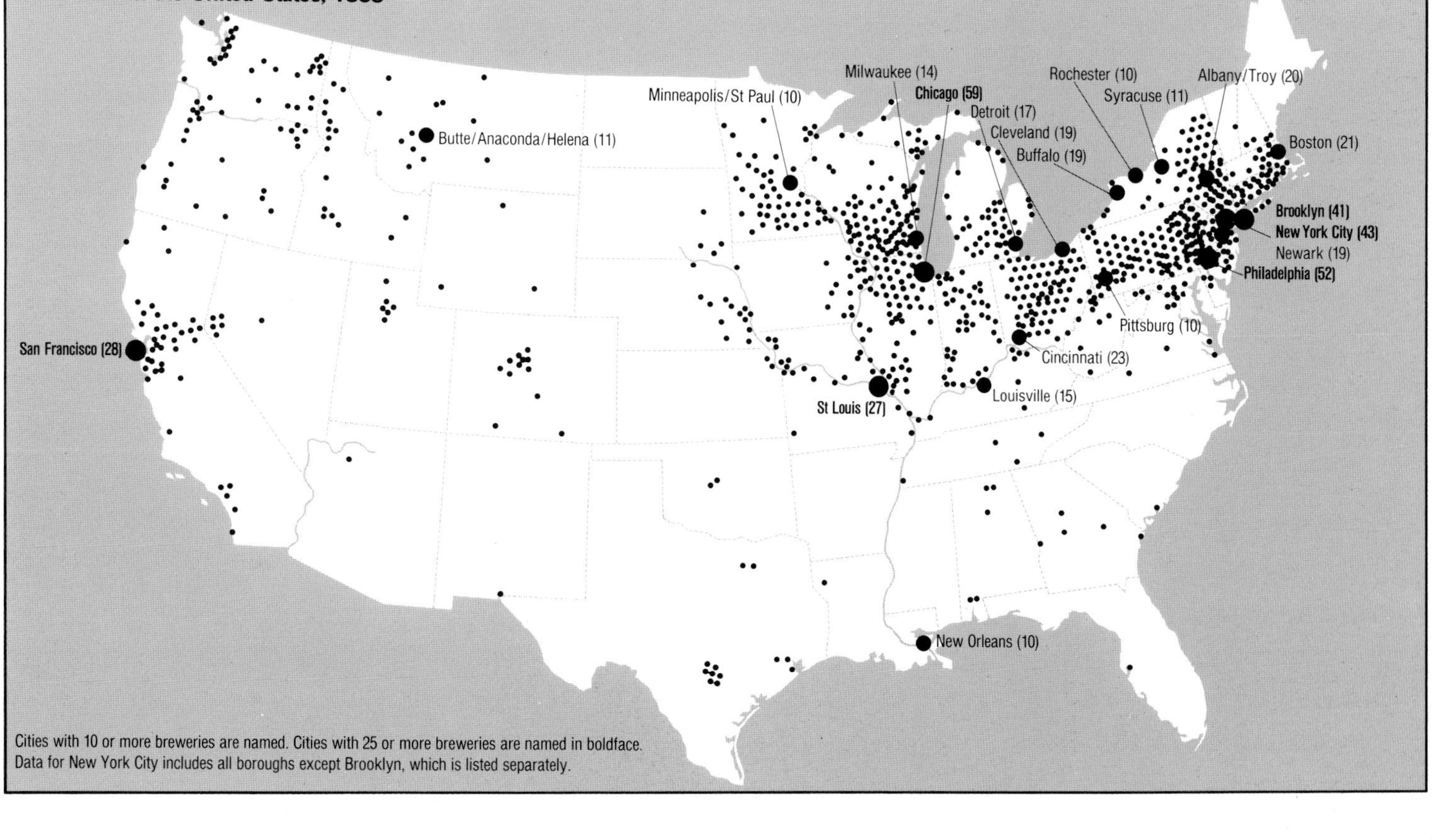

Cities with 10 or more breweries are named. Cities with 25 or more breweries are named in boldface.
Data for New York City includes all boroughs except Brooklyn, which is listed separately.

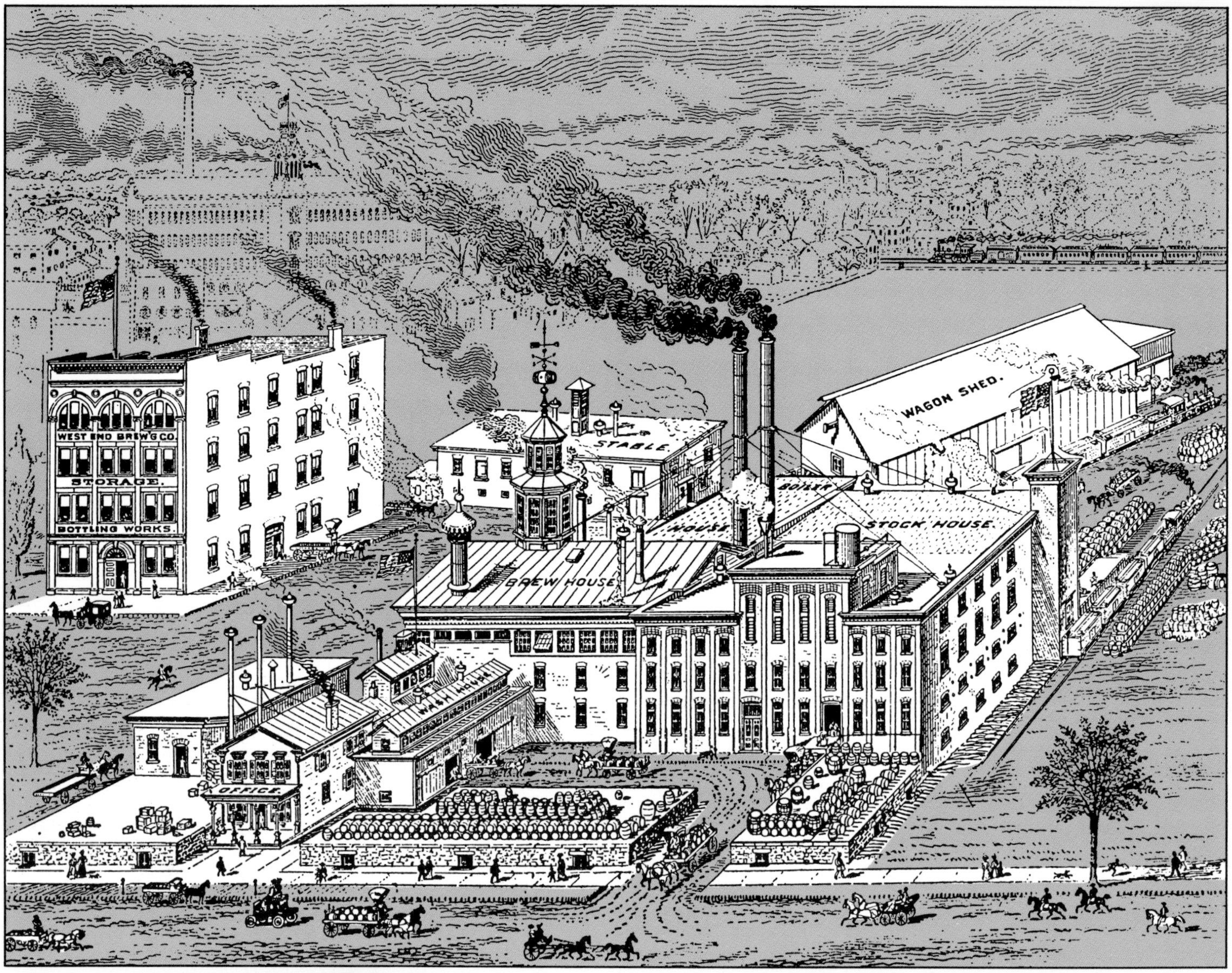

Above: Overall layout of the West End Brewing Company of Utica, New York, a typical North American brewery of 1800s.

Above right: This cutaway shows the layout of that section of a typical brewhouse devoted to the processes that follow mashing and brewing. The vats and casks were still constructed of oak.

Below: Turn-of-the-century brewery equipment includes *(from left)* an improved grader and separator, oak fermeting tanks, a copper brew kettle designed for a smaller-scale brewery than the dreadnaught kettles and a stationary mash machine.

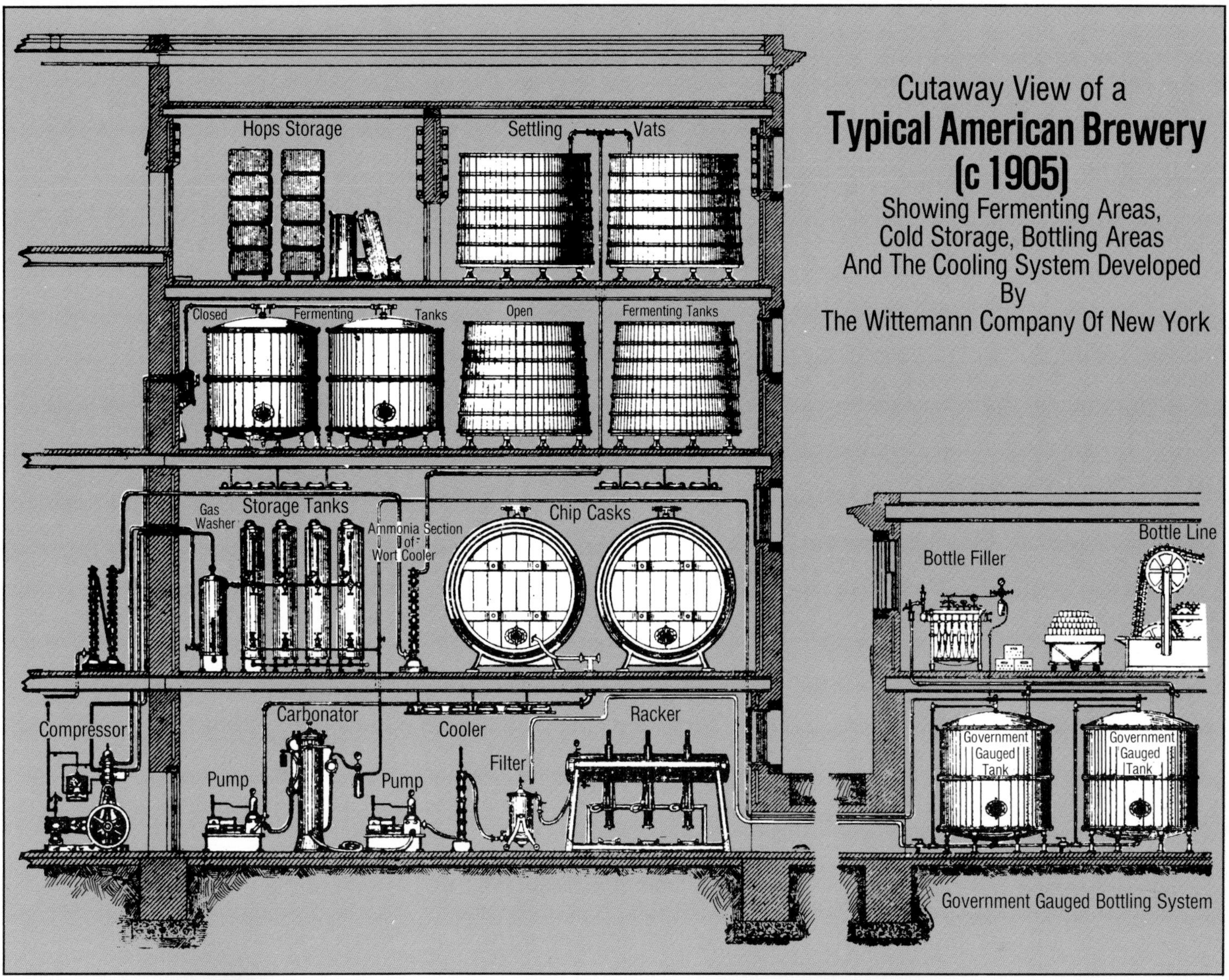
Cutaway View of a
Typical American Brewery
(c 1905)
Showing Fermenting Areas,
Cold Storage, Bottling Areas
And The Cooling System Developed
By
The Wittemann Company Of New York
Hops Storage
Settling
Vats
Closed
Fermenting
Tanks
Open
Fermenting Tanks
Gas Washer
Storage Tanks
Ammonia Section of Wort Cooler
Chip Casks
Bottle Filler
Bottle Line
Compressor
Carbonator
Cooler
Racker
Filter
Pump
Pump
Government Gauged Tank
Government Gauged Tank
Government Gauged Bottling System

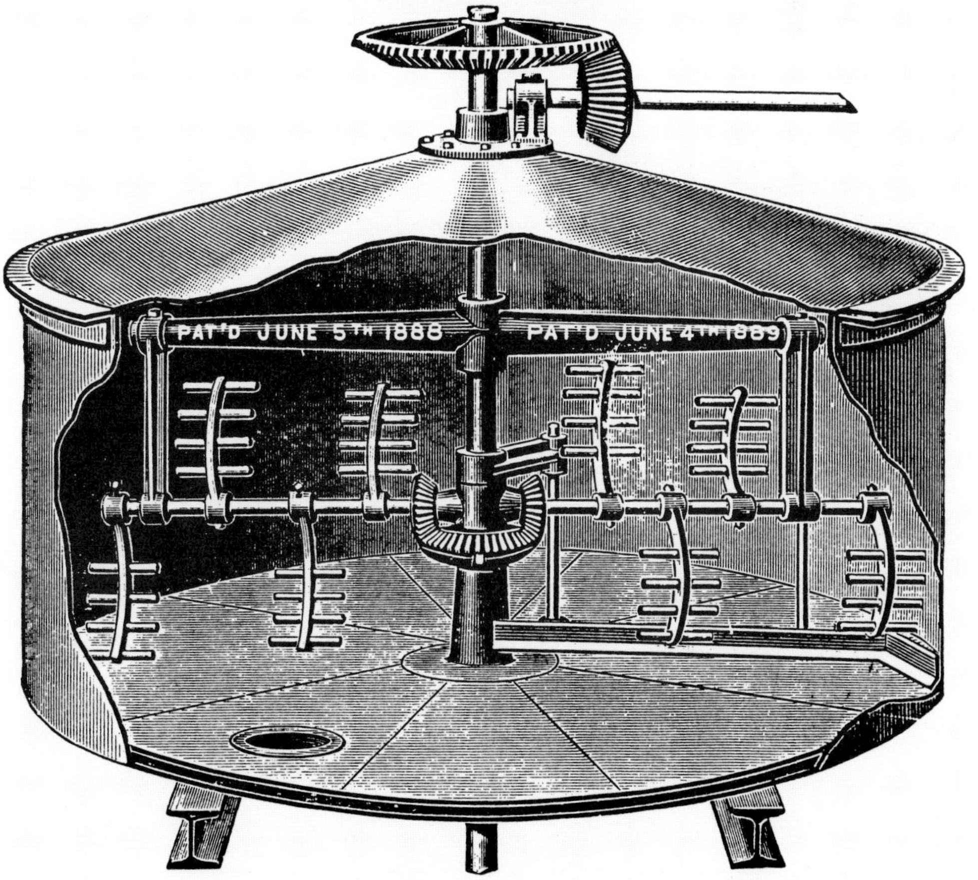
PAT'D JUNE 5TH 1888
PAT'D JUNE 4TH 1889

United States, but only one of its brewers, Schultheiss in Berlin, was in the million-barrel class of America's big three. At that time, Spaten, the largest of the Munich brewers, was brewing 600,000 barrels and Burgerliches Brauhaus at Pilsen in Bohemia was brewing 842,000 barrels of the original Pilsner (Pilsner Urquell). In 1900 Brauberechtigte Burger at Budweis in Bohemia was brewing 121,000 barrels of the original Budweiser while, notably, Anheuser-Busch was brewing eight times that much of the American Budweiser.

BREWING IN MEXICO

North American brewing began in Mexico, first with the Indians and then with the first Spanish brewery or *cervecería* established there in the 1500s. In the ensuing three centuries, however, Mexican tastes paralleled those of Spain just as American tastes paralleled those of England, and this meant an inclination toward wine and distilled spirits such as *mescal* and *tequila* rather than beer (cerveza). There was also *pulque*, a fermented beverage favored in the nineteenth century by Mexican peasants. Even through an influx of German immigrants in the mid-nineteenth century, the tropical nature of much of Mexico prevented the brewing of lager until the latter part of the century when artificial ice-making technology became widely available.

By the turn of the century Mexico had 29 breweries, over half of them brewing lager. The remaining relatively small breweries brewed *sencilla* or *corriente* beer which was similar to lager but fermented for a shorter period of time. Unlike the United States and Canada, most beer sold in Mexico around the turn of the century was bottled rather than put into kegs. A good deal of beer was imported from the United States which probably helps explain the rapid conversion from brown beer to lager in the 1890s. With the exception of the Toluca Brewery near Mexico City and La Perla Brewery in Guadalajara, the major Mexican breweries themselves imported their malt from north of the border.

Above: **Santiago Graf introduced lager brewing to Mexico.** ***Right:*** **A technician checks the storage tanks at the Moctezuma brewery in Guadalajara. Here, beer is aged and readied for bottling.**

The first Mexican breweries of modern times were founded in Mexico City prior to 1845—the Pila Seca founded by Bernhard Bolgard of Switzerland and the Candelaria started by the Bavarian immigrant Frederick Herzog. These breweries survived until the 1880s brewing beer with sun-dried Mexican barley and brown sugar. The quality of these products was unable to measure up to that of lager, which was being brewed in substantial quantities by that time. The arrival of lager brewing in Mexico can be traced to the winter of 1884–85 when the first rail line was opened between Mexico City and El Paso, Texas. One of the first consignments brought south over the new steel was an ice-making machine bound for the Toluca Brewery of Santiago Graf, who had imported the first ice-making machine to Mexico just two years before. The Toluca Brewery, 20 miles from Mexico City, had been started by Augustin Marendaz, late of Switzerland, in 1865 and was acquired by Graf in 1875. Santiago Graf had already established a reputation for brewing a high-quality ale and his new ice machines helped him branch into the field of lager brewing. Lager brewing, in turn, helped Graf to become one of Mexico's largest and most successful brewers. By the turn of the century, he had a glass factory in Toluca, branches in several other cities and a second brewery in Oaxaca. The second Mexican brewer to convert his production from ale to lager was Juan Ohrner, proprietor of the Cervecería La Perla in Guadalajara.

In 1891, the first Mexican cervecería to be built as a lager brewery was opened in Monterey. The Cervecería Cuauhtemoc, which was

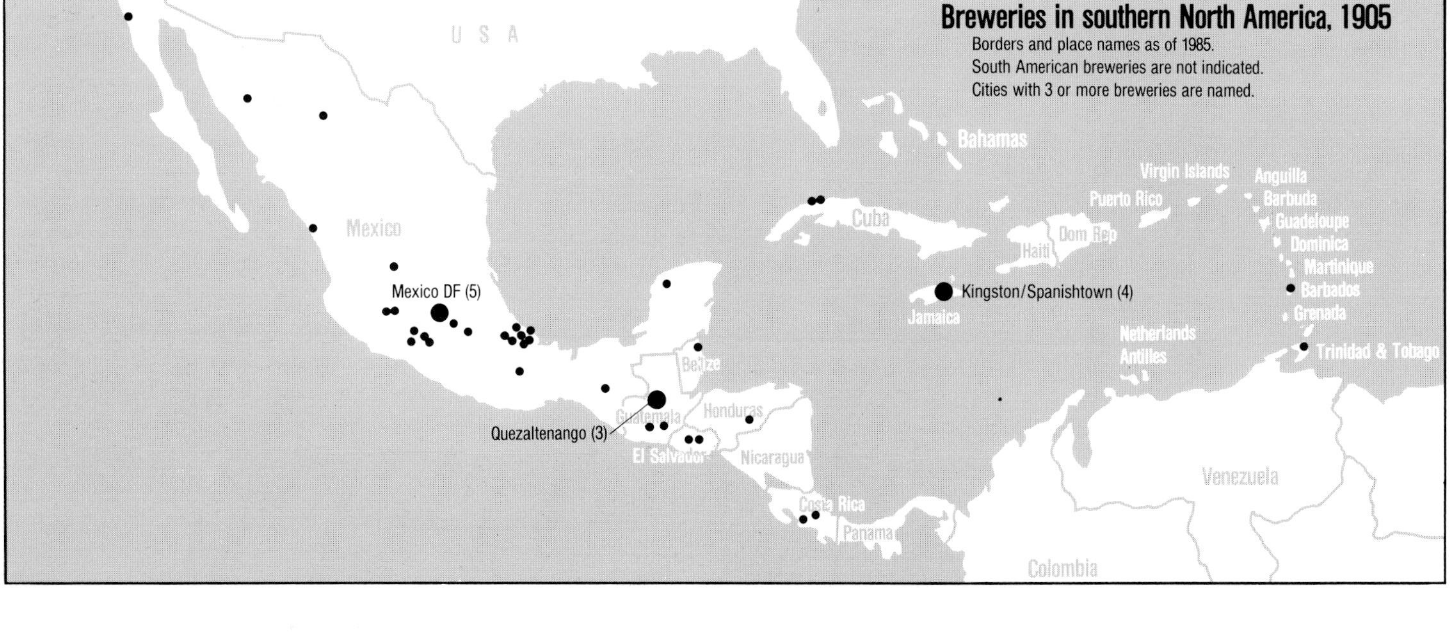

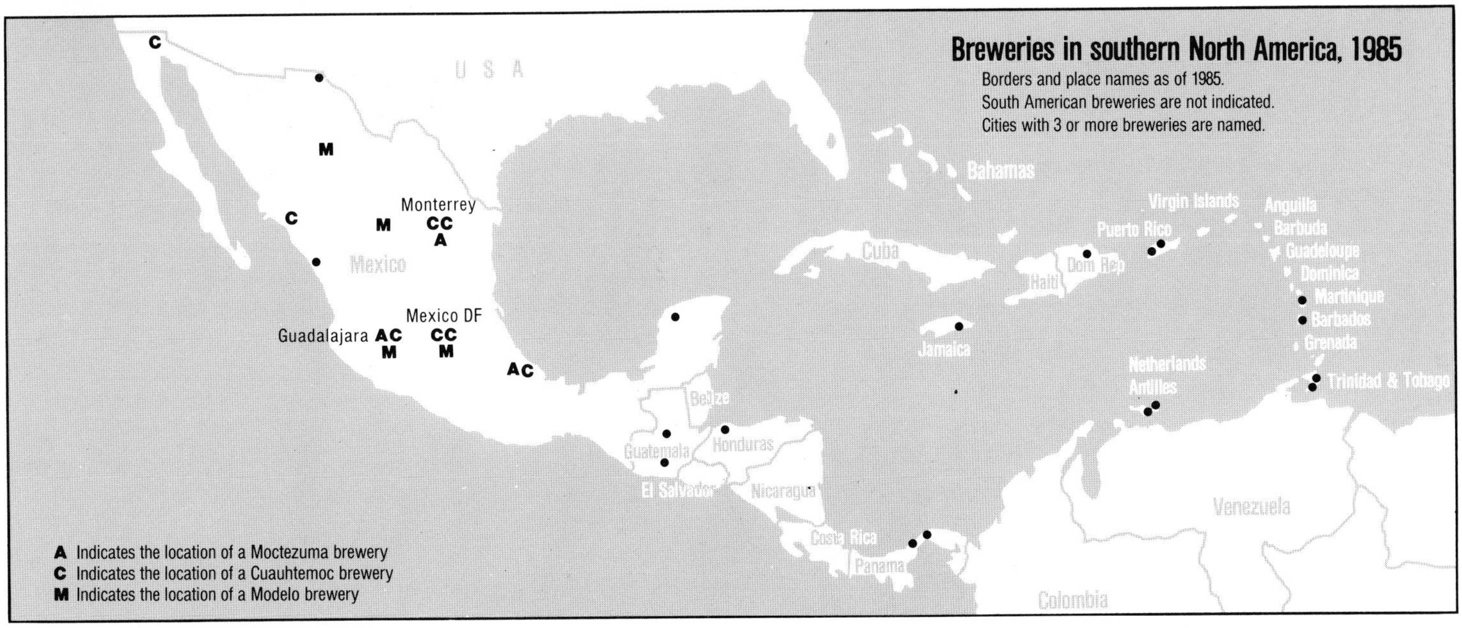

Breweries in southern North America, 1985

Borders and place names as of 1985.
South American breweries are not indicated.
Cities with 3 or more breweries are named.

A Indicates the location of a Moctezuma brewery
C Indicates the location of a Cuauhtemoc brewery
M Indicates the location of a Modelo brewery

founded by Joseph Schnaider, an immigrant from St Louis, Missouri and his partner Isaac Garza, had by 1897 become the largest brewery in Mexico, producing more than 100,000 barrels annually. Though Schnaider left Cuauhtemoc to purchase La Perla later that year, the brewery prospered and today continues to be one of Mexico's three major breweries.

After Mexico City, the state of Veracruz surrounding the great port city of the same name, became the country's second major brewing center. By 1905, six breweries operated in the state of Veracruz and among them was the Cervecería Moctezuma, which would eventually become another of Mexico's three largest. Started in 1894 by Henry Manthy and Adolf Brukhardt along with German brewmaster Wilhelm Hasse, Moctezuma began brewing lager in 1896.

Another relatively early Mexican brewery surviving today is the Cervecería del Pacifico in Mazatlán. Built with American equipment, this brewery was founded in 1900 by Jacob Schuehle who had four years earlier helped to found the now-defunct Cervecería de Sonora in Hermosillo along with the Clifton, Arizona entrepreneur George Grunig.

Unlike the United States and Canada, Mexico did not experience a prohibition in the 1920s. Understandably, those breweries located in the northern part of the country did rather well during the period, and in 1930 the Mexican brewing industry produced 838,000 barrels. Though this was a far cry from the 66 million barrels the United States industry had produced in 1914, it was 838,000 barrels more than were produced in the United States in 1930. The worldwide depression soon took its toll and by 1932 Mexican production had sunk to just 489,000 barrels even though Prohibition was still in effect in the United States.

By 1936, however, the Mexican industry was back on its feet and had just surpassed the million-barrel mark. Four years later Mexican beer production had doubled to two million barrels, although this represented an output only four percent of that of the United States brewing industry. By 1960 Mexican production was up to 10 million barrels and was nine percent of the size of the American industry. In 1975, Mexico reached 23 million barrels and just barely surpassed Canada as the second largest brewing nation in North America. The Mexican brewing industry reached a 32.8-million-barrel peak in 1981, but declined to 27.6 million in 1983 in the midst of its national economic crisis.

NORTH AMERICAN BREWING SOUTH OF MEXICO

Though the Indians brewed beer in the region centuries ago and British ships sailing there certainly carried beer, the brewing tradition in Central America and the Caribbean simply never developed to the extent that it did in the north. A West Indies porter however existed in the early nineteenth century. By the latter nineteenth century there were fewer breweries thoughout the region than in Mexico; imported beer was a major factor. Most of the beer imported to Central America came from Germany and the United States, although British beer was an understandably important import in British Honduras (now Belize). Lager, however, was generally more popular than British-style beers. For example, 75 percent of the beer brought into Costa Rica in 1900 originated in Bavaria. Prosperous Costa Rica was in fact by this time an important early brewing center, with three breweries in San Jose and one at Cartago. By 1905, however, only the Traube Brewery in Cartago and G Richmond's Cervecería Costaricense in San Jose remained. After Costa Rica, Guatemala was the next most important brewing center in the area. By 1905, there were six breweries in the country, half of

Brewing in the Caribbean: Desnoes & Geddes Red Stripe lager on the bottling line *(below)*, and the picturesque Antillian Brewery in Curacao *(right)*, which has won many gold medals for its Amstel beer.

AMSTEL BIER

***Above:* Cerveceria Hondurena, in San Pedro Sula, is the major brewery of Honduras.**

them located in Quezaltenango. The latter three included the rival Cervecería Republicana of Molina Hermanos and the Heussler Brothers' Cervecería Alemana (German Brewery).

In the Caribbean at the turn of the century breweries existed on just four of the islands. Trinidad and Barbados had one each and Jamaica had four including the West India Brewing Company in Kingston. The others were the smaller proprietorships of C M Lindo and J Harris Carr in Kingston and Edwin Charley in Spanishtown. Cuba, prior to its independence from Spain in 1898, had a single brewery, La Tropical, in Havana. Following the American victory in the Spanish-American War, the New York firm of David Obermeyer and Joseph Liebmann (they operated a brewery in Brooklyn) went south to set up a modern American-style brewery in the Cuban capital. Their establishment, the Havana Brewery, was noted for its Cerveza Aguila (Eagle Beer) which was brewed in Cuba until 1924, well into the era of Prohibition in the United States.

In 1918 Eugene Desnoes and Thomas Geddes of Kingston, Jamaica merged their competing soft drink businesses to form a company whose products one day joined the most sought-after beers in the Caribbean. In 1920 Desnoes & Geddes Ltd added their first beer to an otherwise soft drink line. Though Dragon Stout was a short-lived experiment, Desnoes & Geddes were not entirely discouraged. When Prohibition in the United States dried up a major supplier of beer for the Caribbean, the firm returned to the brewing business permanently. Utilizing the talents of brewmasters recruited in England and Germany, Desnoes & Geddes Ltd first brewed their famous Red Stripe beer in 1927. In 1934 one of the original English brewmasters, Bill Martindale, along with Paul Geddes (descendant of the cofounder and the first Jamaican brewmaster), teamed up to alter the Red Stripe formula. The resultant pale lager has been brewed by the company ever since. Red Stripe lager was joined in the Desnoes & Geddes repertoire by another beer product when the company revived Dragon Stout in 1961. Since that time, both products have become available thoughout the Caribbean and have been exported to the United States, and Red Stripe is brewed under license in England.

WINDS OF CHANGE

Even as the American brewing industry was growing and evolving through the period from 1880 to 1910, a dark cloud was growing on the horizon. It was the harbinger of an ill wind that would still forever the happy sounds of many of America's beer gardens.

The idea of temperance is as old as brewing. The Congregational Church formed a temperance society as early as 1808 and the American Temperance Society (formed in Boston in 1826) had 100,000 members by 1829. The objective of temperance was prohibition and, beginning in New England, entire states began to prohibit brewing and selling beer. Between 1846 and 1855 thirteen states followed Maine's lead and experimented with prohibition, but many of these laws were repealed in the years after the Civil War.

By 1910 the boom years for brewing had come to a close, and the pendulum began to swing the other way. By 1912 nine states had gone 'dry' and four years later the number of dry states had increased to 23. Despite the efforts of the temperance societies and the Anti-Saloon League, it took the anti-German hysteria of World War I to push the idea of national prohibition into law. The United States was neutral when the war began in 1914, but by 1917 the tide of sentiment was clearly against Germany on the issue of the latter's barbarous U-boat attacks. The sinking of the liner *Lusitania* was the last straw; the United States declared war on Germany on 6 April 1917. On 10 April the Food Control Act was passed with the stated intention of conserving grain for the war effort. Under the new law the production of distilled spirits was forbidden and severe restrictions were placed on brewers and vintners. President Woodrow Wilson, under powers granted to him under the Food Control Act, moved in December 1917 to restrict brewing and to limit alcohol content in beer to 2.75 percent by weight. Anti-German feelings fueled the prohibitionist fire, and the vast majority of pro-American German-American brewers were signed along with the handful of German nationals who had interests in American breweries. The Sheppard resolution calling for a constitutional amendment for national prohibition was submitted to the state legislatures in December 1917. Caught up in the mood of a nation at war with Germany, legislators across the nation succumbed to the prohibitionist flames.

By 16 January 1919, the 18th Amendment to the Constitution of the United States was ratified. One year later, Prohibition was a reality.

PROHIBITION

Effective on 19 January 1920, 'the manufacture, sale, or transportation of intoxicating liquors within, the importation thereof into, or the exportation thereof from the United States and all territory subject to the jurisdiction thereof for beverage purposes is hereby prohibited.'

With a single poorly worded sentence, the brewing history of the United States changed forever. The Volstead Enforcement Act, passed over President Wilson's veto in October 1919, stood ready to go into force at midnight on 18 January 1920. Some states like California waited until the last minute to submit, but many were already dry when the nightfall of Prohibition descended upon the land. Many small family-owned businesses from the brewers of Milwaukee to the vinters of California's Napa Valley went out of business overnight. What had been normal commercial activity one day was a criminal act the next. Given a year's warning, many breweries attempted to get into other related businesses such as cereal production or industrial alcohol, but many simply closed their doors forever.

Many of the industry's leaders stayed in business, diversifying into other fields and brewing nonalcoholic or 'near' beer. Auheuser-Busch brought out a near beer with the brand name Bevo, while Miller marketed its near beer under the name Vivo. Schlitz, which had brewed the beer that had 'made Milwaukee famous,' now hoped to perpetuate its own fame through a near beer appropriately called Famo. Coors, one of the few brewers left in Colorado, chose the auspicious name Mannah, while industry leader Pabst registered three near beer brand names: Hoppy, Pablo and Yip. In an apparent industry marketing trend toward ending brand names with the letter 'O,' some names got used twice. The Stroh Brewery in Michigan and the Blitz-Weinhard Brewery in Oregon each used the brand name Luxo. In 1921 there were about 10 million barrels of near beer produced versus 23 million barrels of real beer in 1918 and twice that amount four years before.

Above: **Anheuser-Busch diversified into the commercial yeast field during Prohibition to stay in business.**

In addition to near beer, some former breweries kept their plants and bottling lines humming with other types of beverages. Anheuser-Busch produced chocolate-flavored Carcho, coffee-flavored Kafo, tea-leaf-flavored Buschtee, grape-flavored Grape Bouquet and Busch Ginger Ale. Hudepohl produced root beer, and Coors became a giant in the malted milk industry. Prohibition was a golden age for soft drinks and like Anheuser-Busch some brewers were able to make the transition, although it was a field that few would stay in after Prohibition.

For some companies, the forced diversification turned out to be to their long-term benefit. Anheuser-Busch began producing baker's yeast during Prohibition, continued after repeal and eventually became the industry leader. Coors developed its Coors Porcelain Company into what became one of the world's leading producers of scientific and industrial ceramics.

The food conservation and anti-German hysteria that had helped create Prohibition subsided in the early 1920s, and thoughts of repeal soon followed, but it was over 10 years before the national mistake would be rectified. During the Roaring Twenties, while breweries made near beer and malted mild, bootleggers brewed beer and bathtub gin. An industry once controlled by serious businessmen was now the playground and the battleground of organized crime. Attempts to enforce the Volstead Act were expensive and far from effective. Large numbers of otherwise respectable citizens were openly co-operating with criminals in the evasion of the Volstead amendment, and the gang rule created by the entry of organized crime into the alcoholic beverage industry made law and order hard to maintain. With the arrival of the depression in 1929 the problem reached crisis proportions. Public sentiment was clearly against Prohibition throughout the country. The people wanted to see unemployed brewers and bottlers back to work and paying taxes, and they wanted to see the brewing industry out of the hands of mobsters.

Every Canadian province except Quebec had adopted Prohibition during World War I, but had re-

Breweries in the United States, May 1933

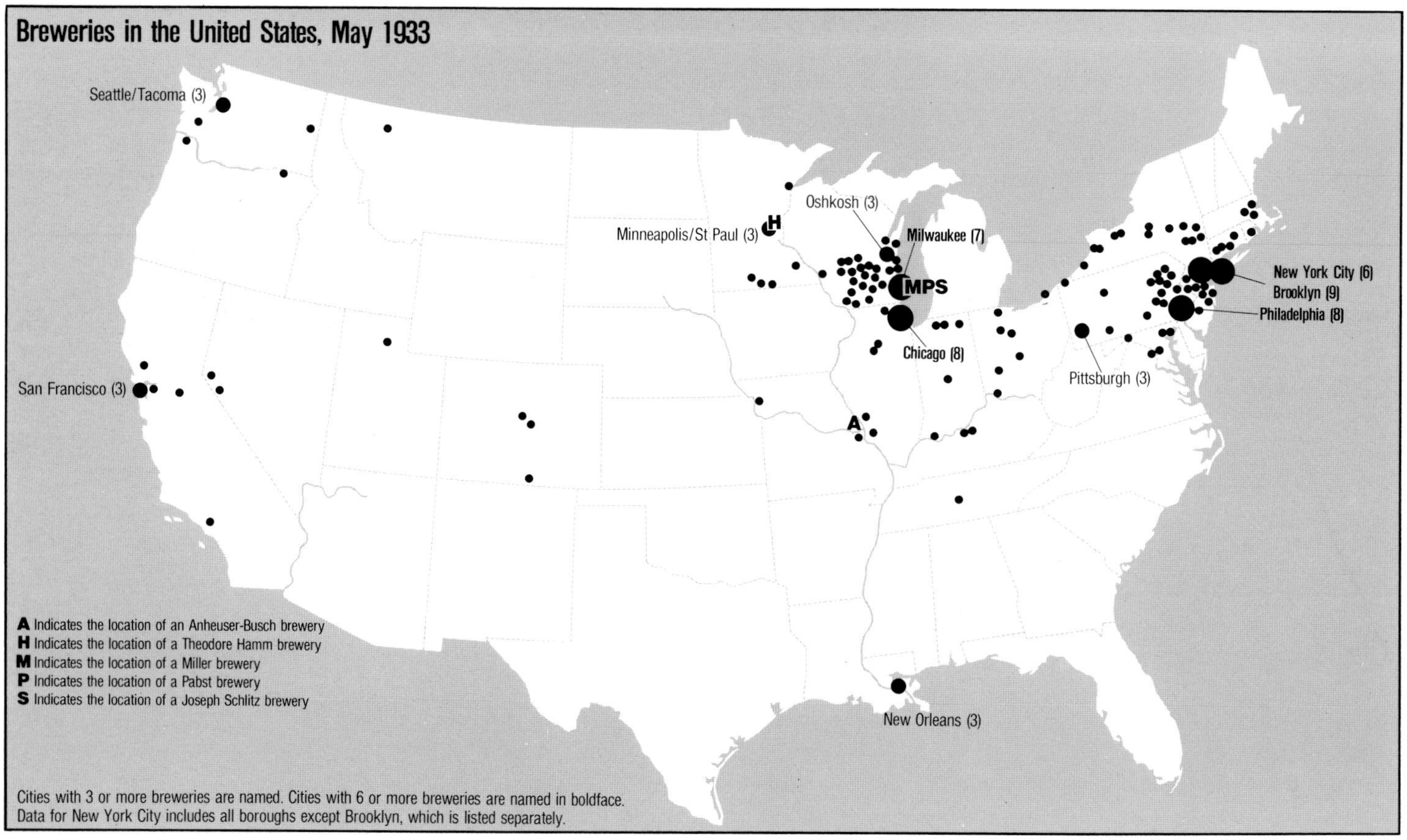

Cities with 3 or more breweries are named. Cities with 6 or more breweries are named in boldface. Data for New York City includes all boroughs except Brooklyn, which is listed separately.

pealed the laws soon after. The people of the United States wanted their government to follow suit. Congressman Volstead of Minnesota, who had authored the 18th Amendment's implementing act, was defeated for re-election in 1922, and in 1926 Montana became the first of many states to repeal its state prohibition enforcement law. Finally, in 1932, Franklin D Roosevelt ran for president on a Democratic Party platform that called for absolute repeal of the 18th Amendment. Roosevelt was elected by a landslide in November and inaugurated the following March. In February 1933 Congress submitted a repeal resolution to the states, and a month later they passed the Cullen Act redefining the phrase 'intoxicating beverage,' thereby permitting the sale of beer with 3.2 percent alcohol before the official repeal of the 18th Amendment.

REPEAL

On 7 April 1933 the headline on the front page of the New York Times read 'Beer Flows in 19 States at Midnight as City Awaits Legal Brew Today.' Within three weeks of President Roosevelt's inauguration the American brewing industry was back in business with temporary permits issued in time to ferment

Left: **General superintendent and brewmaster William Figge of Theodore Hamm Brewing Co draws the first stein of legal beer in St Paul, Minnesota in 1933.** ***Above:*** **The finishing touches are applied to a 14-foot-high brew kettle in March 1933.**

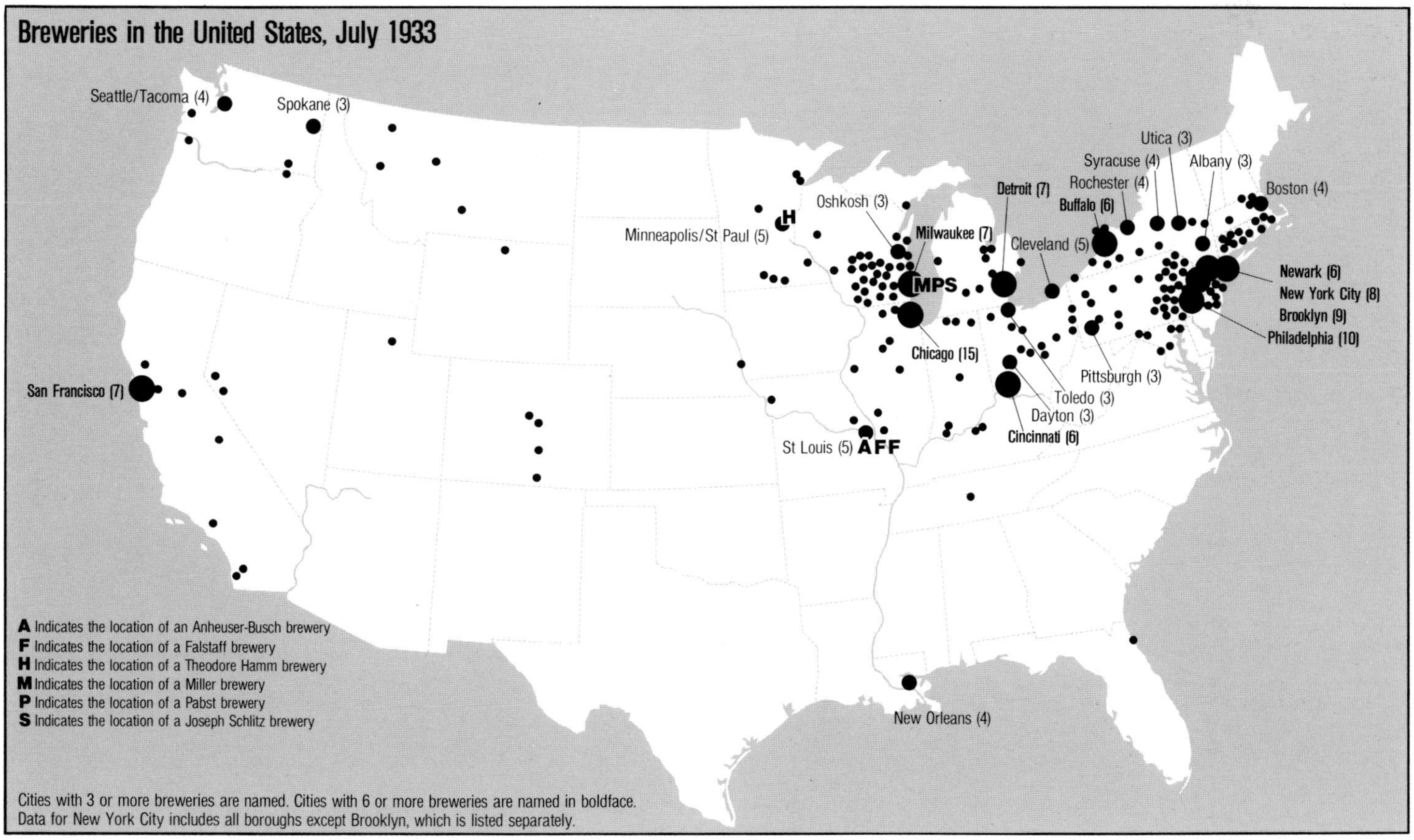

The favorite since 1848
Fauerbach
Badger Club
BEER
MADISON, WIS.
"The Favorite"
Fauerbach
BEER
You'll enjoy
Fauerbach
BEER
Fauerbach
Madison, Wis.
Fauerbach
Madison, Wis.

A Fauerbach Beer Co display *(left)* in 1933. The company ceased operations between 1920 and 1933. *Above:* The General Brewing Co of San Francisco still found a use for horse teams in 1934, but just for show.

their first brew by 7 April. By June 1933 there were 31 brewers brewing beer in the United States out of the 1568 that had existed before Prohibition. A year later the number had risen to 756, but many of these failed in the depression.

In December 1933, when Utah became the thirty-sixth state to ratify the 21st Amendment repealing the 18th Amendment, the production and sale of all alcoholic beverages became legal in the United States for the first time in nearly 14 years. Some states, however, retained prohibition; as late as 1948, Kansas, Oklahoma and Mississippi still prohibited the sale of alcoholic beverages. In 1935 the Federal Alcohol Administration was established by the US Government to control and supervise the American liquor industry—a function absorbed by the Alcohol Tax Unit of the Internal Revenue Service in 1940. Of the states permitting the sale of liquor, 17 adopted laws prescribing a state-controlled sales monopoly. These laws were gradually amended to exclude beer, which then became available at grocery stores.

JUST LIKE RIP VAN WINKLE

When the American brewing industry awoke in 1933–34 from its long slumber, it faced a nation and marketplace much different from those of more than a decade before. The soft drink industry was now firmly established, and consumers were more sophisticated. Consumers could, for example, enjoy Coca-Cola at the soda fountain or take it home in those familiar pale green 'Coke-bottle-shaped' bottles. Perhaps because of Prohibition, a trend grew for packaged beer that could be taken home. At the turn of the century and indeed up to the eve of Prohibition, bottled beer accounted for just a tiny fraction of beer sales. By 1934 a quarter of the beer sold in the United States was in bottles, and by 1941 packaged beer had surpassed draft beer by a 52 to 48 percent margin.

FINE QUALITY
The Result of Expensive Ingredients, Perfect Brewing and Careful Aging
Oertel's
'92
LAGER BEER
SINCE '92
COSTS YOU NO MORE THAN ORDINARY BEERS
OERTEL BREWING CO., INCORPORATED, LOUISVILLE, KY.

Packaged beer in the context of 1934 referred only to bottles, but after 1935 bottled beer was joined on the shelves by a new phenomenon—canned beer. The first canned beer was introduced on 24 June 1935 by the American Can Company and the Krueger Brewing Company of Newark, New Jersey. Schlitz quickly joined forces with the Continental

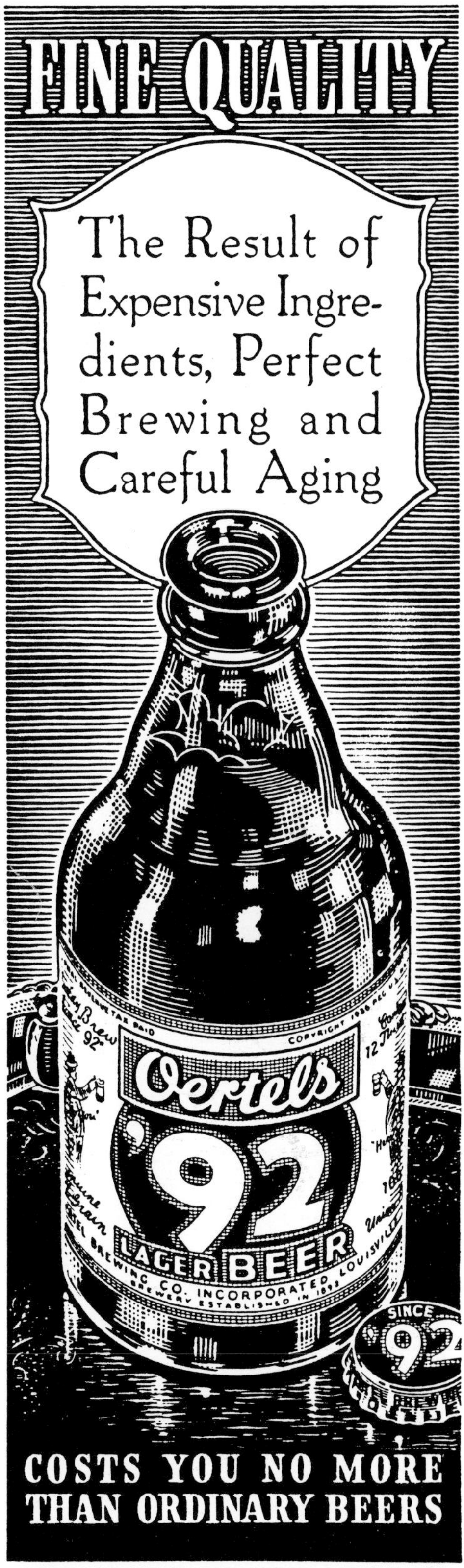

Can Company, introducing a 'cone top' can the same year. The cone top can was just that: a can topped by a cone topped by a bottle cap. It looked something like a metal bottle. Cans were made of first tin, then steel and finally, in 1959, Coors introduced the lightweight aluminum cans that were quickly adopted by the entire

Continued on page 96

BREWERY CLOSE-UP

AMERICAN BREWING IN THE 1940s

ACME BREWING

Above: Acme Brewing began in the nineteenth century in San Francisco and branched out to Los Angeles in 1935. The centerpiece of the company's big expansion of the 1940s was a glass-walled building in San Francisco that Acme called the 'most modern bottle shop in the world' and one that architects and designers described as 'one of the world's most beautiful industrial buildings.'

Below: Sampling the Acme brew on the San Francisco production line.

Above and below: As late as the 1940s, California's central valley was one of North America's leading hop-producing regions. The Acme hop ranch near Yuba City won first place at the California State Fair for two consecutive years. Shirley Kimball, the State Fair's Queen of Hops, was invited to Yuba City for a tour of the Acme ranch.

The vines on the Acme ranch's Hop Avenue *(above left)* reached 18 feet in height. Hops are picked at the peak of ripeness, then cleaned *(above center)*, kiln-dried and bailed in burlap to retain their pungent aroma and flavor. It was not unusual in the 1940s for a brewery to operate its own hop ranch, but today's brewers buy their hops from independent growers. After mashing and straining, the wort that would become Acme beer went into the 450-barrel brew kettle. As the wort was cooked in the big copper kettle, hops from Acme's ranch were added to season it *(above right)*.

Above: After brewing in the brew kettle, Acme's wort was cooled, then fermented in open fermenting tanks to add 'life and sparkle.'

Above: Prior to packaging, Acme beer, like all beer brewed in the 1930s and 1940s, went through a government tax meter.

Above: Based on its faith in the fast-growing West, Acme almost doubled its capacity after World War II. The breweries were sold in 1954, however. The San Francisco plant finally ceased brewing in 1958, and the Los Angeles brewery survived until 1972, spending its last 14 years as a Theodore Hamm brewery.

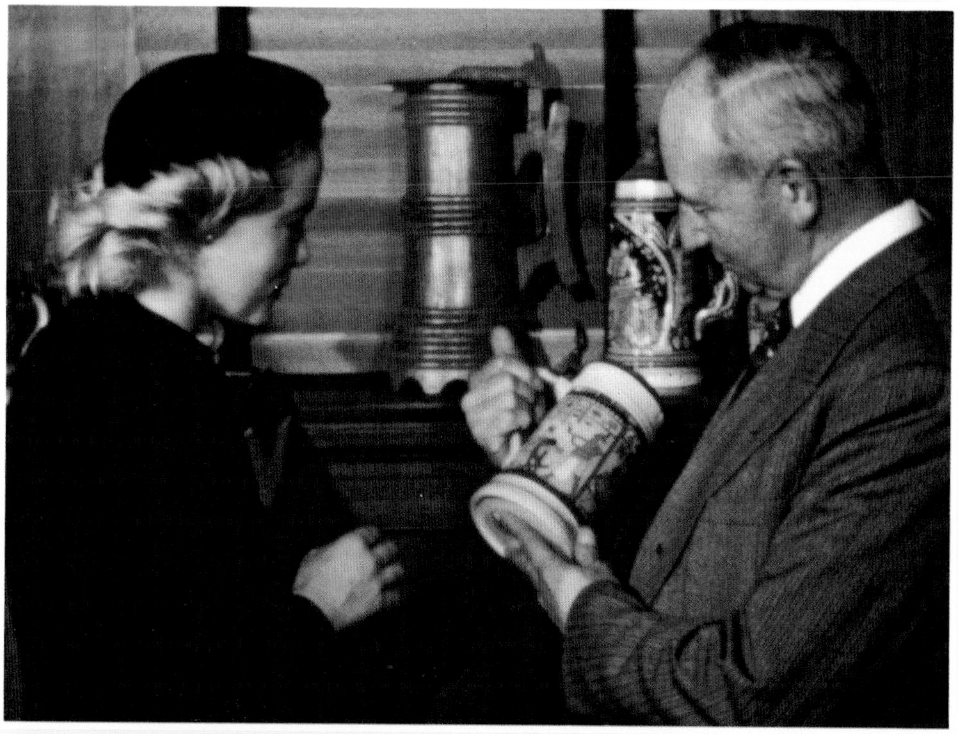

Above: Acme president Carl Schuster invited Queen of Hops Shirley Kimball to his San Francisco office to view the Acme stein collection. Kimball appeared in the film *What's Brewing* (c 1946) which featured Acme Brewing.

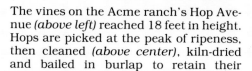

Above: The Sequoia Lodge adjacent to Acme's Los Angeles brewery on East 49th Street was used to entertain dealers, and it could also be rented for civic meetings. Taste tests, some of which were held at the Sequoia Lodge prior to World War II, had determined Acme beer to be 'the West's favorite, ever since repeal.'

industry. Except for the World War II era of tin rationing, sales of beer in nonreturnable cans gained against sales of bottled beer until 1969 when canned beer finally outsold bottled beer for the first time.

Despite the postrepeal resurgence of the industry, growth was slow during the 1930s because of the depression. Annual production went from zero to 53 million barrels between 1933 and 1940, but the 1940 figures were the same as the 1910 figures and well below the 1914 pre-Prohibition peak of 66 million barrels.

WORLD WAR II

Just as the American brewing industry was getting back to its pre-World War I levels, the United States once again found itself at war. In 1941 little of the anti-German sentiment that had been seen at the beginning of World War I existed. This time American brewers, regardless of the spelling of their last names, were thought of as American brewers. Another big change in World War II was that the military establishment had come to realize that the men they were drafting for service liked to drink beer. As a result, the military leadership from Army Chief of Staff George Marshall on down stood by the decision to permit beer sales on military bases.

During the massive mobilization that accompanied World War II, the American brewing industry set aside 15 percent of its output for the troops. Also resulting from the mobilization, young men with long-standing loyalties to hometown brews were exposed to national brands. Their resultant taste for and loyalty to the national brands carried over into the huge expansion of the national brands that followed the war.

The Second World War produced an unprecedented expansion in the American economy, and the brewing industry was certainly part of it. Between 1940 and 1945, the output of beer increased 51 percent to 80 million barrels annually. By comparison, the 26 years before 1940

***Right:* Lucille Knutson stands in front of the glassed-walled million-dollar Acme bottle plant, once dubbed 'one of the world's most beautiful industrial buildings,' for a photograph in March 1942.**

BEER
ACME
BEER

saw a 20 percent decline, and the years from 1945 to 1960 saw just a moderate 11 percent increase. At the turn of the century there were three million-barrel breweries: Pabst, Schlitz and Anheuser-Busch. By World War II these national brands were joined by three more: Ballantine, Ruppert and Schaefer, all in the New York City metropolitan area, and therein lies a tale.

NEW YORK'S BIG THREE

New York City had been the New World's first major brewing center when it was still New Amsterdam, but by World War II it had become the capital of the world. With all of the world's other major cities either under seige or occupied by foreign armies, the world's power and wealth gravitated toward the bustling colossus on the Hudson that was edging past London to become the world's *largest* city as well. In the era before street crime and urban decay, New York represented the hopes and dreams of a war-weary world yearning for a postwar future of peace and prosperity. Manhattan's gleaming skyscrapers, then unmatched anywhere, were like a beacon for the best and brightest from every field whether arts, science or industry. They came not just from America's cities and towns but from throughout the world. Then, as if to crown this great city and confirm its place as the capital of the world, the United Nations established its world headquarters in New York.

It was little wonder then that the world's largest and greatest city should have three of the nation's biggest breweries. They were Ballantine, Ruppert (doing business as Rheingold) and Schaefer, all household words among the households of North America's most populous region.

Ballantine was the first of the big three although Peter Ballantine was one of the last of the English-tradition brewers to set up shop in North America. Ballantine established his shop in Albany in 1833, but moved to Newark, New Jersey across the Hudson River from New York City in 1840. In Newark he joined forces with Erastus Patterson and together they acquired a brewery that had been started in 1805 by General

Below left: **Schaefer was one of the household words in New York City brewing. Frederick and Maximillian Schaefer, founders of the company, were pioneers in lager beer brewing.** ***Below:*** **The Schaefer Brewery in Brooklyn before Prohibition. In 1916 it moved from Park Avenue to the riverfront of Brooklyn and stayed in business during Prohibition by making near beers, dyes and ice.**

The F. & M. SCHAEFER BREWING COMPANY
F. & M. Schaefer
New York
WARDS

Schaefer

John Cumming. In 1847 Peter Ballantine became sole proprietor of the firm, which operated from the location on Front Street until 1920 when Prohibition permanently closed the doors. In 1879, however, Ballantine acquired a second brewery on Freeman Street from the Schalk brothers who had started there in 1852. Also in 1879, Ballantine adopted the legendary three rings logo, its trademark of quality for the next century. When Prohibition ended in 1933, Ballantine reopened at Freeman Street, and in 1943 as wartime demand began to skyrocket, a Plant 2 was opened nearby and it remained in service until 1948. These years were a golden age for Ballantine, whose three rings were omnipresent in the New York area and whose sales placed it among the top brewers in the United States even though it was a regional or, more precisely, a hometown brewery. Ballantine was particularly notable because it brewed top-fermenting ale in an era dominated by lager brewers. In 1960 Ballantine was still the sixth biggest brewer in the nation, but by 1970 it was out of the top 10 and in 1972 the company was sold to Falstaff.

The second of New York's big three breweries was the empire of Jacob Ruppert, Inc, known by its ever-popular Rheingold brand name. Ruppert began operations in 1867 at 1639 Third Avenue on Manhattan's Upper East Side. Over the years the Rheingold brand developed a very loyal following throughout the New York area. Between 1915 and 1939 Ruppert owned the remarkable New York Yankees baseball team. During World War II, with many New Yorkers in the service, Ruppert even set up a Rheingold brewery near the big US Navy yard in Norfolk, Virginia. Originally started in 1896 as Consumers Brewing, the Norfolk brewery was purchased from Southern Breweries, Inc in 1942 and operated as Jacob Ruppert-Virginia, Inc until 1953 when it was sold to the Century Brewery Corp.

The Rheingold flagship remained on Third Avenue through the golden years of the 1940s and 1950s, but the changing nature of the urban landscape in the 1960s cost New York City a good many of its long-established companies. In 1943 New York City (excluding Brooklyn) had eight breweries. In 1953 four remained, and by 1963 only one. In 1964 Ruppert established new satellite breweries in Brooklyn and in Orange, New Jersey. The following year the Third Avenue plant was closed forever. In Brooklyn, Ruppert bought the Liebman Brewery that had been established by Samuel Liebman in 1854 and in Orange the old Orange Brewery (established in 1901) that had been owned by Leibman since 1950. In 1967 Ruppert bought Dawson's Brewery in New Bedford, Massachusetts. By 1976 the changing conditions that led to

Above: Jacob Ruppert, whose Rheingold beer was one of New York City's big three brands. _Left:_ R J Schaefer in 1965, grandson of Maximillian Schaefer, at the height of his kingdom's glory. _Below:_ An ad announcing 1936 Bock Beer Day in New York.

Monday is
BOCK BEER DAY
MARCH
16
MONDAY
Bock Beer makes its annual debut next Monday. For centuries this delightful liquid harbinger of Spring has gladdened the heart of man . . . and this year, we promise you, it will maintain its tradition. Its season is brief. The su,,ly is limited. Try a glass on Monday. Or order a case sent to your home. Sold wherever you see the traditional sign of the goat. To be sure of quality, specify Bock made by one of the brewers listed below.
P. Ballantine & Sons...... Newark, N. J.
Bernheimer & Schwartz Pilsner Brewing Corp. ..... New York
Burke Brewery, Inc. (Ale & Stout) Long Island City
City Brewing Corp. (Tally-ho).... Brooklyn
Peter Doelger Brewing Corp..... New York
The John Eichler Brewing Co.... New York
Christian Feigenspan Brewing Co. (P. O. N.) Newark, N. J.
The Jacob Hoffmann Brewing Co. New York
Horton Pilsener Brewing Co., Inc. New York
G. Krueger Brewing Co. ... Newark, N. J.
Liebmann Breweries, Inc. ....Brooklyn
Lion Brewery of New York City New York
V. Loewer's Gambrinus Brewery Co. New York
North American Brewing Co. (Paramount) Brooklyn
The William Peter Brewing Corp. Union City N. J.
Piel Bros. ....Brooklyn
Rubsam & Horrmann Brewing Co. (R. & H.) Stapleton, S. I.
Jacob Ruppert ....New York
The F. & M. Schaefer Brewing Co. Brooklyn
John F. Trommer, Inc............Brooklyn
BREWERS BOARD OF TRADE, INC.
270 Madison Ave., N. Y.
ANNOUNCING 1936 BOCK BEER DAY

the demise of the old Third Avenue flagship had reached Brooklyn, and in 1977 the Orange and New Bedford breweries closed their doors as well.

Frederick and Maximillian Schaefer, had arrived in New York on the crest of the lager revolution and established one of Manhattan's first lager breweries in 1842. After 67 years in their huge red brick brewery on Park Avenue and East 51st Street, Schaefer was one of the first big Manhattan brewers to move its operations entirely to Brooklyn. Schaefer survived Prohibition by brewing near beer and emerged from those dark days with the motto 'our hand has never lost its skill.' Within five years the company had reached the million-barrel mark. In the expansive decades after World War II Schaefer operated satellite breweries in Albany, New York (1950–1972), Cleveland, Ohio (1961–1963) and Baltimore, Maryland (1963–1978) to help meet the demand for its popular brew. In 1972 when the Albany facility was closed, its production was transfered to a new ultramodern brewery near Allentown in Pennsylvania's Lehigh Valley. By 1976 Schaefer's 60-year-old Brooklyn brewery, no longer economically viable, was closed. The closing of Schaefer's Brooklyn operation in 1976 brought an end to over three centuries of brewing history. It was the last brewery in New York City, North America's original brewing center.

Five years later, the Schaefer operations which had been consolidated in Allentown were sold to Stroh Brewing of Detroit.

MAKE WAY FOR THE NATIONALS

New York's big three brewers would probably have survived as independent brewers had they decided to go national after World War II. They were certainly big enough and had the power, but it was probably for the reason of size that they did not. Why should they expend their energy on national expansion when they were sitting on top of the hemisphere's largest beer market where they could remain hometown brewers and still be part of America's top six, which included the nationals Anheuser-Busch, Schlitz and Pabst? For nearly a quarter century, the theory worked. Though each would attempt briefly to expand as regional brewing companies, they remained essentially hometown New York brewers. As the population center of the United States shifted westward and California overtook New York as the most populous state, the once powerful New Yorkers, who had themselves abandoned Manhattan, were swallowed by out-of-state national brands.

The three rings of quality of Ballantine beer — Purity, Body and Flavor.

A new chapter in American brewing history began to unfold in the years immediately after World War II, but while the strategy was bold and new, the players were familiar. The Joseph Schlitz Company had been early to recognize the importance of distribution and multisite brewing, and in fact the company had built a satellite brewery in Cleveland, Ohio from scratch in 1908 and had operated there for two years. Anheuser-Busch, innovators in mass distribution for over half a century, were also ready to play for a large slice of the national pie. Both companies were looking beyond national distribution and toward a truly national system of satellite breweries unheard of prior to World War II.

When the war ended neither Schlitz nor Anheuser-Busch was based in a major growing market. The major market at the time was, of course, New York which was dominated by Ballantine, Rheingold and Schaefer whose breweries were located there. The first step toward cracking the market was simply to build breweries there. Schlitz was the first by two years when it bought the George Ahret Brewery in Brooklyn in 1949. Anheuser-Busch opted to build a brand new plant in Newark, New Jersey, which opened in 1951. Three years later, in 1954, the two competitors became the first brewers with a coast-to-coast network of breweries as they both opened new facilities in the Los Angeles area. Schlitz, the postwar industry leader, struck next in 1956 by acquiring the former Muehleback Brewery in Kansas City, Missouri, Anheuser-Busch's back yard. In 1959 both of the national giants opened facilities in Tampa, Florida, and by the following year Anheuser-Busch had replaced Schlitz as America's leading brewer.

Over the course of the next 16 years Anheuser-Busch began brewing at six additional locations: Houston, Texas (1966); Columbus, Ohio (1968); Jacksonville, Florida (1969); Merrimack, New Hampshire (1970); Williamsburg, Virginia (1972) and Fairfield near San Francisco, California (1976). During the same period Schlitz expanded into the South with new breweries in Longview, Texas (1966); Winston-Salem, North Carolina (1970) and Memphis, Tennessee (1971). Schlitz also operated the old Milwaukee Brewery in San Francisco as a Schlitz brewery between 1964 and 1969. In 1973 Schlitz consolidated its map of the United States by closing the Brooklyn and Kansas City breweries.

By the mid-1970s Schlitz was still the nation's number two brewer, but by 1980 the once-powerful Milwaukee giant had fallen to number four.

Above: **The Anheuser-Busch team of well-groomed Clydesdales. These magnificent animals are now a part of the company's tradition of excellence.** ***Below:*** **Bottle plant hands busily pack crates of brew at the Anheuser-Busch plant in St Louis.**

An event symbolic of the times for Schlitz came in 1979 with the sale of its two-year-old Baldwinsville, New York brewery to Anheuser-Busch. The final blow came in 1982 when the brewer that brewed the beer that made Milwaukee famous was sold to the Stroh Brewing Company of Detroit.

As World War II ended, Schlitz and Anheuser-Busch represented the top rung in the market, but it was a market with fewer and fewer brewers serving a growing market, opening the door for other national brands.

Pabst was an important contender. The national industry leader at the turn of the century, Pabst emerged from Prohibition to pioneer multisite brewing by reopening in Milwaukee and starting a new brewery at Peoria Heights near Chicago in 1934. After World War II, Pabst had actually gotten into the New York market before either Schlitz or Anheuser-Busch through the purchase of the Hoffman Beverage Company of Newark in 1946. From then on Pabst's expansion was much slower than its two major rivals. In 1958 Pabst bought the Blatz Brewery, one of its original Milwaukee rivals. From its small number of sites, Pabst continued among the top five national brewers without further expansion until 1971 when a new brewery was opened at Perry, Georgia and 1979 when the company bought the Blitz-Weinhard Brewery in Portland. Three years later in 1983 Pabst sold both of its later acquisitions to Heileman and bought the Schlitz Brewery in Tampa, Florida (which became a Pabst Brewery) and the Olympia Brewing Company in Tumwater, Washington which continued to operate under the Olympia name.

Right: **The Burgermeister building at 470 Tenth Street in San Francisco as it appeared in 1951. The largest single brewery west of St Louis when it was built, it cost $1.5 million and had a 900,000 bbl capacity. The site was once occupied by the Milwaukee Brewery, established in 1880** ***(see pages 4-5)*****, and was a Falstaff brewery from 1975 to 1978, when it closed permanently. The building is still standing.**

FALSTAFF

A fourth brewer to emerge as a national power around the time of World War II was Falstaff. The company was started by 'Papa Joe' Griesedieck who purchased two breweries in St Louis between 1911 and 1917. The two breweries, the Independent/Consumers on Shenandoah Avenue and the Forest Park on the Boulevard of the same name were both renamed after their new owner; together they formed the basis for a small empire of breweries formed along the banks of the Mis-

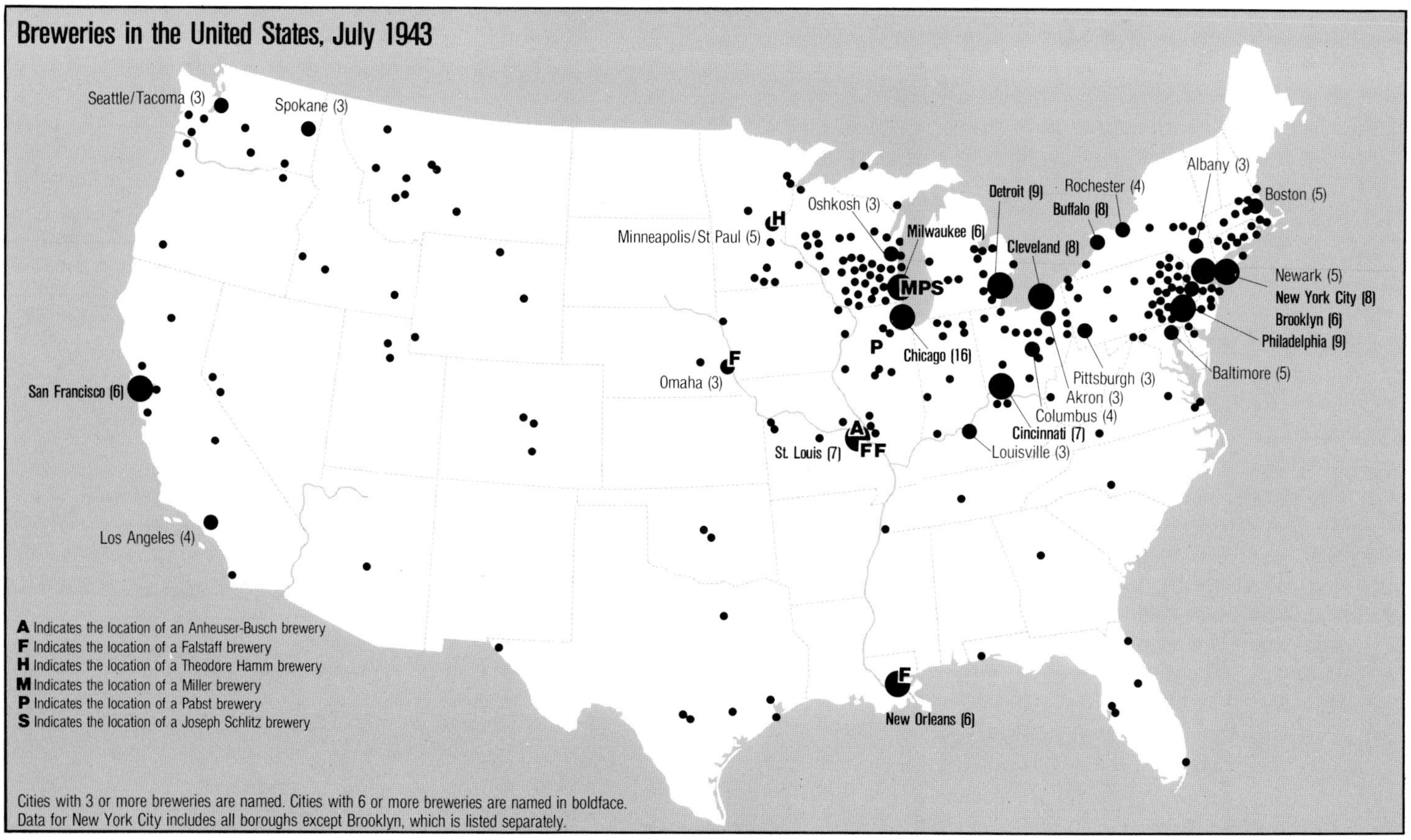

Bürgermeister

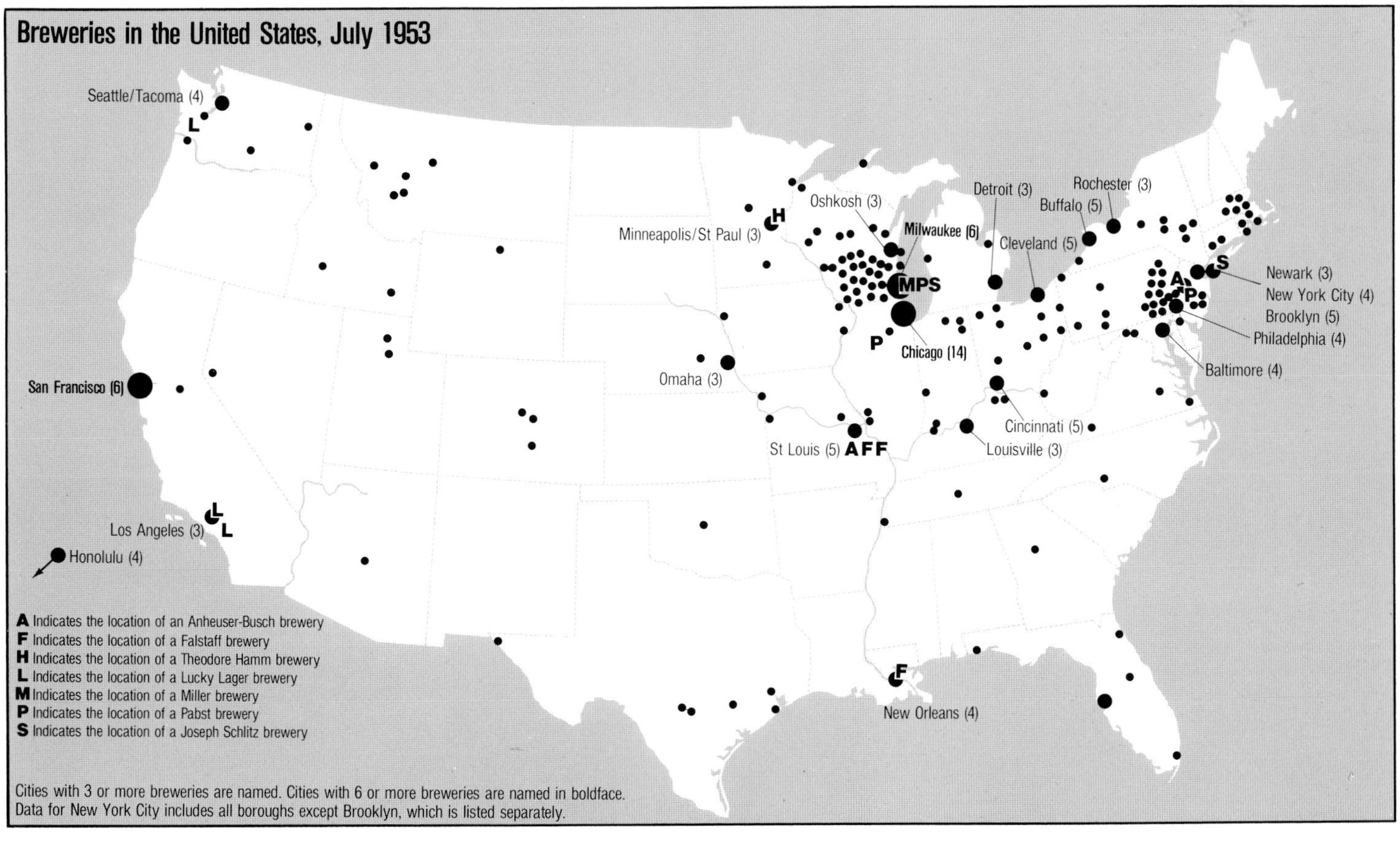
Breweries in the United States, July 1953
Seattle/Tacoma (4)
Minneapolis/St Paul (3)
Oshkosh (3)
Milwaukee (6)
Detroit (3)
Rochester (3)
Buffalo (5)
Cleveland (5)
Newark (3)
New York City (4)
Brooklyn (5)
Philadelphia (4)
Baltimore (4)
Chicago (14)
Omaha (3)
San Francisco (6)
St Louis (5) AFF
Cincinnati (5)
Louisville (3)
Los Angeles (3)
Honolulu (4)
New Orleans (4)
MPS
A Indicates the location of an Anheuser-Busch brewery
F Indicates the location of a Falstaff brewery
H Indicates the location of a Theodore Hamm brewery
L Indicates the location of a Lucky Lager brewery
M Indicates the location of a Miller brewery
P Indicates the location of a Pabst brewery
S Indicates the location of a Joseph Schlitz brewery
Cities with 3 or more breweries are named. Cities with 6 or more breweries are named in boldface.
Data for New York City includes all boroughs except Brooklyn, which is listed separately.

Hom
Pabst
Pabst Blue Ribbon
GMC

Left: A long line of GMC trucks that were part of the huge Pabst delivery fleet in the early 1950s, a striking contrast to the classic Pabst horseless beer wagon *(right)* that delivered Blue Ribbon in New York City just after the turn of the century.

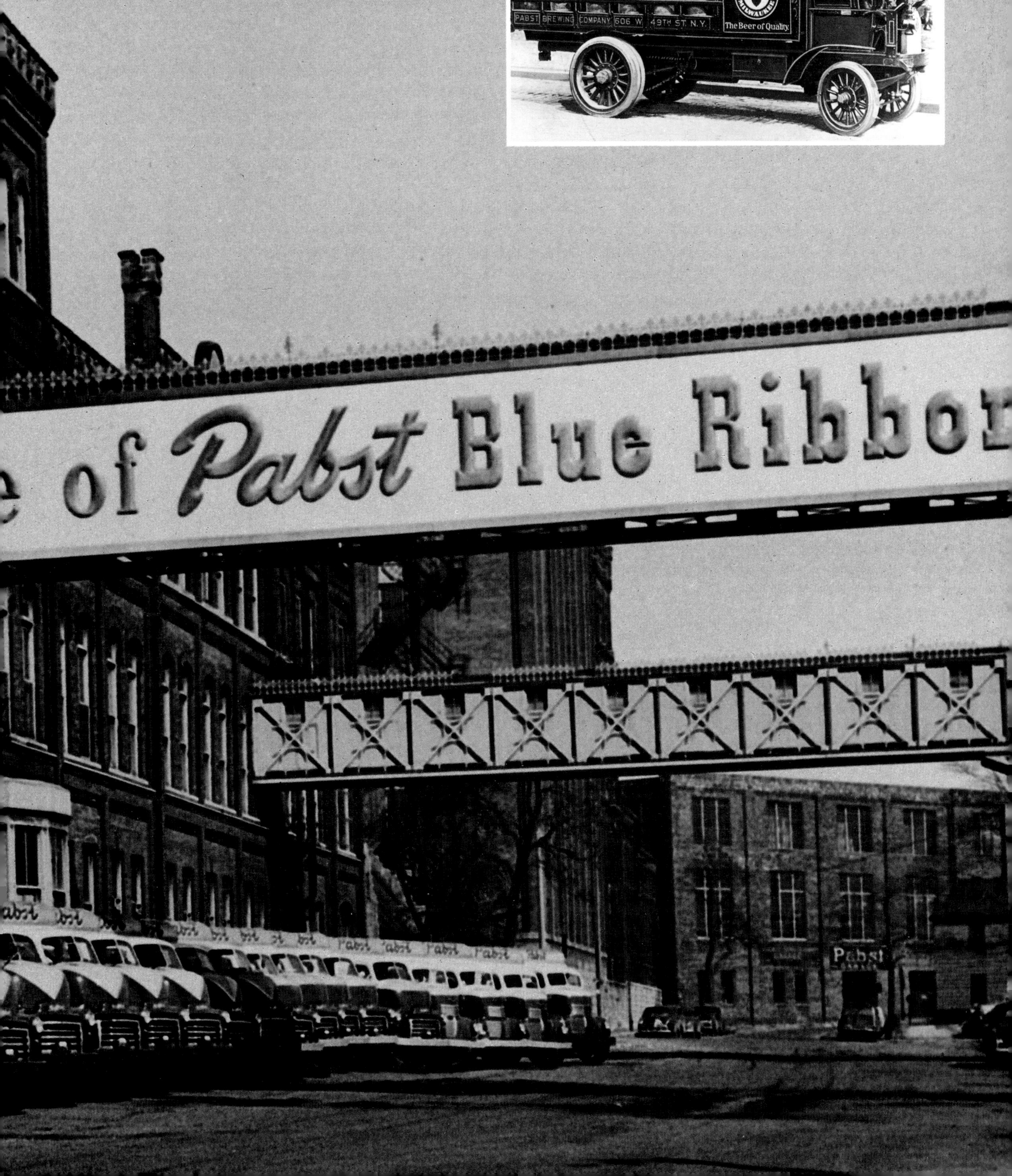

SHINER BEER
HOME OF — SHINER BEER
WELCOME Shiner WELCOME

sissippi and Missouri rivers. During Prohibition, the company was renamed Falstaff after the Shakespeare character, and it whiled away those years brewing near beer and smoking hams.

After Prohibition, Falstaff acquired the former Union Brewery in St Louis in 1933, then went upriver to acquire the former Fred Krug Brewery in Omaha in 1935 and downriver to New Orleans where the former National Brewery was purchased in 1937. Falstaff emerged from World War II with more (albeit smaller) breweries in St Louis than Anheuser-Busch, but while the latter looked forward to a truly national market, Falstaff continued to concentrate on the Mississippi/Missouri River country. In 1948 Falstaff purchased two breweries from Columbia Brewing, one in East St Louis, Illinois and another in St Louis, which gave Falstaff five breweries in the St Louis metropolitan area. Within three years, however, two of these had been closed.

In 1952 Falstaff reached toward the rapidly expanding California market by acquiring Wieland's Brewery in San Jose which had originally been Gottfried Krahenberg's Fredericksburg Brewery (established in 1856), one of the first breweries in California. In doing so, Falstaff was the first major eastern brewer to expand into the Golden State beating both Schlitz and Anheuser-Busch (who were then concentrating on the New York area) by two years.

In 1954, Falstaff purchased the former Berghoff Brewing Company in Fort Wayne, Indiana which today serves as the company's flagship brewery. The next few years saw Falstaff moving into Texas, again ahead of Anheuser-Busch and Schlitz. Falstaff breweries were opened in El Paso in 1955 and Galveston in 1956, but they were closed in 1976 and 1981 respectively. Falstaff also moved deeper into California and briefly operated two breweries in San Francisco, the former Milwaukee (later Joseph Schlitz) Brewery on Tenth Street between 1971 and 1978 and the former Lucky Lager Brewery on Newhall Street between 1975 and 1978.

The K Spoetzel Brewery in Shiner, Texas, one of the Lone Star State's great breweries. It was founded in 1909.

Sick's Lethbridge Brewery Ltd in Lethbridge, Alberta as it appeared between 1955 and 1960. Emil Sick expanded his empire south from Lethbridge into the US, where Sick's breweries extended from Oregon to Montana. His flagship brewery was the former Seattle Brewing & Malting facility and Rainier was the flagship brand. Today Sick's Lethbridge still brews Lethbridge Beer, known as 'bridge Beer, but is owned by Molson of Montreal. Rainier beer and ale were a symbol of Seattle when home-owned and when Sick owned, and continue as such under the present Heileman ownership.

Falstaff closed all of its California plants by 1978 (the San Jose brewery was closed in 1973) and all of its St Louis plants by 1977, leaving the New Orleans, Omaha and Ft Wayne plants brewing the only beer under the Falstaff name. In the meantime, however, Falstaff had acquired Ballantine in 1972 and Narragansett in 1965. The Narragansett Brewing Company in Cranston, Rhode Island had been established in 1890 and had become a popular brand name in New England. For this reason, Falstaff for a time continued operations under the original Narragansett name.

Though it slipped from third place nationally in 1960 to sixth place in 1970, Falstaff, through its 1975 affiliation with General Brewing, remained the ninth largest brewer in the United States in 1985.

THE WESTERN REGIONALS

When it was acquired by Pabst in 1983, Olympia was the last of a breed of independent western brewers that had emerged from Prohibition and survived for many years after the postwar arrival in the West of the major national brands. These western brewers included Olympia at Tumwater, Blitz-Weinhard at Portland, the Sick's Empire that was centered in Seattle and Lucky Lager with locations throughout the West. Both Olympia and Blitz-Weinhard were essentially single-site brewers that passed to their new owners (Pabst and Heileman) with their identities intact. Largely *because* they remained single-site breweries, they had developed strong regional identities. Unlike their two neighbors, Sick's and Lucky Lager represented postwar attempts at creating multisite regional empires that paralleled in geographic scope those being created in the East at the same time by the major national brands. Excluding their California and Texas operations, neither Schlitz, Pabst nor even Anheuser-Busch had breweries spread over a larger area in the East than Lucky Lager had in the West at its peak.

The story of Lucky Lager is thoroughly intertwined with that of the General Brewing Company of Vancouver, Washington which has

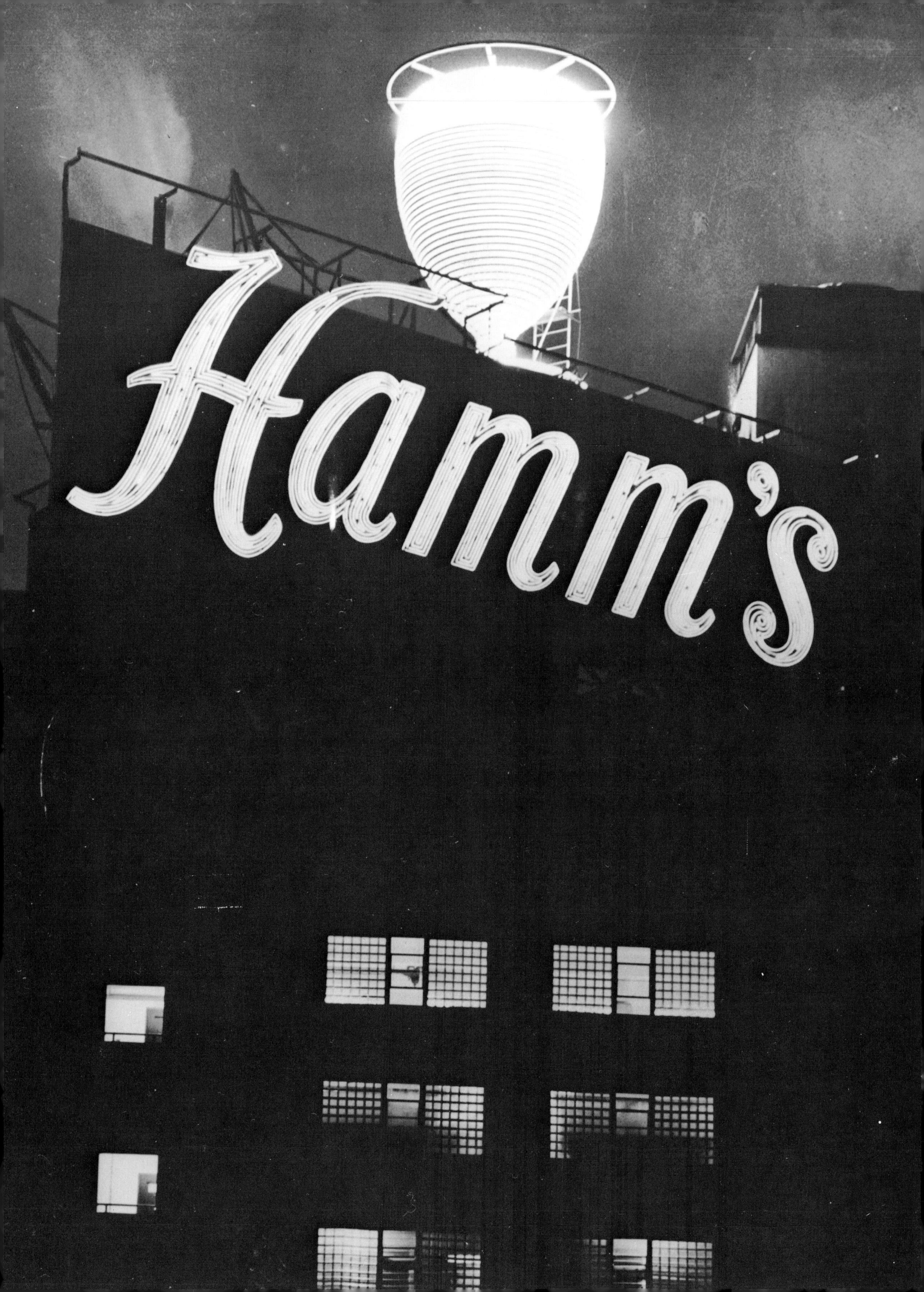
Hamm's

Scenes from the heyday of western regional brewing, General Brewery's Lucky Lager plant *(above)* in Vancouver, Washington in 1970. It was a General/Lucky brewery from 1950 until it closed in 1985. Hamm's *(left)* came from St Paul to build a big brewery in San Francisco, whose most prominent feature was its huge neon beer glass sign. Flashing lights created the illusion of a glass being filled and quaffed, until the plant closed in 1975. *Overleaf:* Turn-of-the-century offices of Seattle Brewing & Malting.

owned the Lucky trademark since 1971. The first Lucky Lager brewery is a case in point. Located on Newhall Street in San Francisco, it was started by General in 1934 and became a Lucky Lager brewery in 1948. It passed from Lucky back to General in 1963 and back again to Lucky in 1969. It was closed in 1978, seven years after Lucky Lager became a General brand. The second Lucky brewery, at Azuza in Southern California, was started in 1949, sold to General in 1963 and then to Miller in 1966. The third Lucky brewery was located in Vancouver, Washington and actually traced its heritage back to the brewery that Henry Weinhard had owned between 1859 and 1864. Restarted after Prohibition as the Interstate Brewery, it was sold to Lucky in 1950, to General in 1964 and back to Lucky in 1969. After General's 1971 purchase of Lucky, the Vancouver brewery served as the flagship brewery, until its closure in October 1985.

Throughout their long courtship both Lucky and General established other widely dispersed satellite breweries in the West, including Los Angeles (General, 1971–1974), Pueblo, Colorado (General, 1971–1975) and in Salt Lake City, Utah (Lucky, 1960–1964 and General, 1964–1967). In the case of Lucky Lager, this move helped establish it as one of the West's most important and widely recognized brand names in the 1960s. Even today, the Lucky Lager name is the General Brewing Company's most prominent brand.

The Emil Sick empire of Seattle had many similarities to the Jacob Ruppert empire in New York. Both produced a very popular beer under a brand name other than their own: Ruppert brewed Rheingold and Sick brewed Rainier. Both were associated with a baseball team: Ruppert with the New York Yankees of the American League and Sick with the Seattle Rainiers of the Pacific Coast League. Both made serious bids toward regional expansion during and after World War II: Ruppert in New York, New Jersey, Virginia and Massachusetts and Sick in Washington, Oregon, Montana and the Canadian province of Alberta.

Like many founders of North American breweries, Emil Sick was not American-born. His father, Fritz Sick, had started the Lethbridge Brewing & Malting Company Ltd in Lethbridge, Alberta, Canada in 1901. Emil took over from his father and used the Lethbridge brewery as a springboard for an American empire.

The Sick empire in the United States traces its ancestry to the post-Prohibition Century Brewing Association which operated breweries on Westlake Avenue and on Airport Way, and which became Seattle

ARE YOU RUN DOWN
Malt Rainier
WILL BUILD YOU UP.
Rainier BEER
AWARDED
TWO
GRAND PRIZES
HIGHEST AWARDS
AND THREE
GOLD MEDALS
SEATTLE BREWING & MALTING CO.

Above: **Rainier beer has been a favorite among beer drinkers in the Northwest since 1878, and Rainier Ale is the largest selling ale in the West.**

Brewing and Malting in the 1930s. There was, however, an earlier Seattle Brewing and Malting, located on Duwamish Avenue which operated between 1892 and 1915 that brewed the Rainier brand between 1906 and 1915. The Westlake and Airport Way breweries became Sick's Century and Sick's Seattle, respectively, in 1944. The two Seattle plants were just the beginning. By the time the Americans beat the Germans in the Battle of the Bulge on Christmas 1944, Sick had staked out a brewing empire that spanned the Northwest. He had acquired the Spokane Brewery (started by Galland-Burke in 1892) in Spokane; the Salem Brewery (started by Samuel Adolph in 1874) in Salem, Oregon; Missoula Brewing (started by George Gerber in 1874) in Missoula, Montana and the Great Falls Brewery (started in 1895 as American Brewing) in Great Falls, Montana.

New brand names like Highlander (brewed in Seattle and Missoula) and Rheinlander were added to their program, but gradually the breweries slipped away. The two Montana breweries left the Sick fold in 1949. The brewery in Salem was closed in 1953, the Century in Seattle closed in 1957 and the one in Spokane closed in 1962. In 1970, only the Airport Way Brewery remained, and by then a majority interest was owned by Molson, the Canadian giant. Molson took over Sick's Lethbridge in 1958, and Emil Sick, then chairman of Sick's Breweries Ltd, became a director on Molson's board of directors. In 1977, Molson sold the Seattle brewery to Heileman of LaCrosse, Wisconsin, who continued to brew Rainier beer and Rainier ale in Seattle.

BREWING IN HAWAII

While it is geographically not part of North America, much of Hawaii's recent economic and cultural history is intertwined with North America because of its long association with the United States. A territory of the United States since 1900 (it was annexed in 1898), Hawaii has been a state since 1959. The first commercial brewery in the Hawaiian Islands, the Honolulu Brewing Company established in 1898, was also the only commercial brewery to be located there prior to Prohibition. With the repeal of the 18th Amendment, which had applied to US territories as well as states, a number of breweries opened in Hawaii. The former Honolulu Brewing reopened as American Brewing in 1933 and another com-

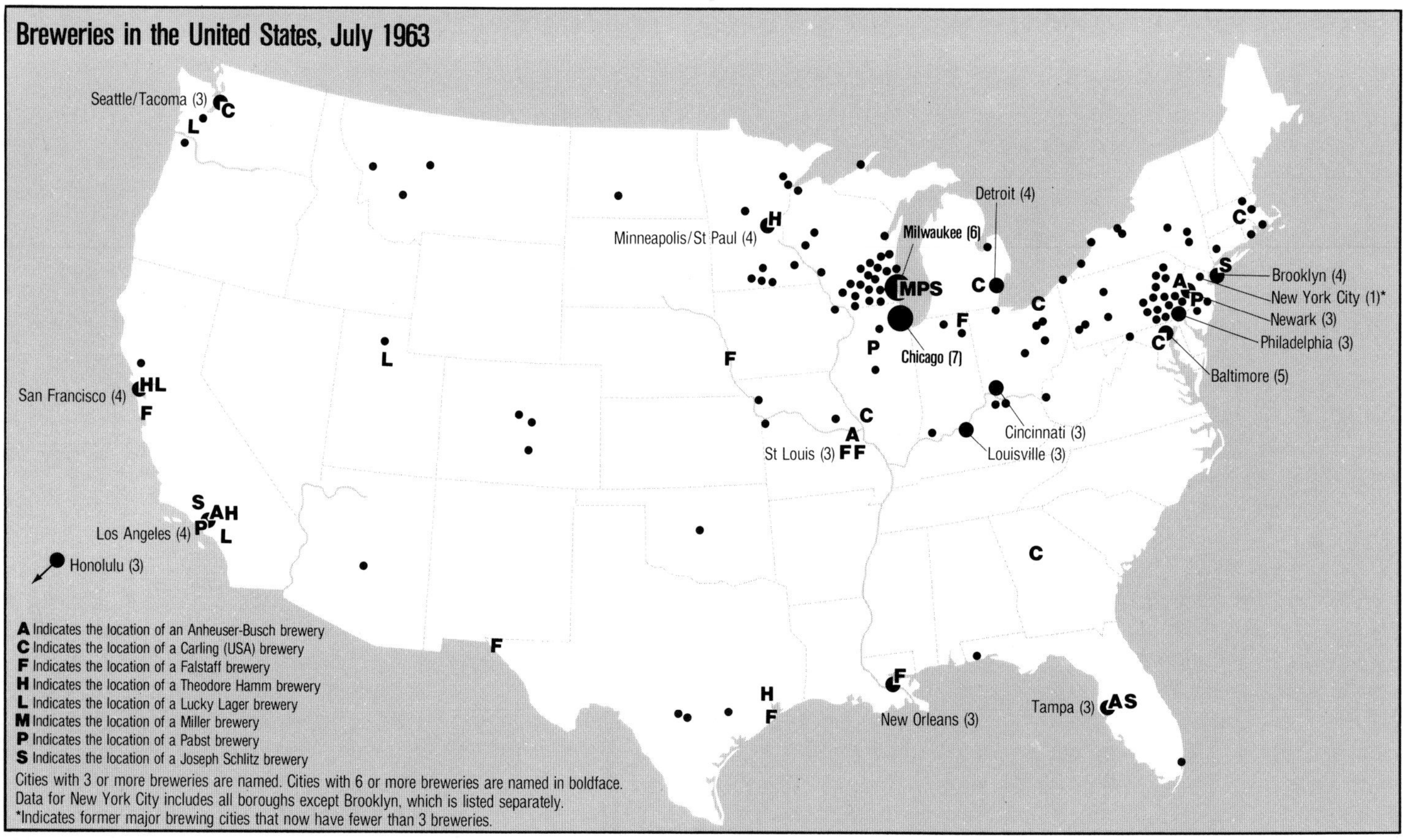

pany, the Hawaii Brewing Corporation opened on Honolulu's Kapiolani Boulevard in 1934.

By the 1930s a sizable portion of Hawaii's population was of Japanese ancestry, and many of them favored the traditional Japanese beverage, sake, which is brewed and fermented somewhat like beer. The major differences are that sake is made with rice rather than malted barley, it is not hopped, it is drunk warmed rather than chilled or at room temperature and it has an alcohol content roughly four times that of most beer. All but two of the breweries in Hawaii's history brewed sake rather than beer.

The first had been a short-lived experiment in 1915, but after Prohibition five sake breweries appeared in Hawaii, two in Honolulu, two in Hilo on the island of Hawaii and one in Kula on Maui. With the Japanese air attack on Honolulu's Pearl Harbor in December 1941, the United States Government moved to close down Japanese businesses on the islands, including all the sake breweries, because many of them had ties to parent companies in Japan. After the war, Fuji Sake in Honolulu and the Kokusui Company in Hilo reopened, but by the time of statehood only Fuji remained, and it closed in 1965.

Above: **Primo Beer was the only beer brewed in Hawaii by the mid-1960s. It is surprising that so few breweries existed in a climate so conducive to cold refreshment, but because of the high percentage of Japanese living on the islands, the preferred beverage was sake. Today Primo is brewed by Stroh in California, but is still the best selling beer in Hawaii.**

America Brewing, Hawaii's original beer brewer, closed in 1962, and Hawaii Brewing was sold to the Joseph Schlitz Brewing Company in 1964. Schlitz went to great lengths to promote the Primo brand, which by this time was the only beer still brewed in Hawaii. The Primo label celebrated the fact that beer had been brewed in the islands since 1897 and noted that 'pure Hawaiian water, naturally filtered through thousands of layers of lava rock (was) combined with the finest quality brewing ingredients to give Primo beer a distinctive light golden taste!'

Though it was a typical American-style lager, Primo became a cult classic and every beer drinker who ventured to the islands during this period sampled the brew, and many returned home with blue-labeled Primo bottles in suit cases. By 1979 the financial woes of the Joseph Schlitz Brewing Company became such that the parent company had to choose between the survival of the Joseph Schlitz Brewing Company and the survival of the last vestige of Hawaiian brewing history. They chose the former and the Hawaii Brewing subsidiary was closed. Schlitz did, however continue to brew Primo 'on the mainland,' making what was once Hawaii's last and proudest brand an import.

Breweries in the United States, July 1973

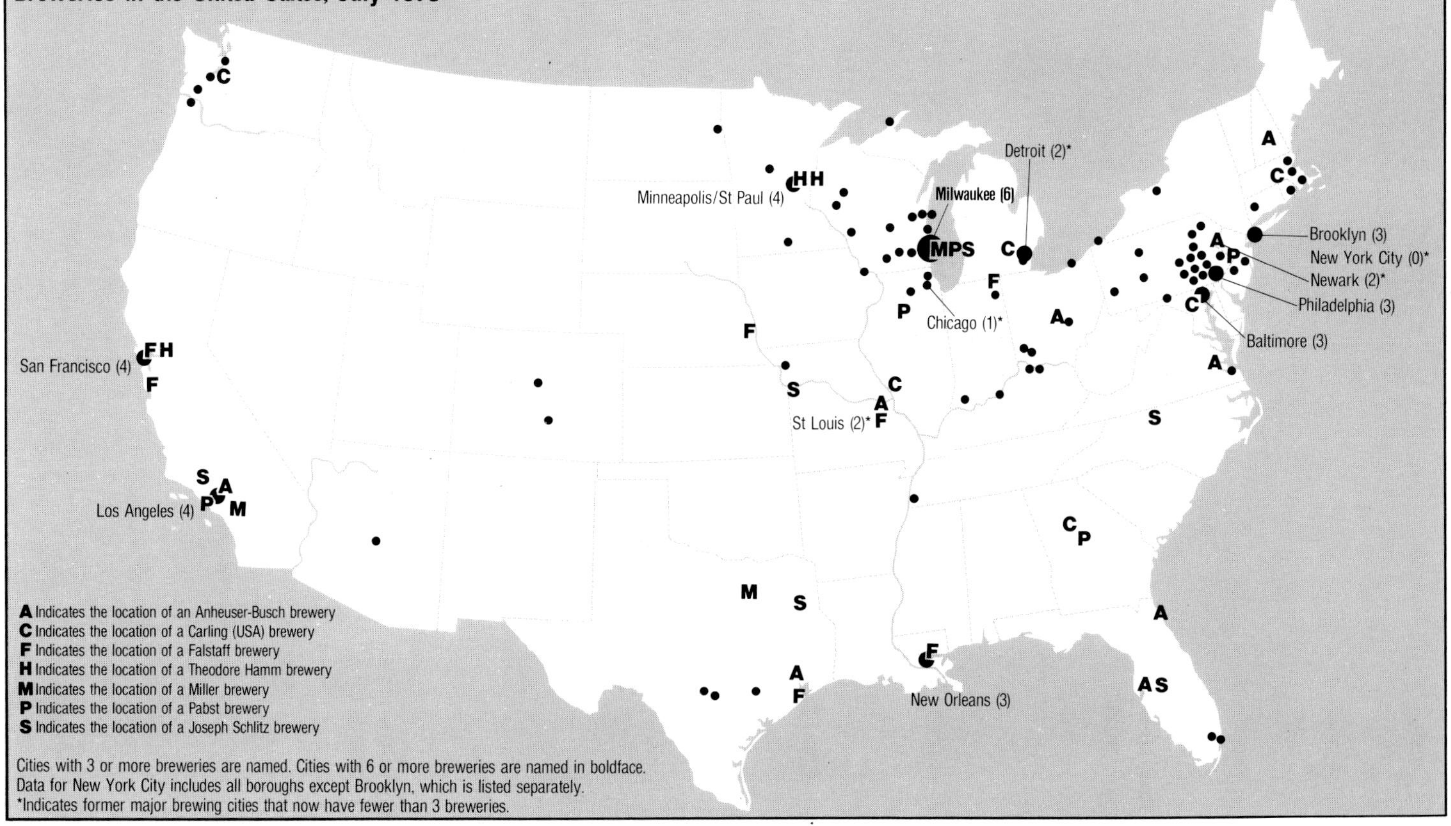

BREWERY CLOSE-UP

A MEXICAN CERVECERIA

CERVECERIA MOCTEZUMA

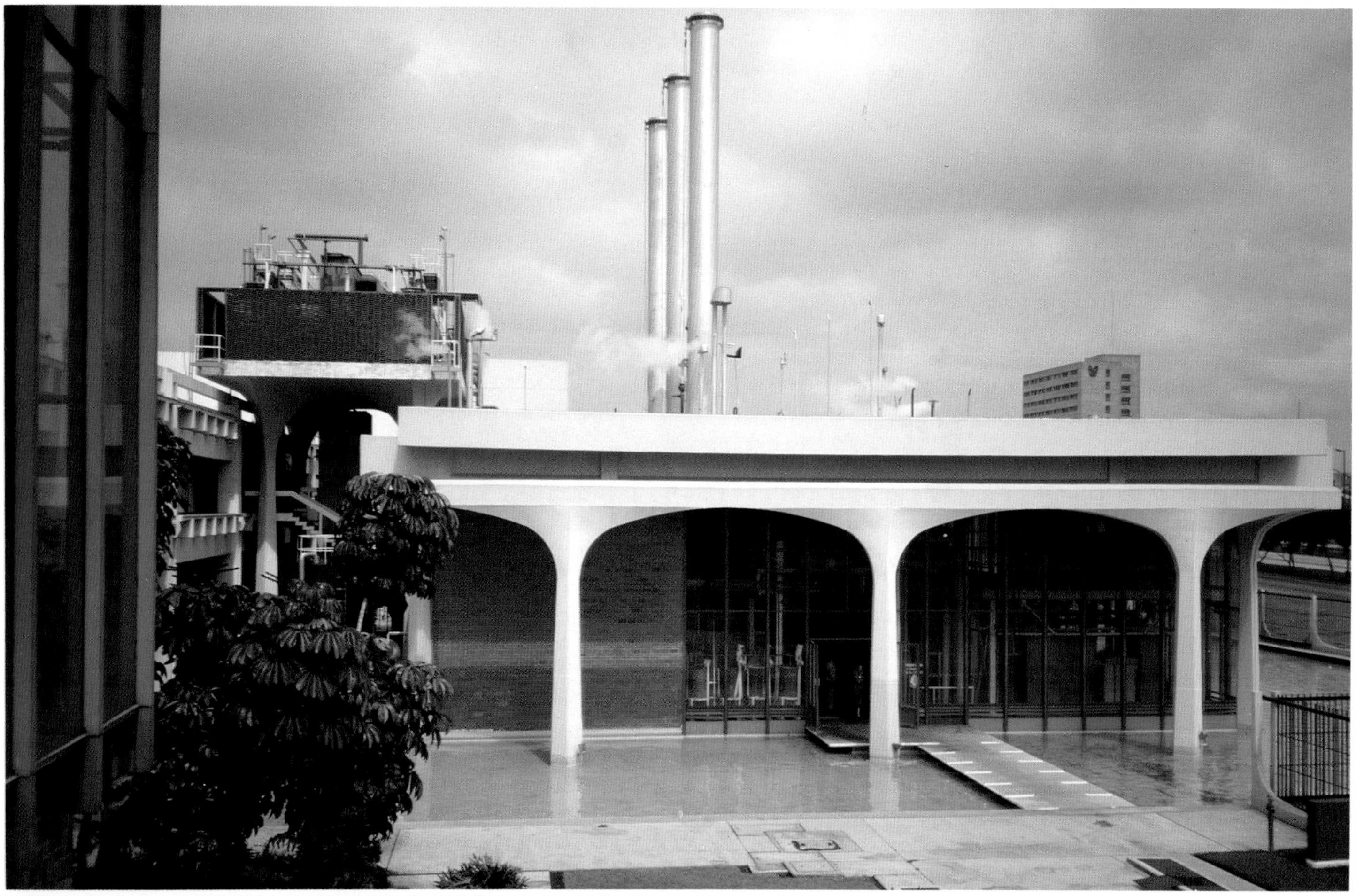

Above: Surrounded by a moat like a medieval castle, the powerplant of Moctezuma's Guadalajara Cervecería is described as the 'heart of the factory.' It provides steam power for the cervecería as well as carbon dioxide to carbonate the cerveza.

Left: Malta (barley malt) is brought in from Central de Malta in Pueblo for milling at the Moctezuma Cervecería. Dark carmel *malta* is used in the brewing of the Dos Equis brand, while lighter *maltas* are used in lighter brands such as Sol.

Top right: The *malta* is heated in the *cocedor* (mash tun) to transform starches into fermentable sugars.

Right: From the *cocedor*, the sweet *mosto* (wort) is piped into the *filtro lauter* (lauter tun) for filtering prior to brewing.

Above: After filtering in the *filtro lauter*, the sweet *mosto* goes into the *paila de cocinientos* (brew kettle) where the brewing takes place. The *lupulo* (hops) will be added at this stage in the form of pellets or oil rather than as whole hops. The hops will transform the *mosto* from sweet to hopped *mosto*. Moctezuma imports its hops from Yakima Valley, USA.

Above: Moctezuma's Guadalajara brewmaster, José Paz Aguirre, confers with American beer columnist Fred Eckhardt in the cervecería's laboratory.

Right: The laboratory at Moctezuma's Guadalajara Cerveceria provides a constant quality control check.

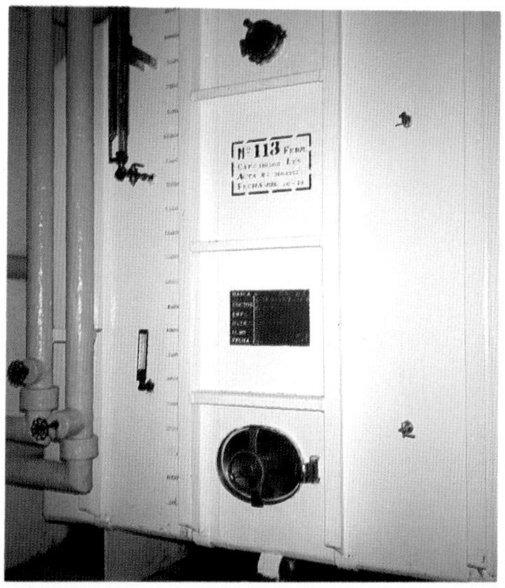

Left: After brewing in the *paila de cocinientos*, yeast is added to the *mosto* and it is placed in large closed tanks for seven days of fermentation at 12°C. As is the case with Anheuser-Busch, the yeast is recycled three times before it is discarded. It is then sold for use in animal food and medical products because of its high Vitamin B concentration.

Right: Used Moctezuma bottles are sterilized prior to refilling. The 60-peso bottle deposit, which is higher even than that in Oregon, has contributed to a high rate of recycling.

Below: Bottles used on the bottle lines at all three of Moctezuma's Cervecerías come from the Moctezuma glass factory at Orizaba.

A cerverama, or cerveza store, in a Mexican village on the north side of Lake Chapala near Guadalajara, well marked with the Tecate and Carta Blanca trademarks of Cerveceria Cuauhtemoc. Cuauhtemoc is one of Mexico's big three brewers and has more breweries than any other brewer in Mexico.

CERVERAMA
TENDEJON
CARTA
BLANCA

BREWERY CLOSE-UP

NORTH AMERICA'S OLDEST BREWERY

MOLSON LTD

Above: The present day Molson brewery (Brasserie Molson) in Montreal, Quebec is located on the same site as the brewery John Molson established in 1786. Today, there are eight Molson breweries located in seven Canadian provinces from British Columbia to Newfoundland.

Above: Unlike most smaller brewers, Molson malts and mills its own barley.

Above: Putting the Molson signature on the back of a Molson delivery truck.

Above and right: The first step in the brewing process is to mix and heat malted barley and water in the mash tun. After mashing, the thick mash mixture is piped to a large lauter tun. Here the mash is carefully filtered through the natural grain bed and the resultant golden amber wort is piped to the brew kettle.

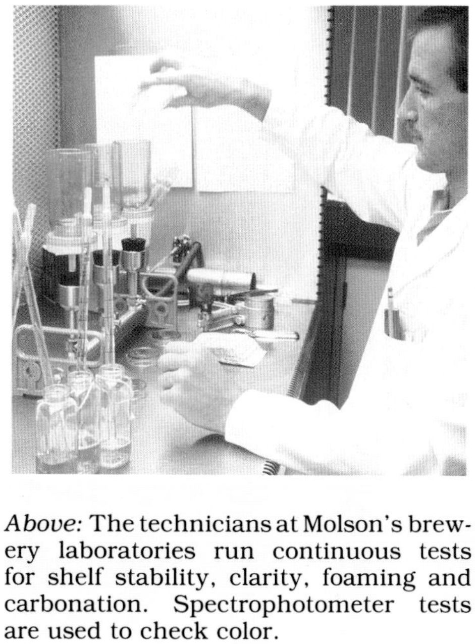

Above: The technicians at Molson's brewery laboratories run continuous tests for shelf stability, clarity, foaming and carbonation. Spectrophotometer tests are used to check color.

BREWERY CLOSE-UP

In big stainless steel *(above)* or copper *(below)* brew kettles, the wort is cooked and the hops are added which will season the brew and give each Molson product its characteristic flavor. The quantities, varieties and even the times that hops are added vary with the type of beer being brewed. The older breweries use copper, the newer ones, stainless steel.

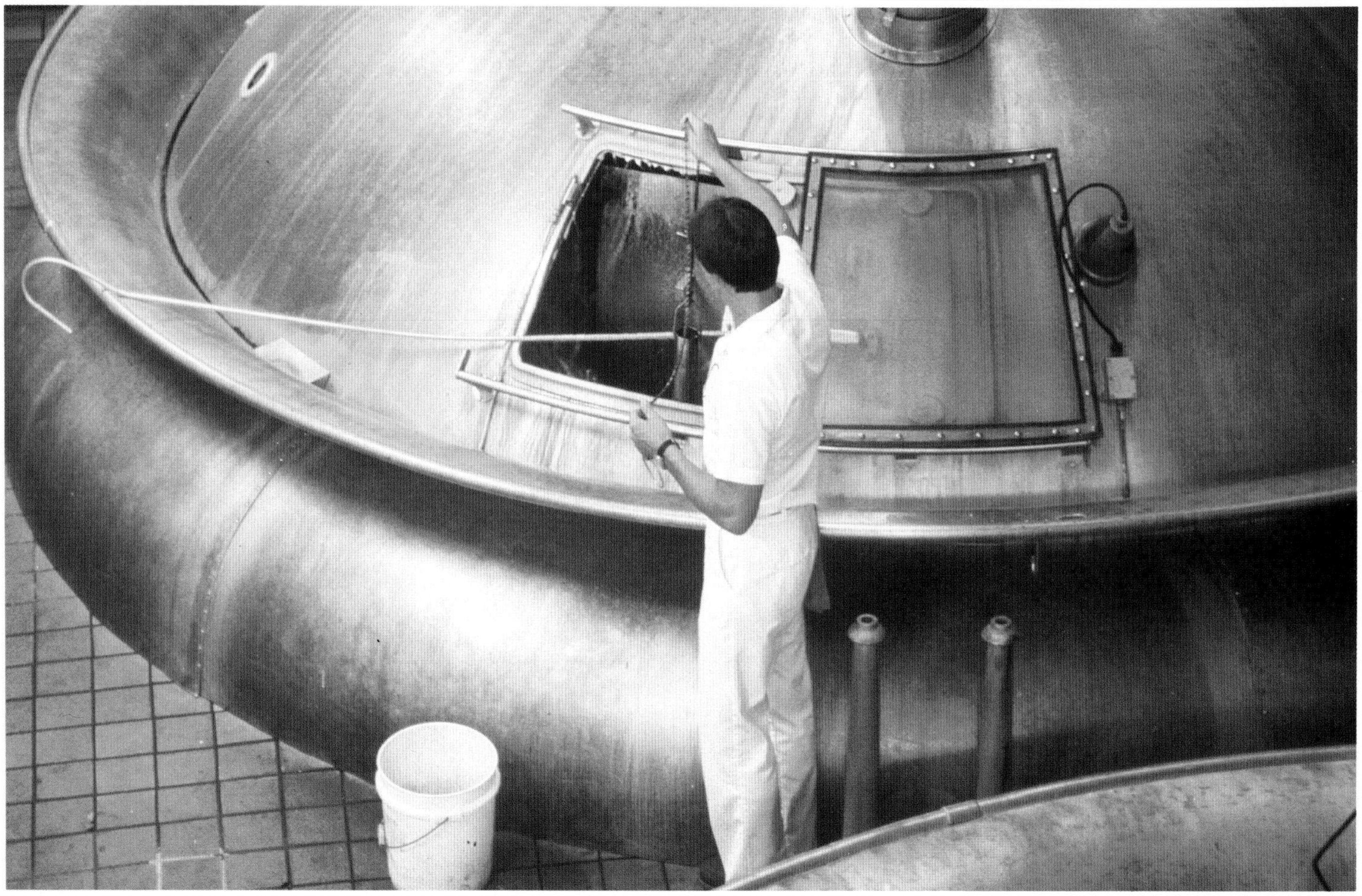

Above: Cooled wort goes into fermentation tanks where Molson brewmasters use both laboratory tests and their own practical experience to monitor the fermentation process. Visual inspections are made at regular intervals, and only when all of the brewmaster's requirements are met is the fermentation deemed complete and cooling started. After leaving the fermentation tanks, the beer passes through coolers, bringing the temperature down almost to freezing. It is then allowed to rest in the primary aging tanks where the yeast will settle out. The beer is then filtered and carbonated using the carbon dioxide produced earlier during fermentation. The beer is then transferred to aging tanks.

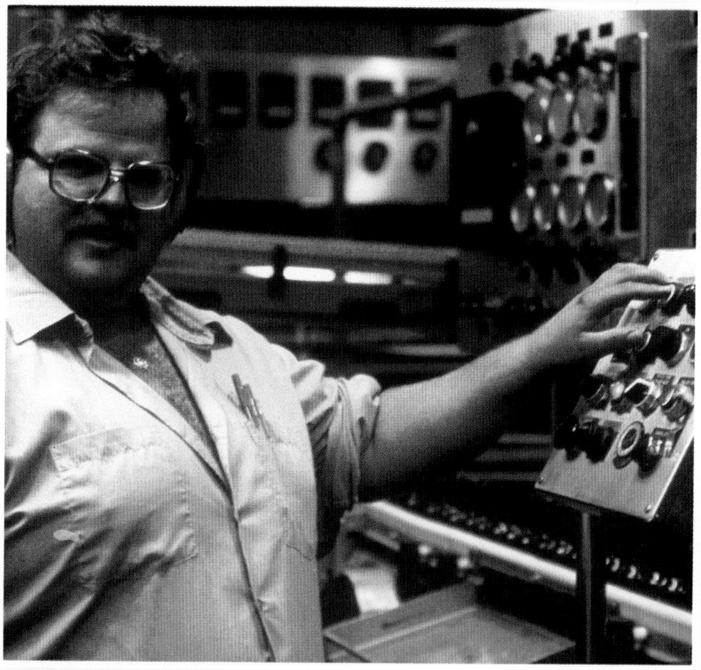

Above left: After secondary aging and final filtration, Molson beer is ready for packaging, pasteurization and labeling.

Left: Deposit-returned bottles are carefully inspected prior to filling.

Above: Filled bottles are inspected at random as a final quality check.

CANADA'S BIG THREE

Just as the big three United States brewers at the turn of the century remained near the top of the heap through most of the century, so it was in Canada. These breweries (Molson, Labatt's and the duo of Carling and O'Keefe) faced marketing conditions quite different from those in the United States. Canada has a larger area but a much smaller population. Its population remained concentrated in the east long after the United States population began to disperse westward. For this reason the big breweries of Quebec and Ontario faced no competition from national brands because outside of these two provinces, there could be no national brand. Even though they constitute just 25 percent of Canada's land area, they contained 75 percent of her population in 1896 and were still home to 60 percent of Canadians in 1980.

By the turn of the century, Canada's 132 breweries were producing 27.6 million gallons of beer of which 54 percent were produced in Ontario, 31 percent in Quebec and

Canada's big three are Carling-O'Keefe, Molson and Labatt. The Carling-O'Keefe brewery in Montreal *(above)*, a Molson's driver happily making his rounds *(below)* and Labatt's Blue and Blue Light, the dominion's biggest seller.

Labatt's
BIÈRE Pilsener BEER
341ml
5% alc./vol.
SYMBOL OF BREWING QUALITY
1828
call for 'Labatt's Blue'
Labatt's
LIGHT Pilsener LÉGÈRE
Blue Light
LIGHT BEER · BIÈRE LÉGÈRE
TWIST OFF
Labatt's
Blue Light
OR USE OPENER

The Molson flagship brewery in Montreal is still located on the same site where John Molson founded North America's oldest brewing company in 1786.

5 percent in British Columbia. The last province had an unusually large number of smaller breweries whose output was 96 percent lager. Eastern breweries, especially those in the maritime provinces, were more apt to produce ale or porter. For the vast plains of central Canada, marketing meant creating a market where none existed. Konrad Witteman, who established a brewery at Prince Albert, Saskatchewan in 1896 (when it was still part of the Northwest Territories), wrote in 1902 that 'when we came here there was hardly any demand for beer, everybody drinking whiskey; but since we started the brewery, the sale of beer has increased right along and the taste here will be cultivated.'

Aside from Canada's vastness and the cultural and economic domination of Ontario and Quebec, Canada's lag in developing national brands as early as the United States probably resulted from her more autonomous provinces. Many of the types of governmental regulations concerning brewing that are written by the federal government in the United States are written by the provincial governments in Canada. Even today, a brewer must operate a brewery within a province in order to sell his beer there.

In 1916, as the United States was beginning to toy with the idea of a national prohibition, Canada's prov-

Above: **The main office of Pelissier's Brewery in Fort Garry, Alberta in 1919.** ***Above right:*** **A 1930 photo of the headquarters for Prince Albert Breweries Ltd, in Prince Albert, Saskatchewan. Small breweries helped cultivate a taste for beer in central Canada where mostly whiskey was drunk. The inset shows an old Labatt label.**

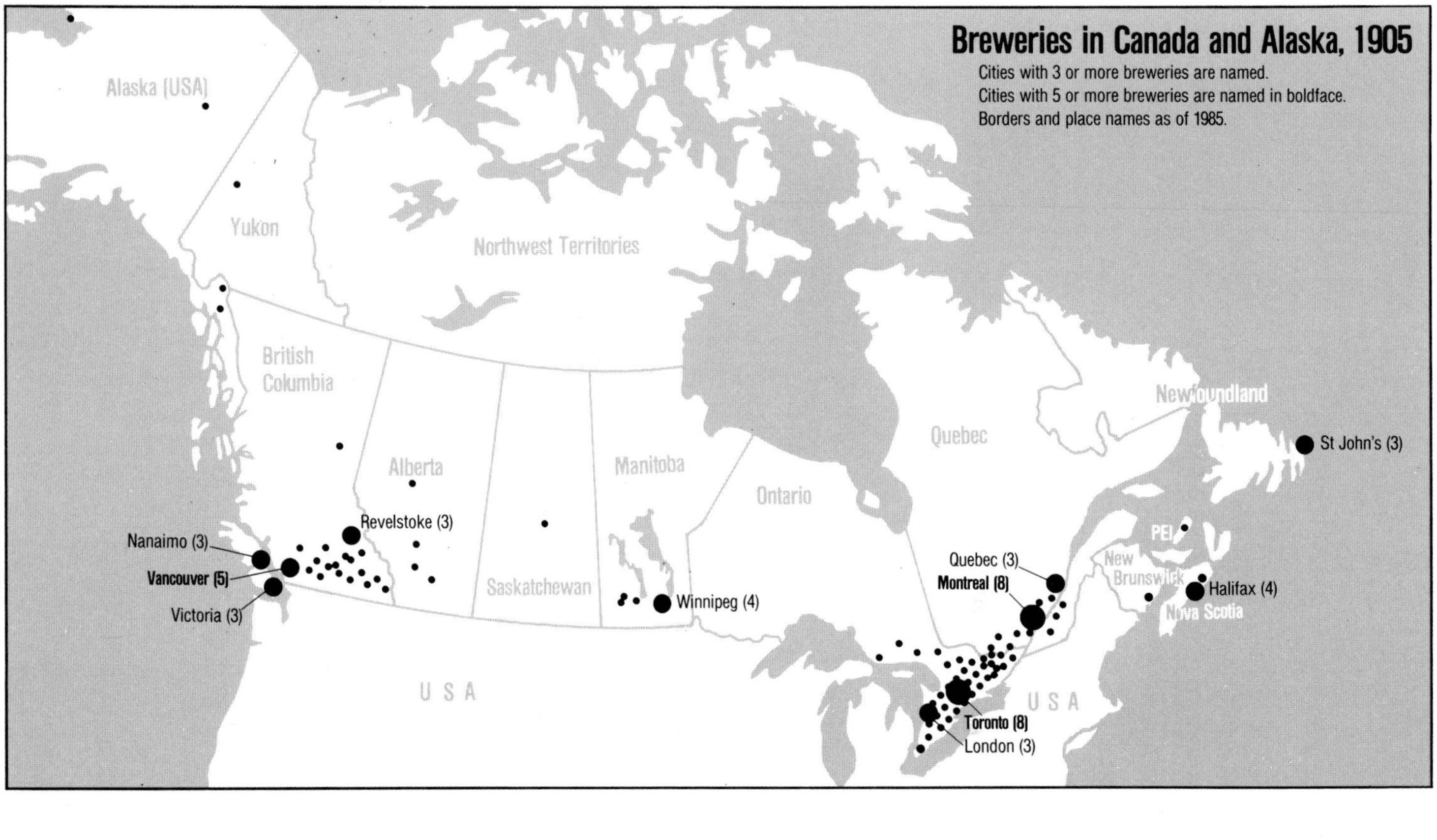

Labatt's
EST. 1832
Crystal
LAGER
L.C.B.O.
JOHN LABATT LIMITED
LONDON · CANADA
LABEL REGISTERED
CONTENTS 12 FLUID OUNCES
HEAD OFFICE
Prince Albert
BREWERIES LIMITED

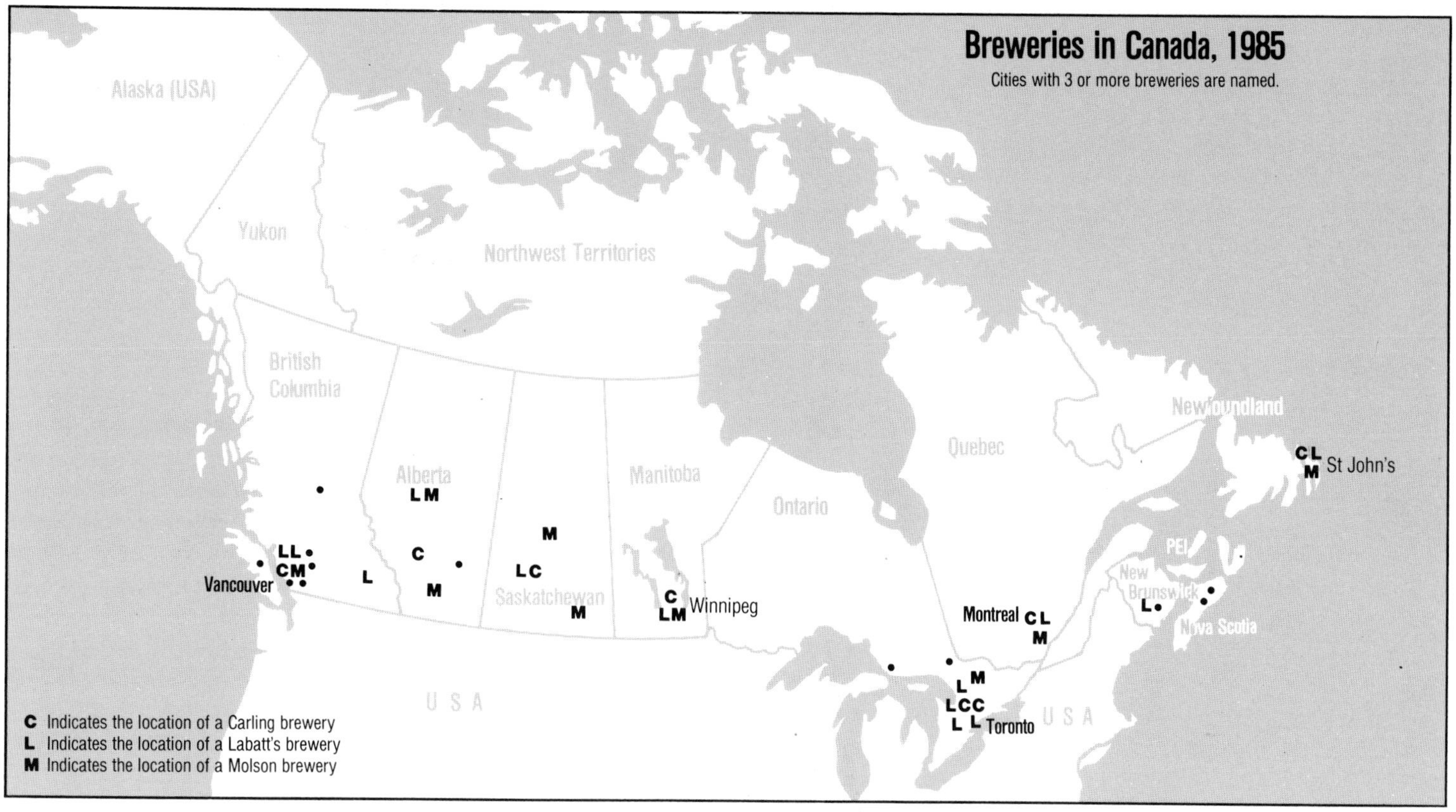
Breweries in Canada, 1985
Cities with 3 or more breweries are named.
Alaska (USA)
Yukon
Northwest Territories
British Columbia
Alberta
Saskatchewan
Manitoba
Ontario
Quebec
Newfoundland
PEI
New Brunswick
Nova Scotia
USA
Vancouver
Winnipeg
Montreal
Toronto
St John's
C Indicates the location of a Carling brewery
L Indicates the location of a Labatt's brewery
M Indicates the location of a Molson brewery

These images from Canada's brewing history include (*above*) a case of Molson's brew coming down the bottling line at the Montreal plant in the 1930s; a sleigh of the type used by Molson's to deliver their brew in Quebec's north country (*below*); and a turn of the century poster (*right*) showing two gentlemen enjoying Labatt's brew at their club.

inces began to adopt provincial prohibition as a wartime measure. By 1919 prohibition was complete except for Quebec which exempted beer and wine. During 1920–21, Quebec was the only place north of the Mexican border where beer could legally be brewed. The other provinces gradually began to repeal their prohibition in 1921, and by 1930 Prince Edward Island, the only province to adopt prohibition before 1916, was the only province to still retain it.

During the years between Prohibition and World War II Canada's big three, like the brewers in the United States, began to improve their distribution system in order to capture larger segments of the market. The most colorful stories belong to Labatt's and begin in 1919. Prior to prohibition in Ontario, the brewery of John Labatt, like that of John Molson, had transported its beer by rail or by horsedrawn wagons by summer and sleds the rest of the year. In 1919 the US Government blocked the sale of some White Motor Company trucks to the revolution-ridden Mexican government. As a result, White found another international customer, and Labatt's had its first motor-driven distribution vehicles.

JOHN LABATT,
BREWER,
LONDON, CANADA.
ALE & STOUT.

By 1932 trucks were commonplace and Labatt's was ready to try the uncommon. In that year the company introduced its bright red Streamliner truck. Designed by the Russian ex-patriate coach designer Count Alexis de Sakhnoffsky, these striking aerodynamic vehicles won 'Best Design' at the 1939 New York World's Fair and earned a place as the most innovative beer truck in the history of North America. Although they were withdrawn from service in 1942, one of the trucks was preserved and today remains as a major company showpiece.

After World War II, Canadian brewers, like American brewers, began to set their sights on multisite operations. Labatt's purchased its second brewery, the former Copland Brewing Company of Toronto in 1946, and Molson, Canada's oldest, opened its second in 1955, just 169 years after its first. Though it would not take Molson as long to open its third, the leader in the Canadian multisite expansion was Carling-O'Keefe. Behind its flagship brand, Carling Black Label, the company was spreading its empire beyond Ontario, where breweries were in operation at Toronto, Waterloo,

Introduced in 1932, Labatt's red streamliner trucks (*above*) were designed by a Russian count who once designed coaches for the Tsar. The streamliners were more distinctive, but no more reliable than vehicles of today, such as the Molson's truck seen below,

winding its way through Montreal bringing the brew to friendly and congenial neighborhood taverns such as the one above.

Sudbury and Thunder Bay. The Carling-O'Keefe group included Golden West and Calgary Export in Alberta, Standard in Manitoba and Four-X Special, a stout brewed in Vancouver, British Columbia.

Carling was not content to remain solely a Canadian brewer either. Through international licensing agreements, Carling Black Label was appearing throughout the world, and the company was plying that huge beer market south of Canada's borders. Carling made its first inroads in the United States in Cleveland, Ohio through the Brewing Corporation of America before World War II. However, it was after the war that Carling moved south in a big way. The Brewing Corporation of America's Quincy Avenue brewery in Cleveland became the Carling Brewing Company in 1953. The following year Carling acquired the former Griesedieck Western breweries in Belleville, Illinois and St Louis. In 1956 Carling added breweries in Natick, Massachusetts and Frankenmuth, near Detroit, in Michigan. Two years later the Canadian-based brewer put out its shingle in Atlanta, Georgia and Tacoma, Washington, making it an archipelago of breweries that was the envy of many American brewers.

During the early 1960s Carling opened breweries in Baltimore, in Fort Worth and Phoenix, but the decade was marked by the company's gradual decline in the market. In 1960 Carling had been the fourth biggest brewer in the United States. By 1970, the Canadian's position had slipped to eighth and by 1975 it wasn't even in the top 10. In the meantime the breweries in Cleveland, Atlanta and Natick were closed or sold. In March 1979 Carling left the United States market, selling its holdings to Heileman which acquired the Carling breweries in Phoenix, Baltimore, Frankenmuth, Tacoma and Belleville, Illinois. Stag Beer was but one of the many brand names that came along with breweries. Carling also sold Heileman two important international brewing licenses. The first was for Carling's products, which Heileman continued to brew in the United States; the second was for Tuborg, a Danish beer for which Carling had acquired the license in 1973, and which had been introduced into the US market amid much fanfare in the mid-1970s.

BREWERY CLOSE-UP

NORTH AMERICA'S LARGEST BREWER

ANHEUSER-BUSCH

Right: All the hardware and procedures in every Anheuser-Busch brewhouse, like the recipes for every Anheuser-Busch beer, conform to carefully prepared corporate specifications to ensure absolute uniformity. A bottle of Budweiser brewed in Fairfield, California should taste exactly the same as a bottle of Budweiser brewed in St Louis, Missouri.

Anheuser-Busch's beers, especially Budweiser, are the most popular in North America. Every year the company's plants fill millions of bottles, cans and draft kegs. In 1984, it produced enough beer to fill 23 billion 11-ounce bottles.

Below: A state-of-the-art laboratory is an important part of every Anheuser-Busch brewery. The lab monitors the characteristics of the beer from brewing to bottling. With modern 'automated beer analysis' it is possible to monitor the fermentation going on in every tank rather than simply relying on spot checks.

Anheuser-Busch brews over 60 million barrels of beer each year at 11 breweries throughout the United States. Even though they are widely separated geographically, the company takes pains to ensure that the products are of uniform high quality.

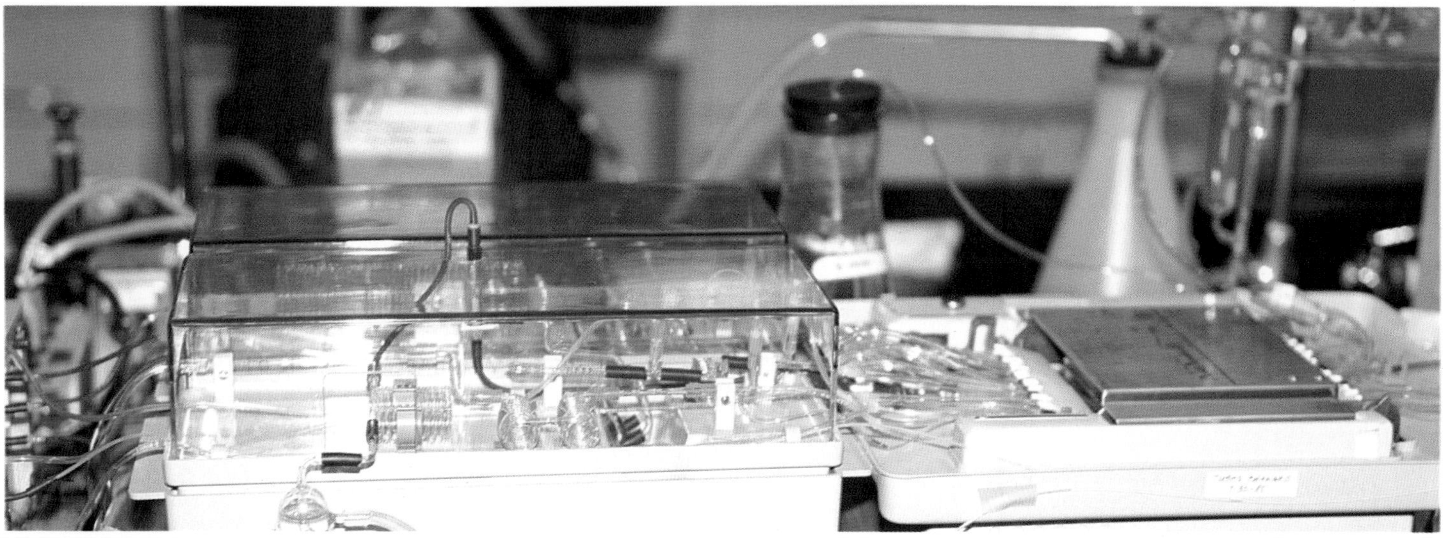

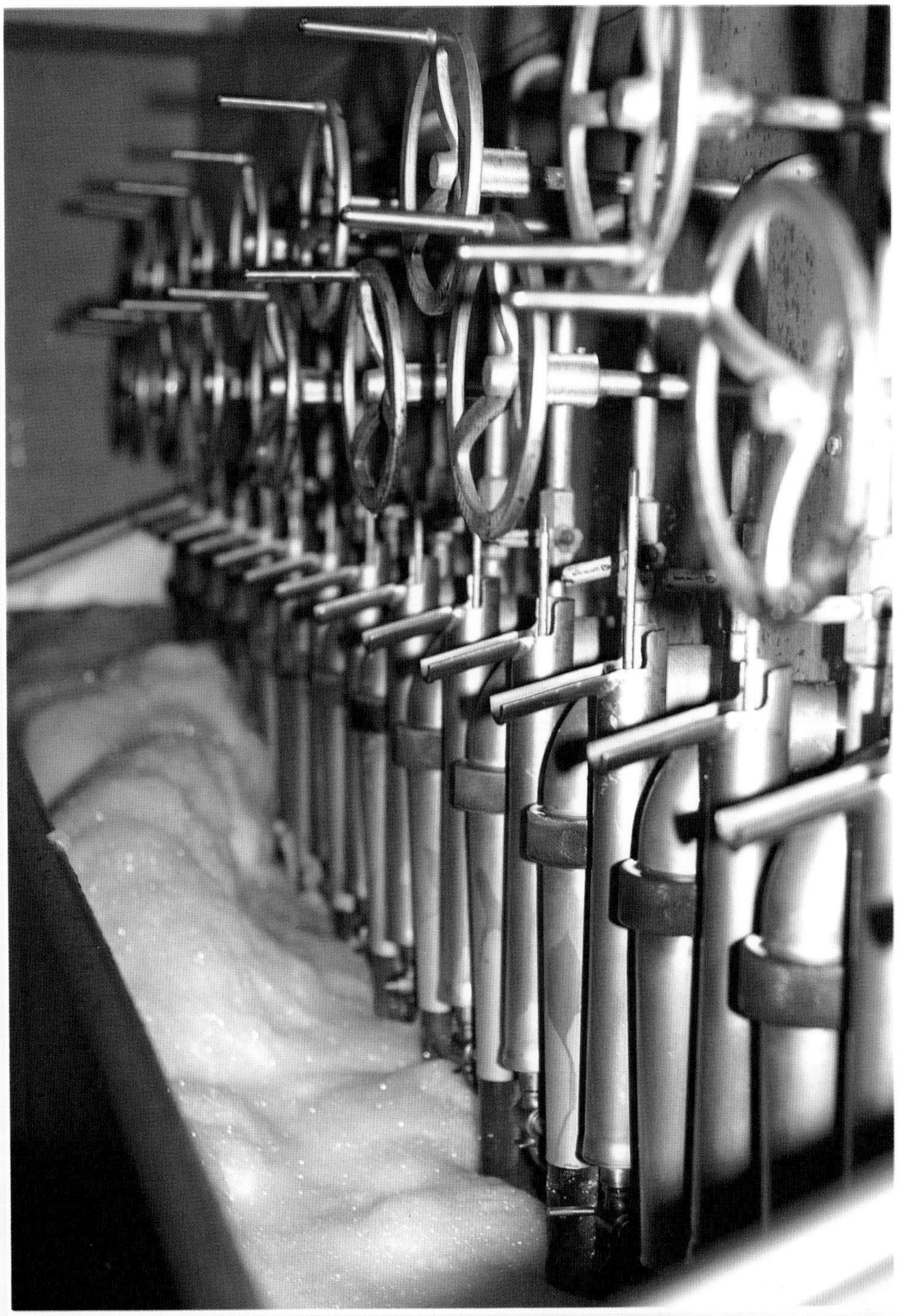

Above: After malted barley and rice are milled the barley is mashed and the rice cooked to change their starches into fermentable sugars. Barley and rice are mixed according to very specific recipes for each Anheuser-Busch product.

The sweet wort, a mixture of cooked rice and mashed barley, is strained in the strainmaster before being placed in the brew kettle. The strainmaster performs the same function as the traditional lauter tun.

Right: After it is strained, the sweet wort moves through the grant, which controls the rate of flow into the brew kettle.

Below: An Anheuser-Busch hop room. A variety of domestic and European hops are used, depending on the particular recipe for each specific Anheuser-Busch beer. Michelob, for example, is made with only European hops.

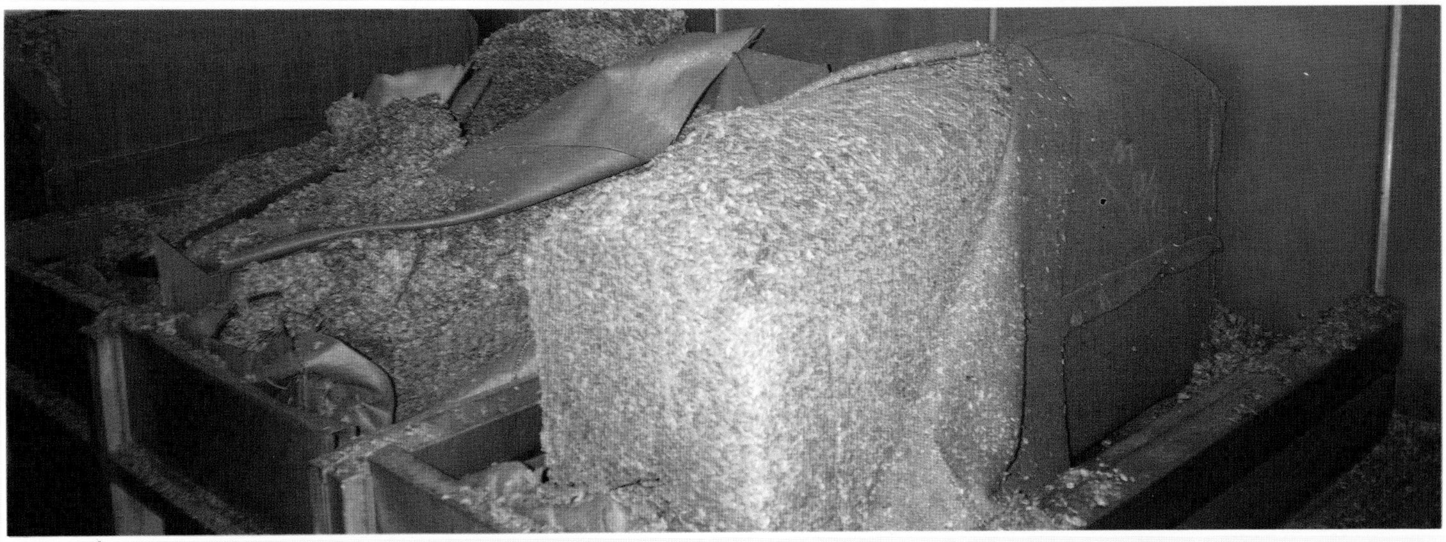

BREWERY CLOSE-UP

Above: Anheuser-Busch hops, ready to be added to the brew kettle.

Right: After the sweet wort is brought to a boil in the stainless steel brew kettle, hops are added, and the resulting hopped wort is boiled for over three hours. In the nineteenth century, brew kettles such as those at the original Anheuser-Busch brewery in St Louis *(below)* were made of copper for even heat conduction, but most modern large-scale brewers now use stainless steel for easier cleaning.

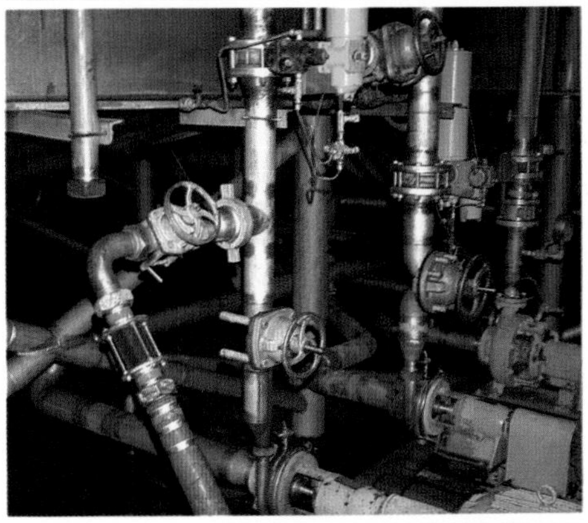

Far left: Anheuser-Busch adds yeast to the hopped wort as it moves through the lines to the fermenting tanks rather than adding it after the wort is in the tanks. To ensure quality and uniformity, the yeast is shipped weekly from St Louis to each Anheuser-Busch Brewery.

Left: The cold wort is placed in Alpha tanks for five to seven days. During this time the yeast converts the fermentable sugars to carbon dioxide and alcohol, and the wort becomes beer.

Far left: Beechwood chips are placed in the second fermentation tanks for the krausening of all Anheuser-Busch beers. The sterilized beechwood is chemically inert, but it serves to help extract the yeast. The beechwood chips themselves are extracted by hand.

Left: After roughly a month in the two fermentation tanks, Anheuser-Busch beers go into the Schone tanks to be clarified. Natural tannin is added, which picks up protein particles and settles them out.

Below: Sophisticated control centers help brewmasters at every Anheuser-Busch brewery carefully monitor every step of the month-long beer-making process, from brewing to finishing.

NORTH AMERICAN BREWING AT THE CLOSE OF THE TWENTIETH CENTURY

The story of American brewing in the third quarter of the twentieth century closely parallels that of the last quarter of the nineteenth, characterized simply as fewer breweries brewing more beer. At the end of World War II, over 450 brewing companies existed in the United States alone, but by 1985 there were fewer than 100 on the entire continent. At the end of World War II multisite brewers or even brewers with two plants were a rarity, but in 1985 such companies as Anheuser-Busch and Heileman were operating 10 or more plants in the United States. Canadian giants like Molson and Labatt's had operations in practically every province.

A major sign of the times during the 1960s and 1970s indicated that many of the great brand names in the United States ceased to exist as independent entities. Miller was acquired by Philip Morris, while the once great Schlitz was acquired by the much smaller Stroh's. Hamm's was acquired by Olympia, which was acquired by Pabst, which was in turn acquired by Paul Kalmanovitz whose holdings already included Ballantine, Falstaff, Lucky Lager, Narragansett and Pearl. Heileman, once a small brewer from La Crosse, Wisconsin worked its way from thirty-first to fourth among American brewers by collecting an extensive roster of formerly independent regional brewers from around the country including Blitz-Weinhard, Blatz, Heidelberg, Lone Star, Schmidt and Rainier.

Even as the American brewing industry was going through this unprecedented torrent of mergers, some of the most important regional brewers in the United States remained independent and successful. These included Yuengling in Potts-

Facing page: **Women such as this young lady in a Molson promotional film became more important as consumers of beer during the 1970s and 80s than at any time in history. Women were an important factor in the decision to begin introducing 'light' beers. Reduced calorie beer, typified by Lite Beer from Miller (*above*) was a major 1970s phenomena, and light beers soon became part of the repertoire of all major North American brewers. Reduced alcohol beer, such as Anheuser-Busch's LA (*below*), introduced in 1984, was less widely accepted by consumers than light beers had been.**

Two small long-established brewers whose products enjoyed renewed popularity in the 1970s and 80s were Stevens Point in Stevens Point, Wisconsin and Anchor in San Francisco. Anchor distributes in the West and part of the East, but Stevens Point only in its corner of Wisconsin. *Right:* Workers unload lager tanks at Anheuser-Busch.

ville, Pennsylvania (the country's oldest brewer), Hudepohl in Cincinnati, Dixie in New Orleans and Anchor in San Francisco. At the same time, the Adolph Coors Brewing company in Golden, Colorado was independent and extremely successful. By 1975 Coors was still a single-site brewery without a complete national distribution system, yet it was the fifth largest brewing company in the United States and the seventh largest in the world. The brewery that young Adolph Coors had started in 1873 in the Colorado Rockies had become the single largest brewing plant in the world.

While the third quarter of the twentieth century was marked by mergers and the decline of many of the old names in American brewing, the final quarter of the twentieth century, particularly the 1980s, was marked by an amazing revival of small regional and even local 'microbreweries.' Spawned by renewed interest in the art of beer-making, these microbreweries represent a phenomenon that has not been seen on such a scale since before Prohibition. For the first time in over a century the number of breweries in the United States was actually increasing!

The microbrewery revolution began in Northern California, but quickly spread to other places throughout the United States. The appearance of microbreweries is certainly due in part to the establishment in 1975 of a brewing course under the Food Sciences Department at the University of California's Davis campus, located halfway between San Francisco and Sacramento. Under the able direction of Dr Michael Lewis, the department turned out brewmasters who have gone not only to the microbreweries

Breweries in the United States, November 1984

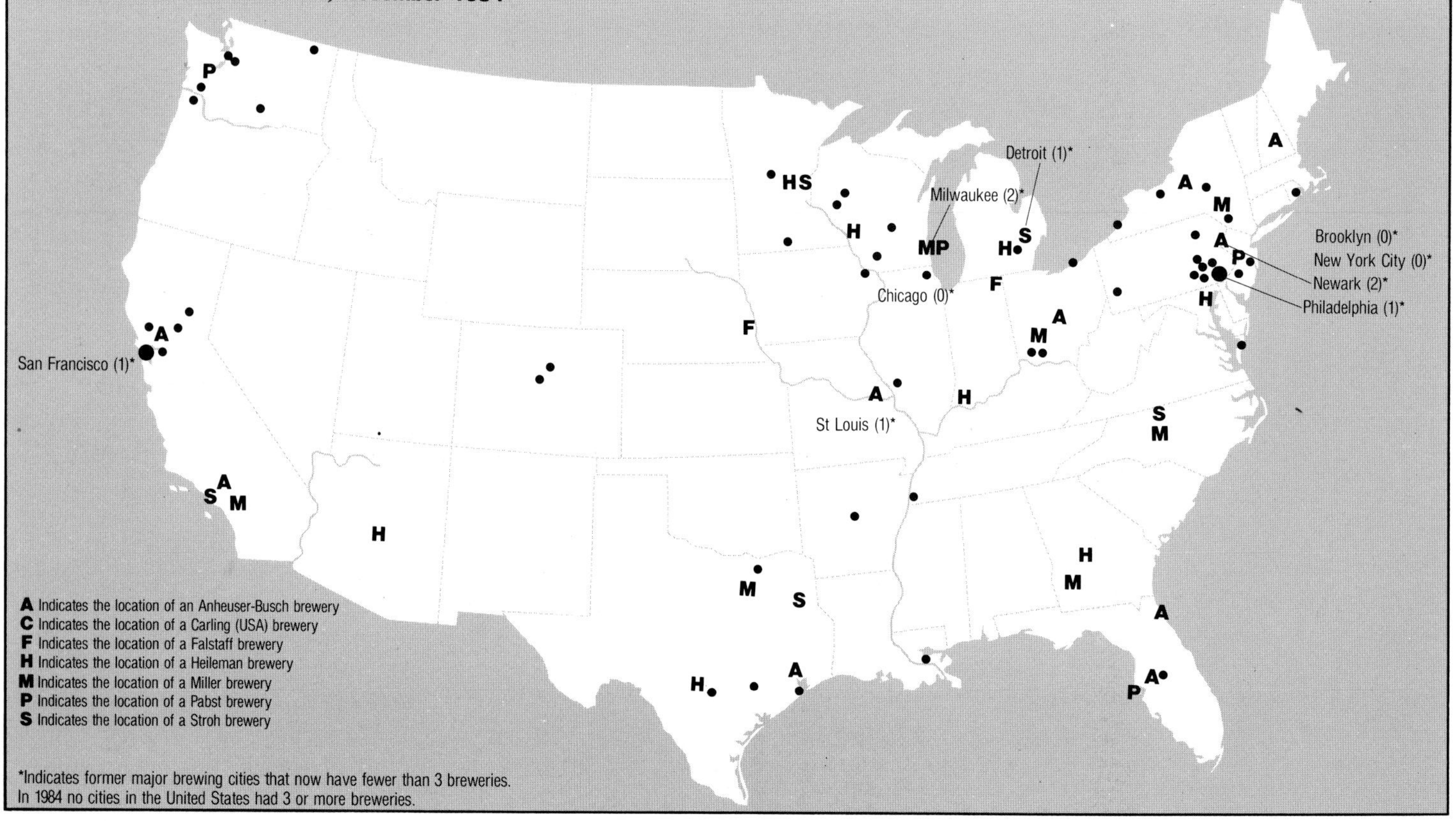

KEEP DOORS
CLOSED

Sierra Nevada of Chico was one of the original microbreweries, precursor of a wave of small breweries that began a new tradition in brewing in the 1980s.

but to the large established breweries as well. Several of the people brewing beer at the Anheuser-Busch facility in nearby Fairfield are, for example, graduates of Dr Lewis's courses.

The first California microbreweries were the Sierra Nevada Brewing Company of Chico and the now defunct River City Brewing company in Sacramento (both of which were started in 1980) and the Thousand Oaks Brewing Company in Berkeley which opened in 1981. It is interesting to note that the last previous breweries in each of these towns had closed their doors in 1902, 1949 and 1915, respectively. The microbrewery movement spread to Colorado in 1980 with the opening of the Boulder Brewing Company and to New York State as William Newman began brewing in Albany the following year. Two microbreweries opened in Washington State during 1982, the Red Hook Ale Brewery in Seattle, and Yakima Brewing in Malting, which is coincidentally located in the heart of the best hop-growing region in North America.

By 1984, Northern California had four more microbreweries, Buffalo Bill's Brewery in Hayward, Palo Alto Brewing in Mountain View, Stanislaus Brewing (St Stan's) in Modesto and Mendocino Brewing, which was appropriately established in the village of Hopland about two hours north of San Francisco. Both Mendocino Brewing and Buffalo Bill's are primarily 'brew pubs' which means that their products are brewed primarily for consumption in the brewery tasting rooms on the premises rather than for packaged sale elsewhere as with products from other commercial breweries.

While Northern California was rapidly on its way to becoming the new Milwaukee, Portland, Oregon was quickly establishing itself as a major new brewing center. Portland was the city where Henry Saxer had started the first western brewery outside of San Francisco in 1852, which in turn had been Henry Weinhard's brewery and later the flagship of Blitz-Weinhard. Eleven breweries had been established in Portland prior to 1905 but when Prohibition

Montana Beverage Co of St Helena revived the name Kessler, Montana's original premier brewer and brought Dan Carey *(above)* from California as brewmaster.

The Stroh's flagship brewery in Detroit, Michigan. Stroh was one of the brewing success stories of the 1980s. Coming from a position of a fairly large regional brewery, Stroh bought the aging giant, Schlitz, in 1982 and became a national brewery and the third largest brewer in North America. In 1985 Stroh closed its Detroit brewery and moved production to more modern breweries it had acquired by purchasing Schaefer in 1981 and Schlitz.

was repealed only Blitz-Weinhard returned. Aside from the Cartwright Brewery which came and went between 1980 and 1982, Blitz-Weinhard had been the only brewery in Portland in the 50 years that followed repeal. Then suddenly between 1984 and 1985 Portland became a four-brewery town for the first time in a century, with all four located within a half-mile area on the city's northwest side. Blitz-Weinhard (now flying the Heileman flag) was joined by the Columbia River Brewery, the new Portland Brewery (an unrelated Portland Brewing Company had existed between 1905 and 1928), and the Widmer Brewing Company. Widmer was the second American brewer to make altbier (German style ale) since Prohibition; Stanislaus Brewing in California had been the first.

The microbrewery revolution that began in 1980 was probably the most important event in American brewing history since Prohibition—perhaps even since the lager revolution of 1840. It came just as the trend seemed to be toward fewer breweries larger than ever and geared to a more homogeneous mass market. Suddenly, a dozen small breweries were established in the space of just five years, each one dedicated to producing a small quantity of high-quality specialty beer. The new specialty beers of the new microbreweries arrived on the scene just as consumers were tiring of the white wine vogue that had begun in the early 1970s. The richness and unusual variety of the new brands appealed to a generation of consumers who were beginning to experiment with imported specialty beers.

F X Matt *(left)*, grandson of the F X Matt who started West End Brewing of Utica in 1888. William Newman *(above)* started his brewery in Albany in 1981. *Below left:* A Newman's keg steaming and *(below right)* a worker shoveling out the mash tun.

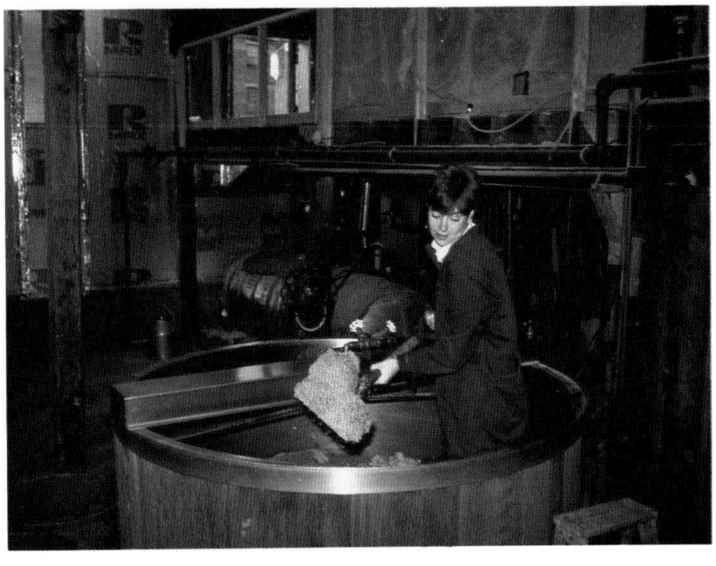

This same generation had also come of age after the heyday of local and regional brands, most of which had closed their doors prior to the 1970s. In a way, the microbreweries were starting up in a market which was, with a few exceptions like Anchor in California and Stevens Point in Wisconsin, almost devoid of small regional specialty brewers. It was almost as though American brewing history was beginning to repeat itself. A new generation was discovering and taking pride in local brews just as their grandparents had.

In a very real sense, American brewing history came full circle on 8 November 1984 in New York City. Over 350 years before, when New York was still New Amsterdam, the Netherlands West India Company had established the first of many breweries which would make the city the Western Hemisphere's first major brewing center. The first New Amsterdam and New York breweries were small, designed to brew small quantities of beer, usually for an adjoining tavern. To describe them in the diction of the 1980s, they were brew pubs not unlike those which had sprung up in California. On 8 November 1984, the Manhattan Brewing Company opened for business at Thompson and Broome streets in New York City, not only brewing beer but serving it in an adjoining taproom and restaurant. It was the first brewery to operate in Manhattan in the nearly 20 years since the Jacob Ruppert Brewery on Third Avenue closed in 1965. With its elegant all-copper brewhouse, the new establishment not only gave America's original brewing capital a working brewery once again, but it gave the city a place to enjoy the local brew in the centuries-old New Amsterdam tradition, combined with the modern brew-pub tradition. Brewing in North America had come full circle and looking to the end of its fourth century in as healthy and vibrant a state as ever.

Portraits of the new American breweries: Boulder Brewing *(left)* opened in the foothills of the Colorado Rockies in 1984 and Manhattan Brewing *(below, both)* began operation in 1984, New York City's first brewery in nearly 20 years.

PART II

THE BREWERS OF NORTH AMERICA

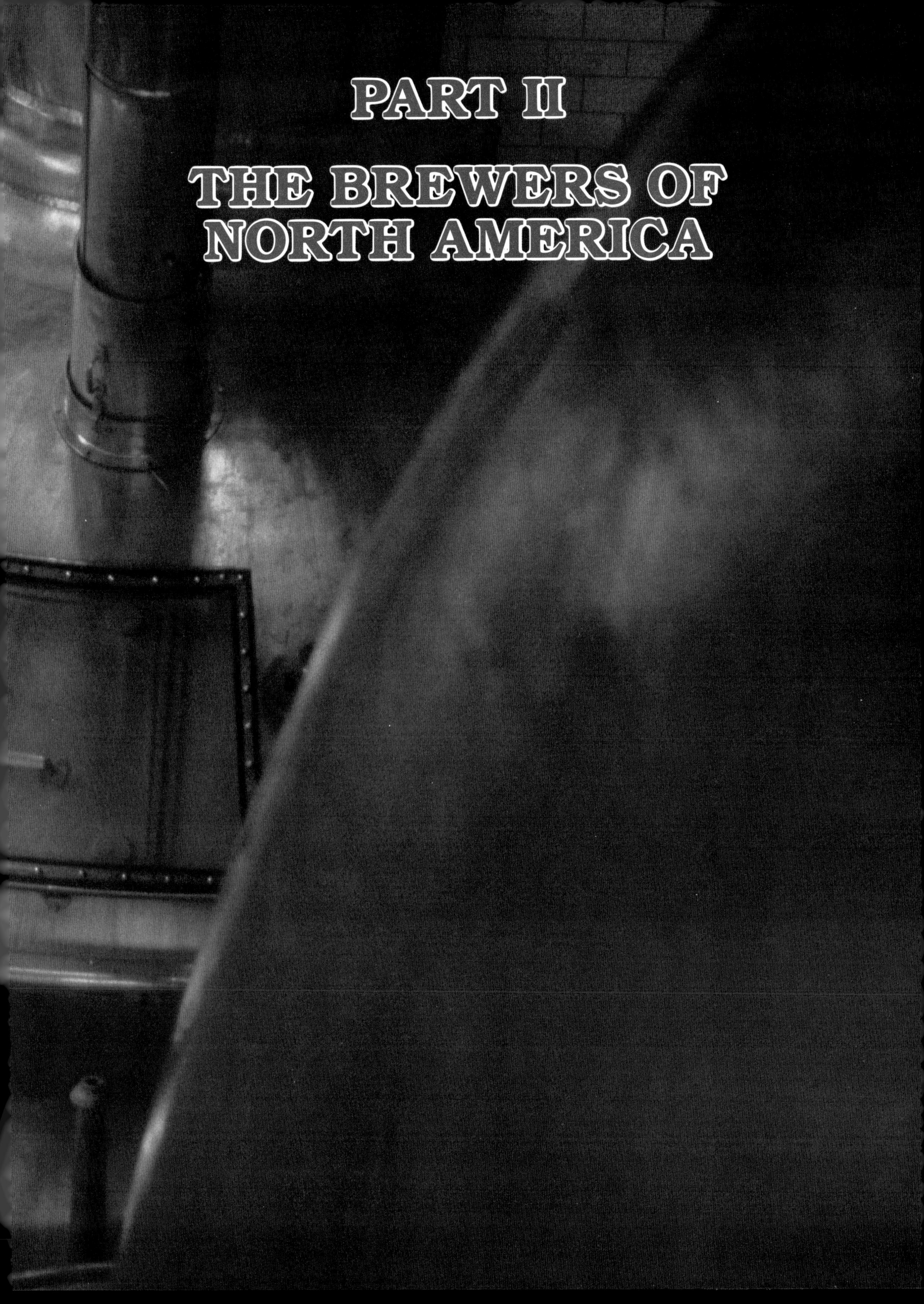

THE BREWERS OF NORTH AMERICA

A FAMILY PORTRAIT

An attempt to catalogue and summarize all the brewers on this great continent is a bit like photographing a moving object. Even though only one frozen moment in time is captured, that snapshot can tell a good deal about the object being photographed—its structure, its past evolution and its present direction. This portrait attempts to capture the brewers of North America for a family photograph circa the middle 1980s. Most of the major family members have held leading positions for many years. Anheuser-Busch has been the number one brewer for more than a quarter century and has been in the top three since the turn of the century. Canada's current top three were in similar positions at the end of the nineteenth century as well. Some of the great old regional brewers have disappeared, replaced by vibrant new microbreweries.

Not only have North America's major brewers become the world's major brewers, but the microbrewery movement has pumped in new life that could not have been predicted as late as the 1970s. In the meantime, the American consumer has finally come to take beer seriously. Major restaurants now have a beer list as well as a wine list, and people entertaining at home are as thoughtful in their choice of a beer as they are with wine.

Consumers are learning to appreciate quality brewing ingredients and a quality end product. This consumer awareness is not lost on the planners within the breweries themselves.

Below: **Filling and crowning bottles on one of Labatt's automated bottle lines. Now Canada's largest brewer, Labatt's has brewing facilities in every province except Prince Edward Island.**

Above: **Enjoying the product of one of North America's brewers and the result of three centuries of brewing heritage.**

Below: **This chart shows the relative size of North America's fifteen largest brewing companies as ranked by millions of barrels produced annually.**

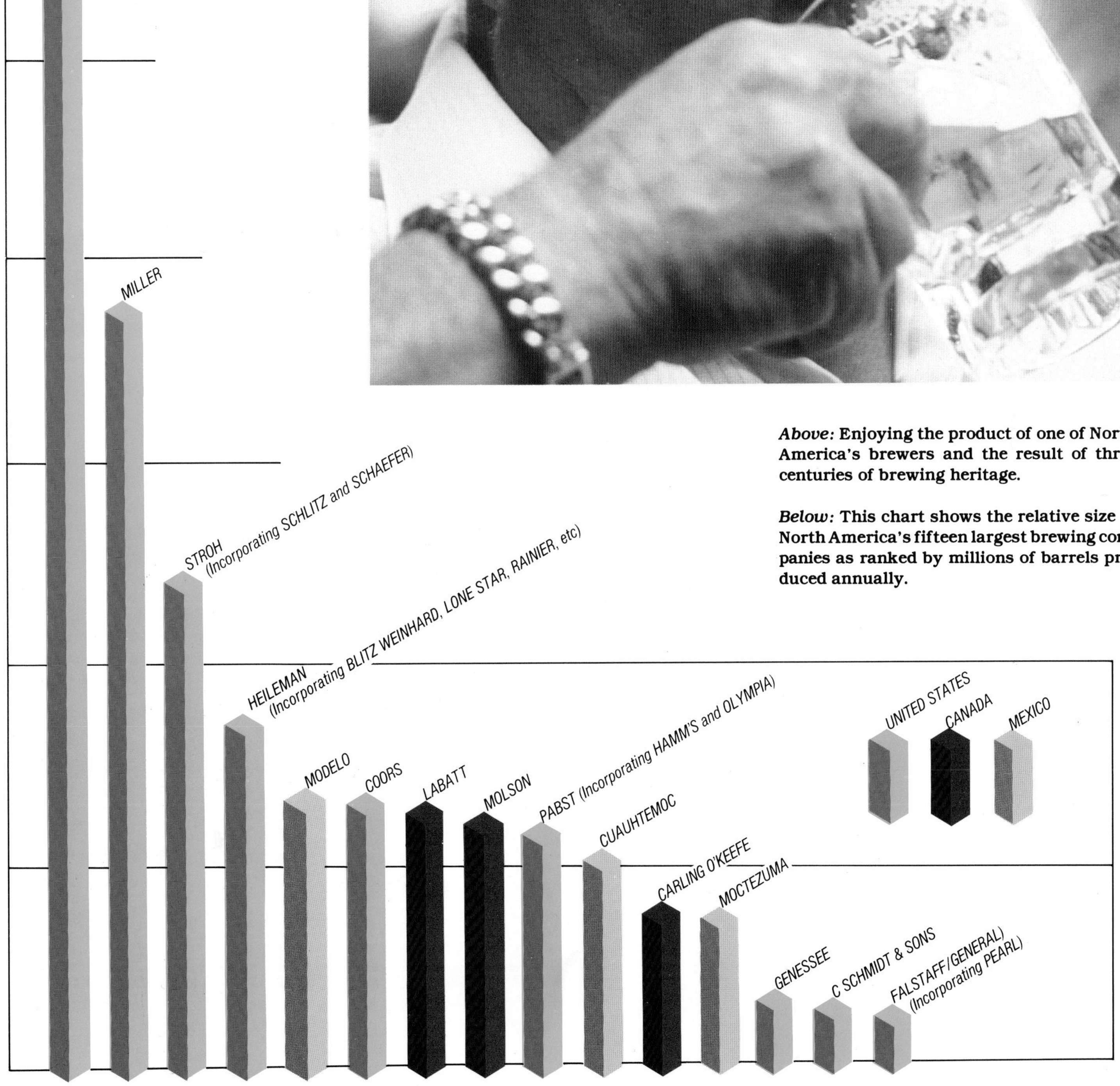

THE UNITED STATES

North America's most populous nation is also the world's biggest brewing nation with an annual output double that of second-place Germany and triple that of third-place Great Britain. The portrait that follows describes the six largest brewers of the United States in order of magnitude and the others in alphabetical order. All of the US brewers were contacted during 1985 and asked to supply labels or product shots. These are included for those brewers that responded.

THE BIG SIX

Anheuser-Busch of St Louis is not only the largest brewer in the United States, but the largest brewer in the world with no close rivals. In 1984 the company brewed 64 million barrels of beer, nearly double that of the second place US brewer, while accounting for 70 percent of the profits within the American brewing industry. While Anheuser-Busch has many popular brands of beer, its most successful is Budweiser which accounts for 70 percent of the company's volume. Budweiser is *so* popular that one out of five alcoholic beverages of all types (wine, beer, hard liquor) consumed in the United States is a Budweiser.

The world's biggest brewing company traces its roots to a small brewery started in St Louis, Missouri, in 1852 by George Schneider and taken over in 1860 by Eberhard Anheuser. Four years later Anheuser's son-in-law Adolphus Busch (1839–1913) joined the firm. A farsighted marketing genius, Busch turned the small city brewery into a national giant. He launched the extraordinarily successful Budweiser brand as a mass-market beer in 1876 and in 1896, he introduced the still-popular Michelob brand as the company's premium

beer. Originally a draft beer, Michelob was not marketed as a bottled beer until 1961.

Today Anheuser-Busch's flagship brewery is still located in St Louis, but between 1951 and 1980, other major breweries were established at Newark, New Jersey (1951); Los Angeles (1954); Tampa, Florida (1959); Houston, Texas (1966); Columbus, Ohio (1968); Jacksonville, Florida (1969); Merrimack, New Hampshire (1970); Williamsburg, Virginia (1972); Fairfield, California (1976); and Baldwinsville, New York (1980). The largest of these are St Louis with a 12.7-million-barrel annual capacity, Los Angeles (10.9 million), Williamsburg (8.7 million), and Houston (8.5 million).

In addition to 'Bud' and Michelob, Anheuser-Busch brews a variety of other beers. Busch, introduced in 1955, is marketed regionally in the eastern part of the United States. In the late 1970s the company introduced a family of low-calorie or 'light' beers. These included Natural Light (1977), Michelob Light (1978) and Bud Light (1982). In 1984

Michelob *(left)* has been Anheuser-Busch's premium beer since 1896, and sold in bottles since 1961. *Below, both:* The company's full product line, bottled and canned. *Right:* The King of Beers!

Anheuser-Busch introduced its third Michelob product, Michelob Classic Dark. Also in 1984, the company became the first major brewer to mass market a reduced-alcohol beer, which they called 'LA' for low alcohol.

Since 1980 the Anheuser-Busch brands have been brewed under license abroad as well. Budweiser is brewed in Canada by Labatt's, in Japan by Suntory, in Israel by National, and in the United Kingdom by the venerable Watney's. Busch brand beer is meanwhile brewed in France by Société Européene de Brasseries.

The industrial side of Anheuser-Busch does more than just brew beer, however. Subsidiaries of the company process barley into brewer's malt, produce baker's as well as brewer's yeasts, manufacture metalized labels for internal use and for sale to other firms, transport beer by truck and by rail, wholesale beer and wine and that recycle aluminum cans. The company's Eagle Snacks subsidiary even produces the likes of pretzels and roasted nuts. Originally designed to be served in taverns to complement Anheuser-Busch and other beers, Eagle Snacks are now available on airlines and in supermarkets.

The nonindustrial side of Anheuser-Busch includes interest in sports. The company was a major sponsor of the 1984 Los Angeles Summer Olympic Games. Anheuser-Busch also owns the St Louis National Baseball Club, Inc—better known as the St Louis Cardinals. Purchased by the company in 1953, the Cardinals have won the World Series three times since, in 1964, 1967 and 1982.

Other Anheuser-Busch sports-related activities include speedboat racing, in which the company sponsors the Miss Budweiser Hydroplane Racing Team and Bill Seebold's Bud Light Powerboat Racing Team. On land the company sponsors auto racing teams and auto races such as the Budweiser Cleveland Grand Prix and the Budweiser Grand Prix of Miami. Other company-sponsored sports events are the Anheuser-Busch Golf Classic in Williamsburg, the Michelob Light Cup women's pro ski races, the Budweiser/Bud Light Hall of Fame Bowling Tournament, the Budweiser United States Soccer Federation Open and Amateur Cup, Chicago's Budweiser Arlington Million horse race, the Busch Pool League and the Bud Light Ironman Triathlon Championship at Kona, Hawaii.

No mention of Anheuser-Busch leisure-time activities would be complete without the company's Busch Gardens theme parks. Located at Tampa, Florida and Williamsburg, Virginia, the parks were opened in 1959 and 1975, respectively, and include family-oriented amusement park activities.

Miller High Life has been the company's chief brand since before Prohibition. Miller's genuine draft beer, Plank Road, was introduced in 1985. Miller is unique among US brewers for using clear rather than brown or green bottles.

Miller Brewing of Milwaukee has been the second largest brewing company in the United States since the late 1970s after a long climb from eleventh place in 1965. The brewery originated in suburban Milwaukee, Wisconsin in 1850 as Charles Best's Plank Road Brewery. It was purchased in 1855 by Frederic Miller who turned it into one of the region's leading breweries. In 1969 the Philip Morris Tobacco Company acquired 53 percent of Miller Brewing and the following year they bought the remaining 47 percent.

Miller Brewing produces 38 million barrels of beer annually at six plants located at Albany, Georgia; Eden, North Carolina; Irwindale, California; Fort Worth, Texas; Fulton, New York; and Milwaukee, Wisconsin. The Milwaukee brewery is the largest, producing 8.5 million barrels annually, but the Eden and Albany plants are close behind with an annual production rate of 8 million each. The company's flagship brand is Miller High Life, a premium national lager brand which has existed since before Prohibition. In 1975, Miller introduced Lite, the first nationally marketed reduced-calorie beer. It went on to become the lead-

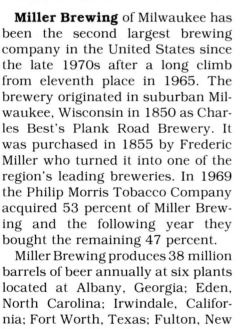

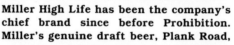

ing reduced-calorie beer in the United States. Miller also markets two budget lager brands (Milwaukee's Best and Meister Brau), a regional liquor (Magnum) and a regional reduced-alcohol beer (Sharp's LA). Milwaukee's Best is a reformulation of a beer originally brewed by A Gettelman in the 1890s. The brewery was acquired by Miller in 1961, but Miller still uses the Gettelman name. In 1985, Miller introduced another 'historical' product. A nonpasteurized draft-style beer, it was called Plank Road after the original brewery acquired by Frederic Miller in 1855.

An important Miller product since 1975 is Lowenbrau, produced under license from the brewer of the same name in Munich, West Germany where it has been produced since 1893. (In Canada Molson brews Lowenbrau.) While Miller brews a German beer in the United States, Miller High Life is brewed in Canada by Carling-O'Keefe and in Japan by Sapporo.

Like industry-leader Anheuser-Busch, Miller Brewing actively sponsors sports. It alone sponsors US Olympic Training Centers in Colorado Springs and Lake Placid, New York. Miller also sponsors the US Hockey Team, the US Rifle Team, the US Track and Field Team and the US Ski Team, as well as a number of auto and power boat racing teams. Among Miller-sponsored sporting events are the Miller High Life 200 and 500 auto races, the Miller High Life National Doubles Bowling Tournament, the Lite Bartender's Cup ski races, the Lite Major League Fun Runs and the Lite Beer World Series of Tavern Pool.

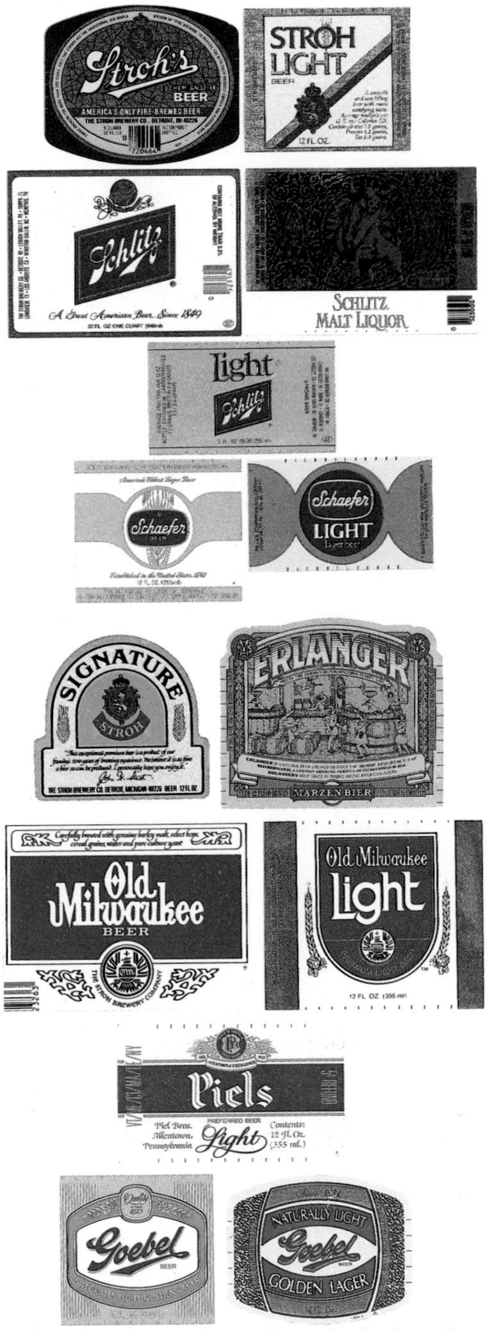

The Stroh product line includes the famous Schlitz and Schaefer brands.

The Stroh Brewery Company of Detroit became the third largest brewing company in the United States in May 1982 when it purchased the much larger, but financially ailing, Joseph Schlitz Brewing Company. Schlitz, whose brand name Stroh retained, had been larger than Stroh and in fact had been one of the two largest brewers in the United States since the nineteenth century.

Started in 1850 by Bernhard Stroh, the company survived Prohibition but remained a regional brewery until well after World War II. The acquisition of Schaefer in 1981 and of Schlitz the following year catapulted Stroh from seventh to third place among US brewers.

The Stroh Brewery company's own brand name products (Stroh's Premium and Stroh Light) have long been noted for the use of direct flame rather than steam in the heating of the brew kettles. The process is used by some European brewers but is uncommon in North America, so the company uses it in its advertising, referring to these two products as 'fire brewed beers.'

Stroh's interesting variety of other products include the upscale Erlanger premium beer and the Signature Super Premium Beer which was first introduced in 1983. From the Schaefer acquisition, the company gained

not only Schaefer and Schaefer Light, but Piel's Draft Style, Piels Light and Goebel Golden Lager. In the Schlitz takeover the Schlitz flagship brand was retained as well as Schlitz Light, Schlitz Malt Liquor and the famous former Hawaiian brand, Primo, which Schlitz was brewing in California. Despite its large repertoire of famous brands, the best-selling brand in the Stroh repertoire by the mid-1980s was the budget brand Old Milwaukee which was complemented, of course, by an Old Milwaukee Light.

The original Stroh brewery in Detroit was finally closed in 1985, doomed to the wrecker's ball by age and inefficiency. This left Detroit's one-time premier brewer with a new corporate headquarters, but no actual brewery in the motor city. With the demise of the old Detroit flagship, America's third largest brewer was left with six breweries: the Allentown, Pennsylvania plant that Schaefer had built in 1972 and which Stroh acquired in 1980; the old Theodore Hamm Brewery in St Paul, Minnesota that Stroh acquired from Olympia by way of Pabst in 1983; and the former Joseph Schlitz

A fanciful view of the Heileman flagship product reminiscent of an Alfred Bierstadt painting *(left)*; samples from all of Heileman's brands *(right)*; and the Blitz-Weinhard family of labels designed by San Francisco designer Prino Angeli.

breweries in Longview, Texas; Memphis, Tennessee; Van Nuys, California and Winston-Salem, North Carolina. Schlitz, the brewer that once claimed to have made Milwaukee famous, had closed its Milwaukee brewery the year before it was acquired by Stroh.

With the Schlitz acquisition behind it, the Stroh company began a spirited marketing campaign that saw a blizzard of new media advertising and the sudden appearance of Stroh's neon signs in the windows of taverns and corner groceries in select markets in California and New York, places far removed from the brewery's earlier midwestern stronghold. By 1984, fire brewing was introduced to the old Schlitz plant at Van Nuys.

The G Heileman Brewing Company of La Crosse, Wisconsin is a unique example of a small regional brewer that grew to national prominence not through the vehicle of a single national brand like Anheuser-Busch or Miller, but through an amazing amalgam of important formerly independent regional brands. Established in La Crosse by Gottlieb Heileman and John Gund in 1858, the House of Heileman remained a small regional brewer until the early 1960s when it began to acquire other smaller regional brewers. In 1960, Heileman was the thirty-first largest brewer in the United States. By 1982 it was fourth.

The House of Heileman is divided into three geographical divisions, the central with five breweries, the eastern with three breweries and the western also with three breweries. Of these 11 breweries, four are former Carling National breweries which were acquired from the Canadian brewing giant in 1979. These plants still operate under the Carling National name and still produce, under license, Carling Black Label Beer, Carling Red Cap Ale and Tuborg, the beer that Carling brewed in the United States under license from Tuborg of Denmark since 1973.

The Heileman Central Division includes two Carling National breweries at Belleville, Illinois and Frankenmuth, Michigan as well as the Heileman flagship brewery in La Crosse. The division also contains Sterling Brewing in Evansville, Indiana and Jacob Schmidt Brewing in St Paul, Minnesota. The beers brewed in the Central Division include Heileman's original brand, their largest seller Old Style, the complementary Old Style Light and the superpremium Heileman's Special Export. The Carling National facilities each brew the Carling products, and the Belleville Carling plant, which is the oldest operating brewery in the Midwest (established in 1851), still brews its famous Stag brand. The Central Division produces other popular brands well known in the Minnesota/Pennsylvania/Kentucky triangle such as Blatz; Falls City; Grain Belt; Red, White and Blue and Wiedemann Bohemian Special. Meanwhile, in the same area, the Schmidt and Sterling breweries still produce beers under their own brand names. In 1986 work began on a unique sixth brewery in the Central Division. Built in Milwaukee, the brewery is named after Valentin Blatz, whose original brewery was one of the major historic Milwaukee brewery until it was closed in 1959. Heileman will operate the new brewery as a specialty brewery—making beer from the original Blatz recipes and under the original brand names.

The Heileman Eastern Division includes a Carling Brewery in Baltimore, Maryland and the brewery at Perry, Georgia that Heileman got from Pabst in 1983. (The town of Perry was known as Pabst, Georgia in the years after 1971 when Pabst built the brewery there, but the name has since reverted to Perry.) The third facility in the Eastern Division is the Lone Star Brewing Company in San Antonio, Texas which was independent until 1976 and owned by Olympia until acquired by Heileman in 1983. Despite its ab-

sentee ownership from Washington and Wisconsin since 1976, the Lone Star brand developed a strong cult following within its home state during the 1970s. Immortalized in the songs of Willie Nelson, Waylon Jennings and Jerry Jeff Walker, Lone Star is reverently known as the 'National Beer of Texas.'

Heileman's Western Division includes a Carling National Brewery in Phoenix, Arizona and two other breweries, which, like Lone Star in Texas, have strong cult followings. The Rainier Brewing Company of Seattle has been around since the nineteenth century, leading the Seattle brewery scene since Prohibition through a variety of owners from Emil Sick to Molson of Canada to the House of Heileman. Rainier Beer is the largest selling beer brand in Washington, Montana, and the Northwest as a whole, and the critically acclaimed Rainier Ale is the largest selling ale in the entire western United States.

Heileman acquired the West's oldest brewery (owned by Pabst for four years) in 1983. The Blitz-Weinhard

Company brewery of Portland, Oregon was around for 10 years when Henry Weinhard became involved in 1862. In addition to the Blitz-Weinhard brand, the brewery produces a limited edition superpremium called Henry Weinhard's Private Reserve (also available in a dark beer) and an 'Ireland-style' ale. Henry's, as it is known to aficionados, ranks with San Francisco's Anchor Steam as one of the West Coast's most sought-after superpremium beers.

Falls City Brewing (est 1905) which Heileman bought in 1978 is notable for having marketed Billy Beer, a product named for the younger brother of President Jimmy Carter. The colorful Billy Carter was noted for his fondness for beer and his ability to distinguish between similar lagers. The idea that evolved at Falls City in 1977 seemed like a good one. They would formulate a product under Carter's specifications and license other regional brewers to produce it. By using a network of regional brewers, Falls City hoped to be the power behind a national brand named for the brother of the president of the United States. It seemed like the most important blending of beer and government since Thomas Jefferson and James Madison were drawn into the National Brewery scheme. As it turned out, Billy Beer was a short-lived phenomenon. It received enormous media coverage but never managed to penetrate the market in the hoped-for quantities, and it was discontinued.

In addition to its own brands, the Carling brands and all the regional brands, the House of Heileman pro-

duces other related products. These include two national brands of higher-alcohol malt liquor (Colt 45 and Mickey's) and a blend of malt liquor and sparkling fruit wine marketed under the name Malt Duck. The company also produces a line of low-alcohol beers under the Old Style, Blatz and Black Label brands. At the opposite end of the spectrum, Heileman is the largest producer of nonalcoholic, or 'near' beer, in the United States. The company's near beers are sold under the Kingsbury, Schmidt Select, and Zing brands.

In other product areas the House of Heileman produces Country Cooler Wine Coolers, La Croix and Cold Spring mineral waters. Heileman produces several brands of snack foods from bakeries in Iowa, Minnesota, Illinois, Michigan and six bakeries in Wisconsin.

Adolph Coors Company of Golden, Colorado, the fifth largest brewer in the United States, is really the antithesis of fourth-place Heileman. Whereas Heileman's product line depends equally on dozens of individual brands brewed in 11 states, Coors depends primarily on a single product from a single brewery. That one brewery is located on the same site high in the Rockies picked out by Adolph Coors in 1873, but the facility itself has grown into the largest single brewery in the world, with an annual output of nearly 14 million barrels.

In 1986, however, the company began work on a new packaging plant in the Shenandoah Valley near Elkton, Virginia. The plant was designed to package beer brewed in Colorado and shipped in refrigerated rail cars to the new facility. In the long term the plant could form the basis for a second Coors brewery.

The Coors product line is headed by the flagship Coors brand and the complementary low-calorie Coors Light. Other products include the distinctively colored George Killian's Irish Red, an ale brewed under license from the original Irish brewer, and two premium beers introduced in the 1980s called Herman Joseph's and Golden Lager. Because Coors products are not pasteurized, the brewery makes a special effort to see that its products are kept refrigerated during delivery and distributor warehousing to ensure freshness.

The Adolph Coors Company has its hand in a number of other activities, the largest of which is the Coors Porcelain Company (CPC) which is in turn one of the world's largest producers of technical ceramics. CPC has three factories in Colorado, one in California and offices in three other states and three foreign countries. Other activities include health care, food products, transportation and recycling. Coors' Container Operations division supplies most of the brewery's cans and bottles, and is the largest aluminum can manufacturing facility in the world.

Pabst Brewing Company of Milwaukee was the largest brewery in the United States at the turn of the century and has remained in the top six ever since. The original brewery was started in 1844 by Jacob Best and later run by Philip Best in partnership with Captain Frederick Pabst. The Captain essentially ran the brewery himself after Philip retired in 1866. Pabst acquired Olympia Brewing in 1983 (which had recently acquired the Theodore Hamm brewery in St Paul, Minnesota) and was itself taken over in February 1985 by the reclusive California millionaire Paul Kalmanovitz who already owned the Falstaff, General and Pearl breweries.

The Pabst breweries include the 6-million-barrel flagship brewery in Milwaukee; satellite Pabst breweries in Tampa, Florida and Newark, New Jersey; as well as the Olympia Brewery at Tumwater, Washington which continues to produce under its own brand name. The major Pabst brand is Pabst Blue Ribbon, one of the oldest name brands in American history. Other Pabst-owned brands include Pabst Light, Pabst Extra Light, Jacob Best Premium Light, Hamm's, Hamm's Special Light, Buckhorn, Buckhorn Light, MAXX Special Lager and Old English 800 Malt Liquor. The former Olympia Brewery at Tumwater (now known as a Pabst Brewery) brews Olympia, Olympia Light and Gold Light. In October 1985, Paul Kalmanovitz closed the General Brewery at Vancouver, Washington and transfered production to the Tumwater Pabst plant of those beer products listed below under General Brewing.

Highlights of the Pabst family *(above)* include Olympia, Hamm's and Blue Ribbon.

Coors' leading product in a chilled mug *(left)* and the whole product line *(below)*.

THE SMALLER UNITED STATES BREWERS

Anchor Brewing Company was originally established in San Francisco in 1896. Appliance-heir Fritz Maytag bought the company in 1965 when it was on the verge of collapse and turned it into the very model of an efficient smaller regional brewery. Despite Maytag's relentless quality control and insistence on high-quality ingredients, such as expensive pure malted two-row barley instead of a mix of cheaper cereal grains, the brewery turned a profit by 1975. Over the years he increased the brewery's output from 600 barrels to 30,000 barrels annually. The company's flagship product is Anchor Steam Beer, one of the West's most prized premium beers, which was developed by master brewer Maytag himself and loosely based on what is known of the legendary

'steam' beers produced in gold rush days. Other Anchor products include Anchor Porter, Anchor Liberty Ale and an annual Anchor Christmas Ale. In 1985, the brewery became one of the few American brewers to produce a German-style wheat beer.

August Schell Brewing of New Ulm, Minnesota was established in 1860 and has existed as a small regional brewery ever since. The brewery's 40,000-barrel annual output is divided among Schell's, Schell's Light, Schell's Export, Ulmer Lager and Ulmer Brown.

Boulder Brewing Company of Longmont, near Boulder, Colorado, which began operations in 1980, is the second largest brewer in Colorado although as its vice-president, George 'Skip' Miller, points out, 'We're not trying to be Coors. . . . Coors brews about three times as much beer in an average day as we will in a year.'

Boulder Brewing developed from an interest in home brewing and, like many of the smaller breweries that started in the 1980s, the company is dedicated to heartier European-style beers and does not brew a lager. The product line at the

10,000-barrel brewery (Coors has a 13-million-barrel capacity) includes Boulder Beer Bitter, Boulder Beer Stout, Boulder Beer Porter and Boulder Extra Pale Ale.

Buffalo Bill's of Hayward, California became one of the first three brew pubs to open in the United States since Prohibition when brewmaster Bill Owens opened for business in September 1983. The unique concept of the brew pub, feeding draft beer directly from the brewery to the taps at the bar, ensures the freshest possible product. Unlike the beers of most microbreweries, Buffalo Bill's unique unpasteurized lager is available only at the Hayward brew pub, whose annual capacity is less than 2000 barrels.

Owens has, however, indicated that he might open a second Buffalo Bill's in the San Francisco Bay Area, which could make it America's first multisite microbrewery.

Champale Incorporated of Trenton, New Jersey (owned by Iroquois Brands of Greenwich, Connecticut) evolved out of the brewery that Colonel A R Kuser established in 1891. The name evolved from Trenton Brewing to Peoples Brewing to Metropolis Brewery before becoming Champale in 1967. Over the years a wide variety of brands have emanated from the million-barrel plant, including Banner and Rialto in the 1970s; and Class A, Colony House, Gilt Edge, Hornell, Old Bohemian and Tudor in the 1960s. Today's

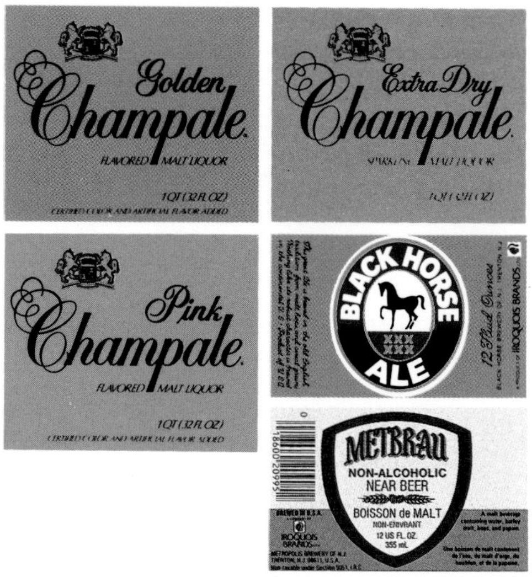

brands include Black Horse Ale (dating from 1973), nonalcoholic Metbrew and three varieties of Champale Malt Liquor: Golden, Pink and Extra Dry.

Cold Spring Brewing of Cold Spring, Minnesota dates back to the brewery started by George Sargel in 1874 and evolved to its present name by 1898. With a 350,000-barrel annual capacity, it is the largest of the two remaining locally owned Minnesota breweries *(see* August Schell Brewing). The brewery's products include Cold Spring, Cold Spring Export, Cold Spring Light, Fox Deluxe, Kegle Brau, North Star, White Label and Wester Cold Spring Sparkling Mineral Water.

Columbia River Brewery in Portland, Oregon is one of three breweries to open their doors in that city during 1984–85. Under the direction of owner Dick Ponzi and University of California-trained brewmaster Karl Ockert, the 4000-barrel brewery has developed a stout and a Bridgeport Ale, named in honor of Portland's nine bridges.

C Schmidt & Sons of Philadelphia (not to be confused with Jacob Schmidt of St Paul, Minnesota) is the last brewery in a city that was one of the two original great American brewing towns and a city that has had more brewers in its history (271)

***Opposite, from left:* Some of the beers of Anchor Brewing, Boulder Brewing and Champale Incorporated. The 12 brands *(above)* are only a third of the C Schmidt & Sons line. *Below:* Dixie's flagship brand.**

than any other except New York City (279 if you include Brooklyn). The brewery originated with Robert Courtrenny in 1859, was acquired by Christian Schmidt in 1863 and has used its present name since 1892. In 1954 the company bought Scheidt Brewing (later Valley Forge Brewing) of Norristown, but closed the facility in 1975. A former Schaefer of Ohio brewery in Cleveland was purchased in 1964 and is still in operation.

The flagship brewery at Philadelphia has today grown to a 3.5-million-barrel capacity. Under the Schmidt name, the company brews Schmidt's Beer, Schmidt's of Philadelphia Light Beer, Schmidt's of Philadelphia Tiger Head Ale, Schmidt's Bock Beer, Schmidt's Oktoberfest Beer, Schmidt's Bavarian Beer, Christian Schmidt Golden Classic and Christian Schmidt Select. The Valley Forge brand of the old Norristown brewery is still being brewed as are Rheingold Extra Dry and Rheingold Extra Light (two brands late of the old Ruppert empire in New York City) that Schmidt has been brewing in Philadelphia since the 1970s.

The Schmidt, Valley Forge and Rheingold brands may be the highest flags flying from the Philadelphia flagship, but a host of other brands are on hand to give the brewery the largest roster of names in the United States. These others include Bergheim Beer, Casey's Lager Beer, Classic Golden Hawk Malt Liquor, Coqui 900 Malt Liquor, Duke Ale, Duke Beer, Erie Light Lager, Gablinger's Extra Light Beer, Kaier Beer, Knickerbocker Beer, Koehler's Beer, Kool Mile Malt Liquor, McSorley's Cream Ale, Ortlieb's, Prior Double Dark Beer, Prior Golden Light Beer, POC Beer, Ram's Head Beer, Reading Premium Beer, USA Beer and Yacht Club as well as two nonalcoholic brews, Birell and Break Special Lager.

Dixie Brewing of New Orleans was established in 1907 and is the only remaining brewery in the Louisiana city that once was the brewing capital of the entire South. The flagship brand of this 300,000-barrel brewery is Dixie Beer, which is complemented by a Dixie Light. Other brands include Battlin Bulldogs Beer, Beier Beer, Fischer, Gold-

en Brau, Golden Brau Light, K & B, K & B Light, Krewes, Mizzou and Razorback. Two budget brands are Mr Thrifty and Super Stop.

Dubuque Star Brewing in Dubuque, Iowa, was established as Star Brewing in 1898 and took the name of its home town in 1904. With an 85,000-barrel annual capacity, it is the only remaining brewery in a state that has boasted 249 licensed breweries through the years. The company's brand names include Dubuque Star, E & B, Edelweiss and Weber.

Eastern Brewing of Hammonton, New Jersey was established as Eastern Beverage Corporation in 1933 at the end of Prohibition and has brewed under a wide variety of brand names over the ensuing years. These have included Circle, Colonial, Colony House, Dawson, Fischer, Fox Head, Garden State, Hampden, Hedrick, Polar, Tube City, Waukee and San Juan Cerveceria. Brands being produced at the 400,000-barrel brewery in the mid-1980s included Canadian Ace, Milwaukee Premium and Old German.

Falstaff Brewing of Fort Wayne, Indiana traces its roots to the Forest Park Brewing company of St Louis, Missouri, established in 1910 and taken over by 'Papa Joe' Griesedieck in 1917. Renamed Falstaff (after the Shakespeare character) during Prohibition, the company expanded to become one of the Midwest's strongest multisite regional brewers. After World War II, Falstaff became a leading national brewer, and by 1960 it was the nation's third largest brewer behind Anheuser-Busch and Schlitz. Through its complicated association with General Brewing of Vancouver, Washington, the Falstaff brand became prominent in the West. After the 1960s, however, Falstaff's market position gave way to other brands such as Miller and Coors. Many of the company's breweries were sold or closed. By the early 1980s, when the company came under the control of Paul Kalmanovitz, only the Fort Wayne and Omaha, Nebraska breweries remained. Because of the long-standing relationship with General Brewing (now also owned by Paul Kalmanovitz), Falstaff's flagship brand, Falstaff Beer, and General's flagship brand, Lucky Lager, have been brewed by the breweries of both companies. In addition to these two brands, Falstaff, at its Omaha plant, brews two budget lagers, Scotch Buy and Valu Time.

F X Matt Brewing of Utica, New York evolved from the Columbia Brewery established by Charles Bier-

bauer in 1853. The company was taken over in 1888 by F X Matt I (grandfather of the current president, F X Matt II) and organized as West End Brewing. The brewery was renamed for F X Matt in 1980, 22 years after his death, by which time it had reached a 800,000-barrel capacity and ranked among the top 15 brewers in the United States. The brand name Utica Club was introduced for the soft drinks produced by the company during Prohibition and became so popular that it was retained afterward for West End's beer products. The brewery's brand names today include Utica Club, Utica Club Light, and Utica Club Cream Ale as well as Matt's Premium and Matt's Premium Light. Other products include Maximus Super, a high-alcohol malt liquor and Choice, a low-alcohol beer introduced in 1984. F X Matt also brews small batches of dark beer and ale for local draft consumption and a Season's Best Amber Beer for sale in December. One other unique product is Fort Schuyler Beer, a product that was brewed by the Old Fort Schuyler Brewery (later named Utica Brewing) between 1886 and 1937.

General Brewing, also known as **Lucky Lager Brewing,** was born on Newhall Street in San Francisco in 1934 and grew to become one of the West's largest multisite brewers in the years following World War II. It had seven breweries operating under one or the other of its two names in four western states, and Lucky Lager was one of the West's most recognized brand names. Like Falstaff, with whom it became associated, General faced serious com-

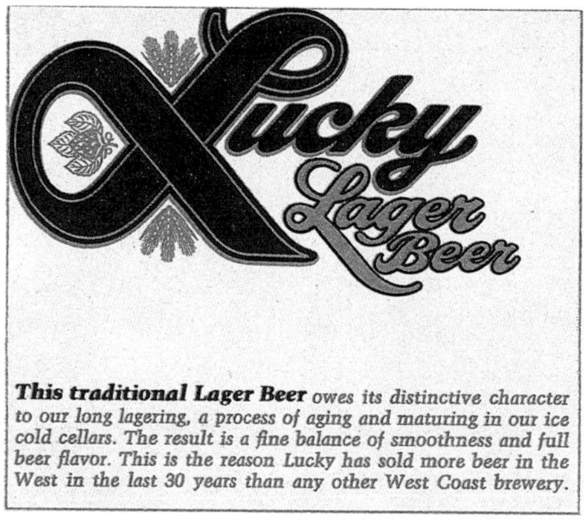

petition from national brands and gradually began to sell or close its breweries in the 1960s. In 1978 the company's two large breweries in San Francisco were closed, leaving only the historic facility at Vancouver, Washington.

The General brewery in Vancouver began as the Muench Brewery in 1856 and was taken over in 1859 by one of the true giants of western brewing, Henry Weinhard. Weinhard sold out to Anton Young five years later when he moved across the Columbia River to Portland, Oregon. It operated as the Star Brewery from 1895 to 1939 and as the Interstate Brewery until 1950 when it became part of the General/Lucky archipelago. Thirty years later and shortly after General's heyday, General and its Vancouver plant, along with Falstaff, became part of the holdings of Paul Kalmanovitz. In October 1985 Kalmanovitz closed his 720,000-barrel Vancouver brewery and transfered production to the Pabst (formerly Olympia) brewery that he had recently acquired in the nearby town of Tumwater.

Prior to its closing, the General plant at Vancouver brewed both Lucky Lager and Falstaff, as well as a host of budget brands including Regal Select and generic beer. General also brewed a number of private label brands including Brown Derby for the Safeway grocery chain.

Genesee Brewing of Rochester, New York is the seventh largest brewer in the United States. Among the nation's regional brewers it is second only to Coors, although the latter produces four times as much beer and distributes to a larger part of the country. The company traces its heritage back to the brewery established on North St Paul Street in 1855 by Jacob Rau. This business evolved into the Genesee Brewing Company in 1878, and in the latter years of the nineteenth century Genesee's Liebot Schaner Beer was famous throughout western New York State. After Prohibition, the company was reorganized under the same name but under the new management of a former Genesee assistant brewmaster, Louis Wehle. Genesee was one of the first breweries in operation after repeal in April 1933 and was the winner of the first postrepeal taste test. After World War II, as regional breweries collapsed throughout the country, Genesee flourished. Between 1960 and 1965, for example, the company went from twenty-eighth to nineteenth place nationally.

By 1985, the Rochester brewery was producing 3.5 million barrels annually and storing its lager in

9000-barrel storage tanks, the largest such tanks in the world. The company's brands include Genesee Lager, Genesee Light, Genesee Cream Ale, Genesee Cream Ale Light and Genesee Twelve Horse Ale.

On 28 February 1985, Genesee bought the Fred Koch Brewery of Dunkirk, New York and moved production of the latter's Golden Anniversary Beer and Black Horse Ale to the Rochester plant. The Fred Koch Brewery, established in 1888, had been owned and operated by the Koch family for 97 years and had grown to a 70,000-barrel annual capacity.

***Opposite:* Representatives of the FX Matt Brewing and General Brewing product lines. *Above:* When Walter Brewing changed hands in 1985, Hibernia beers joined ranks with the original Walter brands. *Right:* Hudepohl's assorted brands.**

Geyer Brothers Brewing of Frankenmuth (near Detroit), Michigan grew out of the Heubisch & Knaust Cass River Brewery established on Main Street in 1862. Taken over by John G Geyer in 1874, the brewery operated under his name until 1908, at which time it became the Geyer Brothers Brewery. The brewery has a 30,000-barrel annual capacity. Its brand names include Geyer's Lager, Frankenmuth Bavarian Light and Park, and Frankenmuth Oktoberfest.

Hales Ales, Ltd is a microbrewery located in Colville north of Spokane, Washington. Established in 1984, the company produces Hale's Pale American Ale, Special Bitter and Celebration Porter.

Hart Brewing Company of Kalama, north of Vancouver, Washington is another of the many microbreweries that sprang up in the Northwest during 1984 and 1985. Among Hart's products are Pyramid Pale Ale and Wheaten Ale, the first draft wheat beer produced in the United States since Prohibition. Hart Brewing itself is the first brewery in Kalama since Prohibition. Kalama's previous brewer closed in 1880.

Hibernia Brewing of Eau Claire, Wisconsin began as Henry Sommermeyer's Dells Brewery in 1878 and became John Walter's City Brewery in 1890. Known simply as Walter Brewing from 1933 to 1985, the company was another rare example of a small family-owned brewery with Karl Walter as chairman, Charles Walter as president, William Walter as vice president and John J Walter as chemist and master brewer. On 5 May 1985 Michael Healy purchased the brewery from the Walter family and renamed it Hibernia Brewing, after the latin name for Ireland. The list of brand names from the former 100,000-barrel Walter Brewery, which includes Walter's, Breunig's, Bub's, Master Brew and West Bend Old Timers Beer, was thus expanded to include Hibernia's product line—Winter Brau, Dunkel Weizen, Oktober Fest and Eau Claire All Malt lager beer.

Honolulu Sake Brewery & Ice Company of Honolulu, Hawaii dates back to 1934 and survives today as the only commercial sake brewery in the United States. The brewery brews two brands of beer's closest relative, Takara Masamune and Takara Musume.

Hudepohl Brewing of Cincinnati originated with Gottfried Koehler in 1852 and was taken over as the Buckeye Brewery of Ludwig 'Louis' Hudepohl and George Kotte in 1885. The company became Hudepohl Brewing in 1899, and in 1934 a second Cincinnati brewery was added. In 1935 Hudepohl became one of the brewers that pioneered use of cans for its beer. During World War II, Hudepohl Beer was selected by the U S War Department for use by American troops in the South Pacific. Special crates were developed for Hudepohl's cone-

topped cans so that the beer could be dropped by parachute to soldiers in the field.

The Hudepohl brewery, with an annual capacity of nearly a million barrels, produces a variety of brands in addition to the flagship Hudepohl brand. These include Burger, Burger Light, Hofbrau, Hudy Delight and Pace, a nonalcoholic beer. In 1982 the company introduced Christian Moerlin, a superpremium brand named for one of Cincinnati's first great brewers whose famous brewery was started on Elm Street in 1853 but did not survive Prohibition.

Jacob Leinenkugel Brewing of Chippewa Falls, Wisconsin was built in 1867 by its namesake and John Miller who was Leinenkugel's partner for the next 16 years. Located on top of Big Eddy Springs, the brewery was known as the Spring Brewery until 1898. Still family owned under the presidency of Bill Leinenkugel, the 95,000-barrel brewery produces Leinenkugel Beer, Leinenkugel Light Beer (Leinie's Light), Leinenkugel Bock Beer, Bosch and Chippewa Pride.

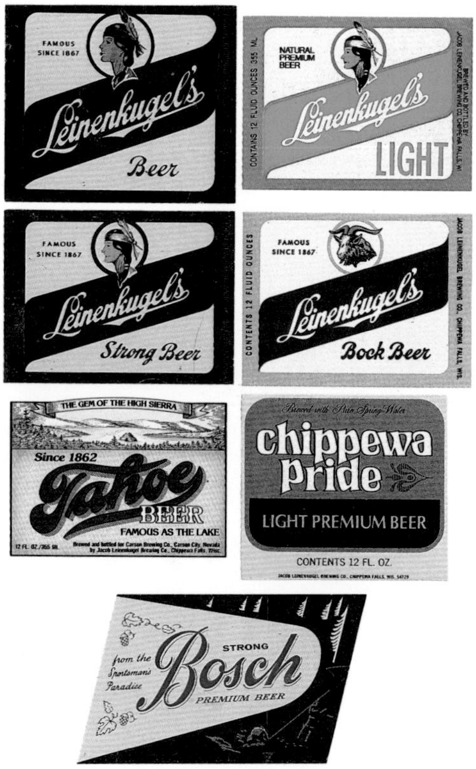

***Left to right:* Sample products of the Jacob Leinenkugel, Jones Brewing and Joseph Huber Brewing companies. Latrobe Brewing puts out Rolling Rock, and The Lion makes beer, ale and porter. *Far right:* Products of the Manhattan and Mendocino Breweries.**

Jones Brewing of Smithton, Pennsylvania was established by Welsh immigrant William B 'Stoney' Jones in 1907 as the Eureka Brewing Company. The brewery's original brand was Eureka Gold Crown, but because Stoney Jones habitually made personal sales calls to taverns in the area, it came to be known unofficially as 'Stoney's Beer.' The brewery lost little time changing the official name. Today the brewery is still family owned and operated under the presidency of William B. 'Bill' Jones III. The company subscribes to the notion that 'the beer most in demand is a product brewed in the traditional fashion (and) that this is why foreign or imported beers are gaining an increasing share of the market . . . as Americans become more and more disenchanted

with American "fad" beers. The Jones Brewing Company, therefore, has chosen not to get involved in fads and gadgets, but instead will brew the finest natural (or traditional) beer possible!'

Because direct contact is still part of company policy the products of the 170,000-barrel brewery are still distributed in a very small area. Those products include Stoney's, Stoney's Pilsener and Stoney's Gold Crown, as well as Fort Pitt Beer, Old Shay Golden Cream Ale and Esquire Premium Beer.

Joseph Huber Brewing of Monroe, Wisconsin evolved from the Bissinger Brewery established in 1845. Between 1848 and 1906 it operated successively under the names John Knipschilt, Ed Ruegger, Jacob Hefty, Fred Hefty and Adam Blumer. It survived as Blumer Brewing until 1947 when it became Joseph Huber Brewing. The brew-

ery's products include Huber, Bavarian Club, Gold Label, Golden Glow, Hi-Brau, Regal Brau, Rhinelander, Wisconsin Club and Wisconsin Gold Label.

Kalmanovitz, Paul of Corte Madera, California, a few minutes north of San Francisco, is neither a brewer nor a brewmaster but he is nevertheless important in any consideration of brewing in the 1980s. By the time he made headlines with his 1985 acquisition of Pabst, Kalmanovitz had already assembled an impressive collection of breweries that included Pearl Brewing of San Antonio; General Brewing of Vancouver, Washington; and Falstaff of Fort Wayne, Indiana (which in turn owned the formerly independent East Coast brand names Ballantine and Narragansett). The cost-cutting and brewery closings that came in the wake of Kalmanovitz's takeover of these three breweries angered many in the industry, but the measures did enhance the profitability of the breweries. The reclusive multimillionaire ruffled more feathers when he bought the ailing Pabst Brewing and eliminated white-collar jobs and public tours at Pabst's big Milwaukee brewery.

Together the Pearl/General/Falstaff group constitutes the ninth largest brewery in the United States with a more-than-2-million-barrel output despite a reduced number of brewing sites. Sixth-ranked Pabst (which includes formerly independent Olympia and Hamm's), meanwhile, has an annual output of 11.6 million barrels of beer.

Kemper Brewing on Bainbridge Island in Washington's Puget Sound is another of the microbreweries founded in the Northwest in 1984. Unlike many microbreweries which tend toward top-fermenting beers, Kemper brews a lager appropriately named Thomas Kemper Beer.

Latrobe Brewing of Latrobe, Pennsylvania was established in 1893 at a time when the town's only other brewery was located at St Vin-

cent's Abbey and operated by Benedictine monks. The brewery at St Vincent's closed in 1898 after 42 years of operation, but the brewery that took the name of the town survives to this day. With its present 750,000-barrel capacity Latrobe Brewing produces beer under the Rolling Rock brand name.

The Lion, Incorporated, also known as **Gibbons Brewery,** in Wilkes-Barre, Pennsylvania was founded in 1905 as the Luzerne County Brewing Company and became Lion Brewing in 1910. It was reconstituted as The Lion, Incorporated after Prohibition and has used

the Gibbons Stegmaier and Pocono brand names ever since. The 300,000-barrel-capacity brewery today produces beer, ale and porter under both the Gibbons and Stegmaier names as well as a Bartel's Beer and a Liebotschaner Cream Ale.

Manhattan Brewing of New York City opened its doors in November 1984, marking a return of brewing to the borough of Manhattan which hadn't had a brewery operating within its borders since 1965. Located in a former Consolidated Edison substation on Thompson Street, the brewery has an annual brewing capacity of 40,000 barrels, but initial fermenting capacity was much less. Manhattan Brewing was also the first brew pub located east of the Rockies and one of the largest in the United States with a full-scale

restaurant operating within a few feet of the huge German-made copper brew kettles. Though Manhattan Brewing will be remembered in the history books as the first brewery in Manhattan in 19 years and, the first brewery in New York City in 8 years (Schaefer's Brooklyn plant closed in 1976), it was known in the mid-1980s for its horse-drawn beer wagons, the first of their kind to make regular deliveries to Manhattan taverns since the turn of the century.

The **Mendocino Brewing Company** in Hopland, California was formed by Michael Laybourn, Norman Franks and John Scahill in 1982. Its Hopland Brewery, a microbrewery, is California's first brewpub since Prohibition and it produces less than 10,000 barrels a year. Its

brands are Peregrine Pale Ale, Blue Heron Ale, Red Tail Ale and Black Hawk Scout.

Montana Beverages of Helena, Montana was established in 1982 by Dick Bourke and Bruce De Rosier. In 1983 they hired brewmaster Dan Carey, a 23-year-old graduate of Dr Michael Lewis's brewing school at the University of California at Davis. In 1984 the first beer was produced under the brand name Kessler, a reference to Helena's old Kessler brewery. The original Kessler brewery had been started in 1865 by Luxembourg native Nick Kessler and had grown into one of Montana's most important breweries. By 1957 the market for small breweries in Montana, as in most of the rest of the United States, had been reduced to

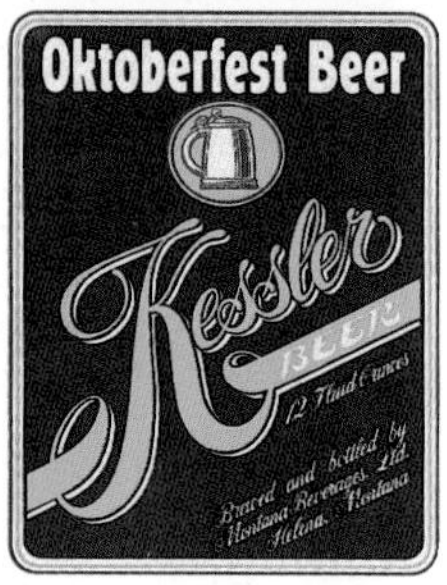

the point where it was no longer economically viable. Kessler Brewing closed, and its copper kettles were shipped to South America. When Montana Beverages revived the Kessler brand 27 years later it was an entirely new beer and an entirely new market. A new generation of Americans was ready for local brews produced on a smaller scale and Montanans were particularly ready for a 'Made in Montana' beer. By the end of 1985, the annual production of the Montana micro had reached 3000 barrels, and four new products (Bock Beer, Holiday Beer, Oktoberfest Beer and Wheat Beer) had joined the original Pale Lager.

Old New York Beer Company is headquartered on Washington Street in New York City, but its New Amsterdam Amber Beer is actually brewed under contract by the West End Brewing Company in Utica, New York. Introduced in 1982, New

Amsterdam Amber is available only in New York City at specialty food stores, restaurants, and what the company describes as 'society' saloons.

Palo Alto Brewing of Mountain View, California was founded in 1983. While many of the microbreweries founded in the early 1970s produce ales, Palo Alto Brewing was established for the specific purpose of brewing English-style ale. The brewery's London Real Ale is produced with ingredients imported from England such as two-row barley malt from Mistley-Manningtree, Fuggles hops from Hereford, East Kent Goldings hops from Tonbridge and Ale Yeast from London.

Pearl Brewing of San Antonio, Texas developed out of the brewery started by J B Behloradsky in 1881 and which evolved into San Antonio Brewing in 1883. The company became Pearl Brewing in 1952, al-

though the Pearl brand name had been used earlier by San Antonio Brewing. Having become a subsidiary of General Brewing in 1978, Pearl is now among the Paul Kalmanovitz holdings. The 1.9-million-barrel-capacity San Antonio brewery produces Pearl Premium, Pearl Light and Pearl Cream Ale as well as Country Club Malt Liquor, 900 Super Premium Malt Liquor, Texas Pride, and Jax Beer, a brand once used by now-defunct Jackson Brewing of New Orleans. The Pearl brewery also produces Pale nonalcoholic beer and General's Lucky Lager.

Pittsburgh Brewing on Liberty Avenue in Pittsburgh, Pennsylvania dates back to the brewery established by Edward Frauenheim and August Hoevler. By 1888 it had evolved into the Iron City Brewing Company. In 1899 Iron City Brewing was one of 21 companies brewing companies to merge into the Pittsburgh Brewing Company. As a result each of the 21 became a 'brewery' of the Pittsburgh Brewing 'Company.' Iron City Brewing thus became the Iron City Brewery of the Pittsburgh Brewing Company. Today the former Iron City site is the only remaining brewery of the old Pittsburgh Brewing consortium, but because it uses the Pittsburgh Brewing name it is technically the descendant of *all* 21 of the formerly independent breweries in the consortium, even though the other 20 have since passed from the scene. For the sake of historical interest, some of the other breweries that joined Pittsburgh Brewing in 1899 were Baeuerlein Brewing (originally established in 1845 and survived as part of the consortium until 1934); Eberhardt & Ober Brewing (1852, 1952); Ernst Hauch's Sons (1849, 1904); Isaac Hippley & Son's Enterprise Brewery (1859, 1899); Keystone Brewing (1887, 1920); Philip Lauer (1874, 1899); John Nusser's National Brewery (1852, 1900); Frank Ober & Brothers (1858, 1904); Phoenix Brewing (1845, 1920); John Seiferth & Brothers (1865, 1899); Herman Straub (1831, 1920); Wainwright Brewing (1818, 1920), and Michael Winter & Brothers (1874, 1920).

Today's Pittsburgh Brewing is the tenth largest brewer in the United States, up from twenty-seventh in

1960. The Liberty Avenue brewery, with its 1.25-million-barrel capacity, still uses Iron City as its flagship brand, producing an Iron City Beer, Iron City Light Beer and Iron City Dark Beer as well as American Beer, Old Dutch Beer, Old German Beer, and Robin Hood Cream Ale.

Red Hook Ale Brewery of Seattle, Washington was established by Paul Shipman in 1982 in the city's Ballard district. This microbrewery's 5000-barrel annual capacity is divided among its original Red Hook Ale,

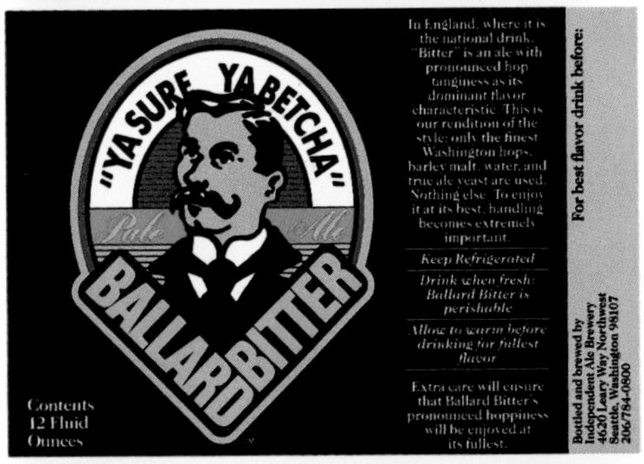

Beer labels representing some of the brand names produced *(left to right)* by Montana Beverages, Old New York Beer Company, Pearl Brewing, Red Hook Ale Brewery, Sierra Nevada Brewing, Spoetzl Brewery and Stanislaus Brewing Co.

Black Hook Porter and the more recently introduced Ballard Bitter. For the first three years of its operation, the brewery's products were available only in draft form, but a bottle line was installed in 1985, in time for the introduction of Winterhook Christmas Ale.

Schoenling Brewing of Cincinnati was established in 1934 on the heels of Repeal under the name Schoenling Brewing & Malting, a name which was quickly changed to Schoenling Brewing & Ice as the firm apparently decided that the ice-making was more lucrative an enterprise than the malting of barley. Schoenling dropped the reference to ice in 1937, the same year that it picked up the Top Hat brand name. Today the brand names at the 400,000-barrel Schoenling plant include Schoenling Beer and Top Hat Beer as well as Big Jug Beer and Little King's Cream Ale.

Sierra Nevada Brewing of Chico, California was founded in 1980 by Paul Camus and Ken Grossman as one of the nation's first microbreweries. As with most microbreweries, Sierra Nevada uses only pure malted barley, Yakima Valley hops and top-fermenting yeast. The firm's major

products are Sierra Nevada Pale Ale, Sierra Nevada Porter, and Sierra Nevada Porter, and Sierra Nevada Stout, but also includes Sierra Nevada Draught Ale (a 'keg-conditioned' version of the Pale Ale), an annual Sierra Nevada Celebration Ale and a barley wine-type ale called Bigfoot Ale that was introduced in 1985.

Spoetzl Brewery of Shiner, Texas evolved from the Shiner Brewing Association started in 1909. Taken over by the Petzold and Spoetzl partnership in 1915, it emerged from

Prohibition as the Spoetzl Brewery and Ice Factory. The Ice Factory tag dropped from the name in 1934. By the 1980s, Spoetzl had 60,000-barrel annual capacity for its Shiner Premium Beer, and was the last remaining home-owned brewery in Texas.

Stanislaus of Modesto, California was established by Garith Helm, who began commercial production in 1984. The 'patron saint' of Stanislaus Brewing is 'St Stan,' a berobed public relations man whose character is based on an apocryphal monas-

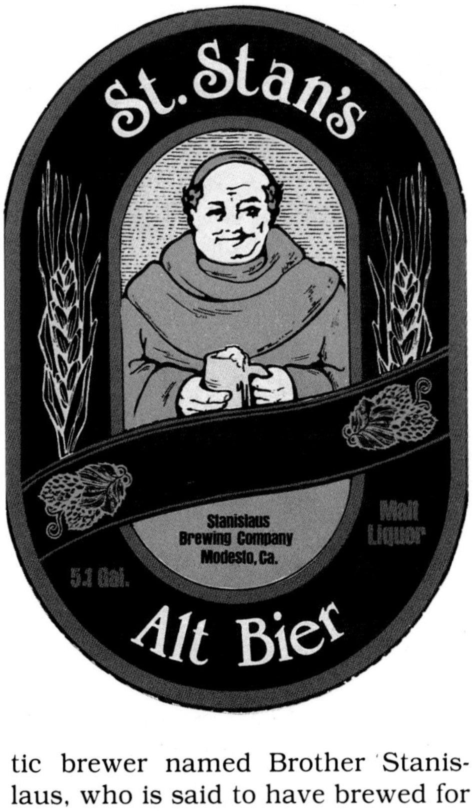

tic brewer named Brother Stanislaus, who is said to have brewed for Frederick the Great a beer inspired by divine intervention.

Stanislaus Brewing produces only altbier, a German-style top-fermented brew similar to ale. Production at the 1040-barrel brewery is divided between the St Stan's Amber and St Stan's Dark brands, available only in California.

Stevens Point Brewery of Stevens Point, Wisconsin dates from the brewery established prior to 1857 by Frank Wahle and George Ruder. By 1902 the brewery had taken its present name. Soon afterward, the Stevens Point Brewery began producing beer under the brand name Pink's Pale Export, a reference to general manager Nick 'Pinky' Gross and his decision to 'export' the beer to faraway Amhearst Junction, Wisconsin. Felix 'Phil' Shibilski joined the company at the end of Prohibition and worked his way to the presidency. Today he is chairman of the board while his son Ken is president and general manager. During his tenure with the company, Felix Shibilski has watched the number of small breweries in Wisconsin dwindle from 44 in 1948 to 4 today.

The success of the Stevens Point Brewery and its Point Special Beer is due at least in part to its decision to limit distribution to a very narrow geographical area, permitting demand to exceed supply. The popularity of the brewery was ensured in 1973 when *Chicago Sun-Times* columnist Mike Royko held a taste test in which Point Special was judged to be the best beer in the United States and second best in the world. Since then, the company's decision to sell beer no more than 100 miles away has been tried many times. It has become a cult favorite in Chicago, but the brewery will not distribute that far afield. A distributor from Colorado sent only a semitrailer truck and was sent a couple of cases because the brewery didn't want to disrupt regular shipments to nearby Hatley and Polonia. Distributors from as far away as Hong Kong have been rebuffed in their attempts to obtain international distribution rights, but Stevens Point doesn't even distribute outside of Wisconsin. Trans World Airlines wanted to serve Point Special aboard its flights, but its order for 200 cases was politely declined.

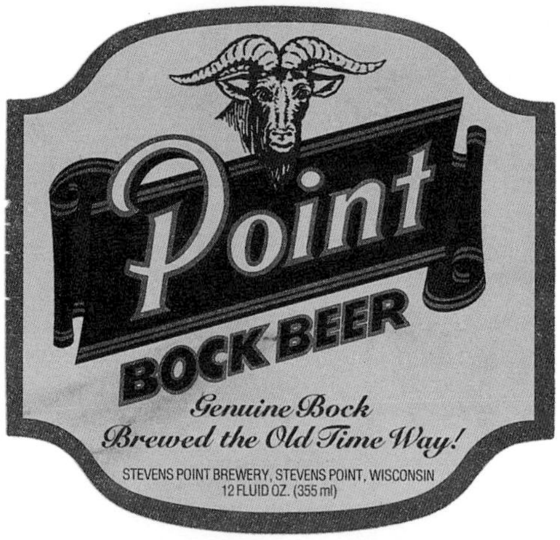

The brewery in the little white hop-covered building at the corner of Beer and Water streets has a 55,000-barrel annual capacity for its Point Special and Seasonal Point Bock Beers and clings tenaciously to the image and reality of a successful small-town American brewery. As the slogan goes, when you're out of Point, you're out of town!

Straub Brewery in St Mary's, Pennsylvania was started by Charles Volk in 1872 and was taken over by Peter Straub in 1876. Thereafter, except for two years (1911–1913) as the Beuzinger Spring Brewery, the brewery has carried the Straub name. The brewery is still a family affair. James Straub is president, general manager and master brewer; Gilbert Straub is executive vice president; Carl Straub is treasurer and Herbert Straub manages sales and

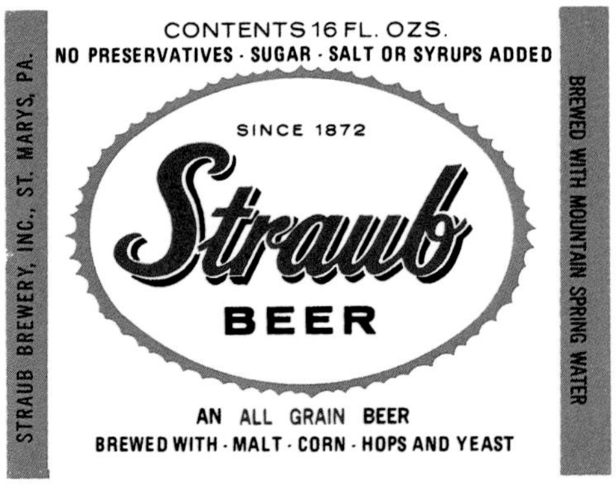

advertising. The name Straub is also the only brand name used by the 40,000-barrel brewery.

Thousand Oaks Brewing of Berkeley, California was started in 1981 and ranks as one of the smallest microbreweries in the United States with an annual capacity of less than a thousand barrels. Located in the home of Charles and Diana Rixford, the brewery also qualifies for distinction as North America's only commercial home brewery. Despite its size, the brewery's products, which include Golden Gate Malt Liquor, Golden Bear Dark Malt Liquor and Thousand Oaks Lager, are widely available throughout the San Francisco Bay Area.

Widmer Brewing of Portland, Oregon was established by Kurt Widmer in 1984. It was the second microbrewery to be established in Portland and the second brewery (after Stanislaus in California) to brew altbier, or German style ale, outside Germany since Prohibition.

William S Newman Brewing, established in Albany in 1981, was the first microbrewery in the East and, incredibly, the first new company to establish a brewery in New York State since Prohibition. Older breweries had changed hands or built new plants during that period but all of the more than 700 previous breweries in New York had roots before 1934, and the majority of those had both opened and closed prior to Prohibition.

Serving as head brewer, William S Newman himself brews the company's products in a brewhouse whose 6500-barrel capacity make it certainly one of the nation's smallest. Brand names include Newman's Pale Ale, Newman's Winter Warmer Ale and Albany Amber Ale.

Yakima Brewing & Malting was established in 1982 in Yakima, Washington, in the heart of North America's greatest hop-growing region. Under the direction of founder Herbert Grant, the 5000-barrel brewery produces only draft products. The brands include Grant's Scottish Ale, Grant's Christmas Ale, India Pale Ale, Light American Ale, Light American Stout, Russian Imperial Stout and Grant's Hard Cider.

Yuengling & Son was established in 1829 by David G Yuengling. It stands as the oldest brewery in the United States and, after Molson in Canada (1786), as the second oldest in North America. The 200,000-barrel Yuengling brewery is today still family owned and operated under president and general manager Richard Yuengling. Its brand names include Yuengling Premium, Yuengling Porter ('brewed expressly for tavern and family trade'), Bavarian Premium Beer, Old German Beer and Lord Chesterfield Ale.

***Left:* Stevens Point Brewery distributes only in Wisconsin. *This page:* Products of Straub Brewery, Thousand Oaks Brewing, William S Newman Brewing, Yakima Brewing & Malting and Yuengling & Son, the continent's oldest brewery.**

CANADA

Long the second biggest brewing nation in North America, Canada lost that distinction to Mexico in the mid-1970s. Canada can, however, boast the oldest brewer in North America in Molson, which was established in 1786. Canadian brewing is overwhelmingly dominated by its big three, Carling-O'Keefe, Labatt's and Molson. Labatt's is Canada's largest brewer and Molson has the largest share among Canadians of the lucrative United States export market. Despite the dominance of the big three, several smaller breweries still exist and new microbreweries have been started in British Columbia and Nova Scotia since the mid-1980s. The big three are, however, the only brewing companies with breweries in more than one province and as a result they are the only brewers with national distribution.

An interesting aside to the big three is that each has a flagship or most popular brand which is identified by a color. These are Carling-O'Keefe's *Black* Label, Labatt's Pilsener *Blue* and Molson *Golden*.

Carling-O'Keefe Ltd (**Brasserie O'Keefe Ltee** in Quebec) is the result of the nineteenth century merger of the breweries of Sir John Carling (established by his father, Thomas Carling, in 1840) and Eugene O'Keefe (established in 1862). In the 1950s and 1960s Carling O'Keefe expanded its operations into the United States through its subsidiary company, **Carling National Brewing,** which once operated 14 breweries in 11 states south of the border. Carling National was, in fact, the fourth largest brewer in the United States in 1960. After that high point the market share of the American subsidiary declined, and Carling, like many other brewers, was forced into plant closing. In 1979 the Carling National Brewing subsidiary, four remaining breweries and a license to brew Carling Black Label Beer and Carling Red Cap Ale were sold to the G Heileman Brewing Company of La Crosse, Wisconsin.

Carling-O'Keefe Ltd is headquartered in Toronto with breweries located in Calgary, Alberta (478,000-barrel capacity); Vancouver, British Columbia (846,000-barrel capacity); Winnipeg, Manitoba (473,000-barrel capacity); St John's, Newfoundland (245,000-barrel capacity); Toronto, Ontario (2-million-barrel capacity); Montreal, Quebec (3-million-barrel capacity) and Saskatoon, Saskatchewan (288,000-barrel capacity).

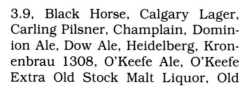

The company's flagship brand is Black Label Beer, which is brewed at all seven Carling-O'Keefe breweries across Canada. Other brands in regional distribution include Alta 3.9, Black Horse, Calgary Lager, Carling Pilsner, Champlain, Dominion Ale, Dow Ale, Heidelberg, Kronenbrau 1308, O'Keefe Ale, O'Keefe Extra Old Stock Malt Liquor, Old Vienna, Standard Lager, Trilight and Toby. In addition to its own brands Carling-O'Keefe brews Colt 45 under license from G Heileman in the United States, Miller High Life under

license from Miller Brewing in the United States and Carlsberg under license from the Carlsberg Breweries of Copenhagen, Denmark.

Granite Brewery of Halifax, Nova Scotia was established in 1985 and was the first Canadian micro-brewery and brew pub outside British Columbia. Head brewer Kevin Keefe is also the proprietor of neighboring Ginger's Tavern. Keefe opened the brew pub after noting the resurgence of interest in ale brewing in North America and Britain.

Granville Island Brewing in Vancouver, British Columbia is among the largest of the new smaller breweries that have opened in the province since the early 1980s. Its brands include Island Lager Beer and Island Bock Beer.

Horseshoe Bay Brewery (and Troller Pub) in Horseshoe Bay, British Columbia became Canada's first brew pub when the trend first crept north from the American Northwest in 1982. The Horseshoe Bay products are available only in the adjacent Troller Pub and include the original Bay Ale, Royal Dark Ale and Royal Light Ale.

Carling's domestic brands *(left)*. Carling also produces foreign brands *(above)* by license. Labatt's export brands *(below right)* and its domestic brands *(above right)* are led by Labatt's Blue.

Island Pacific Brewing of Victoria, British Columbia is another of the province's newer brew pubs. Well situated in the provincial capital, Island Pacific is noted for its Goldstream Lager.

John Labatt Ltd (Brasserie Labatt Ltee in Quebec) was founded by John Labatt in London, Ontario in 1853, and still maintains his corporate headquarters there although the brewing headquarters for the company are in Toronto. The brew-

eries of Canada's largest brewing company are located in Edmonton, Alberta (552,000-barrel capacity); Creston, British Columbia (365,000-barrel capacity); New Westminster, British Columbia (926,000-barrel capacity); Winnipeg, Manitoba (647,000-barrel capacity); St John's, Newfoundland (300,000-barrel capacity); Waterloo, Ontario (757,000-barrel capacity); Weston, Ontario (1.4-million-barrel capacity); Montreal, Quebec (2.7-million-barrel capacity) and Saskatoon, Saskatchewan (266-million-barrel capacity).

Labatt's flagship brand and the leading single brand of beer is Labatt's Pilsener which is better known (because of its label) as 'Labatt's Blue.' As with many United States brews, Labatt's leading brand is complemented by a low-calorie beer appropriately named Blue Light. The company's other brands fall into three categories: other company-owned national brands (like 'Blue' and Blue Light); foreign brands brewed under license by Labatt in Canada and company-owned regional brands which may be brewed only in one or two provinces. The national brands include Labatt 50 Ale (introduced as a special promotion in 1950), John Labatt Classic superpremium Labatt Lite and Labatt Select. The latter are two low-calorie beers introduced in 1978 and 1984, respectively. The first foreign brand to be brewed under license

was Guinness Extra Stout for which Labatt and Guinness Ltd of Dublin formed Guinness Canada Ltd in 1965. In 1980 Labatt's entered into agreement to brew Anheuser-Busch's Budweiser, the world's most popular beer, in Canada. When Labatt's Edmonton brewery started brewing Budweiser, it was the first American beer to be brewed in Canada. Since 1980, Budweiser has been joined at Labatt's by Anheuser-Busch's Michelob premium brand, and both have become national brands in Canada.

Labatt's major regional brands are Kokanee Pilsner Beer which is extremely popular in British Columbia, Club Beer in Manitoba, Crystal Lager Beer in Ontario, Blue Star in Newfoundland and Alexander Keith's India Pale Ale which is the largest selling brand of beer in the Maritimes. Other Labatt's regionals are Cervoise, Columbia Pilsner, Cool Spring, Country Club Stout, Extra Stock Ale, Grand Prix, Jockey Club Beer, Kootenay Pale Ale, Legere Light, Old Scotia Ale, Schooner Beer, Velvet Cream Porter, Velvet Cream Stout and White Seal Beer.

In addition to its activities in the field of brewing, John Labatt Ltd owns five packaged-food companies, agricultural products companies and Labatt Importers which imports its brewery products into the United States. John Labatt also has a 60 percent interest in McGavin Foods, a baked-goods company in western Canada and a 45 percent partnership interest in the Toronto Blue Jays baseball club of the American League.

Molson Breweries (Brasserie Molson in Quebec) is Canada's and North America's oldest brewing company. The original brewery was established on its present site in Montreal, Quebec in 1786. The headquarters and the flagship 4-million-barrel brewery are located in Montreal, and the company's other breweries are located in Edmonton, Alberta (552,000-barrel capacity); Vancouver, British Columbia (996,000-barrel capacity); Winnipeg, Manitoba (360,000-barrel capacity); St John's, Newfoundland (276,000-barrel capacity); Barrie, Ontario (1.9-million-barrel capacity); Prince Albert, Saskatchewan (240,000-barrel capacity) and Regina, Saskatchewan (228,000-barrel capacity).

Molson's flagship brand is Molson

John Labatt Ltd, Canada's largest brewer, produces national brands, regional brands and foreign brands under license. Labatt's Pilsner, or 'Labatt's Blue,' is the company's foremost brand and sports distinctive packaging.

Golden, which is a national brand in Canada and the biggest selling Canadian export brew in the United States. Other Molson beers include Molson Canadian Lager, Molson Light, Molson Export Ale and Export Light Ale. Special regional beers brewed by Molson's western breweries (British Columbia, Alberta, Manitoba and Saskatchewan) are Bohemian, Brador, Edmonton Export Lager, Frontier Beer, Lethbridge Lager, Lethbridge Pilsner, Old Style and Royal Stout. Regional beers brewed by Molson in eastern Canada include Molson Bock, Molson Cream Porter, Molson Diamond, Molson Oktoberfest India Beer and Laurentide Ale. Molson also brews Lowenbrau, a famous Munich lager, under license. Lowenbrau is also brewed under license by Miller Brewing in the United States.

Moosehead Breweries Ltd of St John, New Brunswick was founded by a family of Anglo-Swedish descent named Oland, who also founded Oland Breweries Ltd now owned by Labatt's. Thanks in part to a successful export marketing campaign in the early 1980s, Moosehead's products are now extremely popular in the United States. They are in fact more popular south of the border than they are in Canada, where they are virtually unknown outside New Brunswick. Except for the Quebec and Ontario breweries of the big

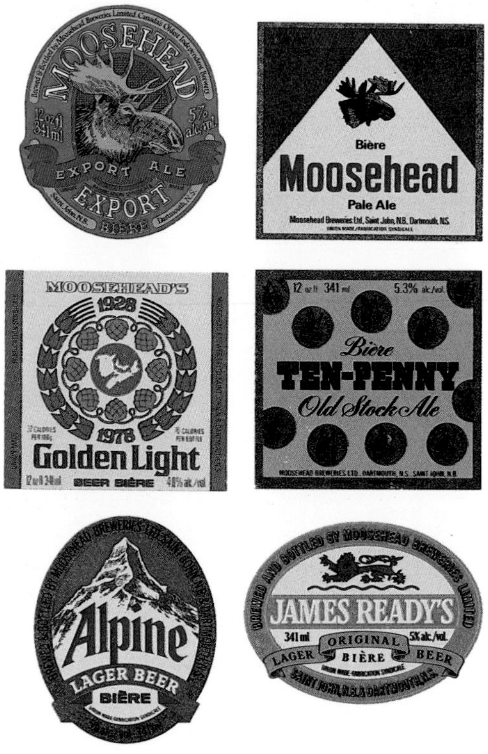

three, Moosehead's single brewery with a 1.2-million-barrel capacity is the largest in Canada. The company's flagship brands all carry the company name and the distinctive Moosehead logo. These include Moosehead Canadian Lager, Moosehead Pale Ale, Moosehead Golden Light, Moosehead London Stout and Moosehead Export Ales. Other products of the brewery are Alpine Lager Beer and Ten-Penny Old Stock Ale.

Mountain Ales, of Surrey, British Columbia was another of the small breweries that started in the Vancouver area in the early 1980s. The brewery and bottle line are designed after the English model as are the products, which include Mountain Amber Ale, Mountain Dark Ale and Mountain Light Ale.

Northern Breweries Ltd has more breweries in Canada's largest province than any other brewing company, although it is among Ontario's smaller breweries. Northern is headquartered in Sault Sainte Marie where it operates a 60,000-barrel brewery. Its other three Ontario breweries are in Sudbury (120,000-barrel capacity); Thunder Bay (50,000-barrel capacity) and Timmins. The latter two breweries brew only draft, with Thunder Bay brewing only Superior Lager and Timmins brewing only Northern Ale. Sudbury brews and bottles Northern and Encore Beer, while the Sault Sainte Maria plant brews and bottles Superior Lager, Northern Extra Light, Edelbrau, 55 Lager, Kakabeka Cream and Silver Spray.

Oland Breweries Ltd of Halifax, Nova Scotia was founded by the same Oland family that founded Moosehead. The Oland Breweries were sold to Labatt's in 1971. It is interesting to note that by the mid-1980s S M Oland held the presidency of Labatt Brewing Company Ltd (a division of John Labatt Ltd) and Philip W Oland was chairman of Moosehead, while J R McLeod was president and general manager at Oland Breweries Ltd.

Two Oland breweries operate; the one at Halifax is called Oland Brewery and the one at St John, New Brunswick is called Labatt's New Brunswick Brewery. The annual capacities of the two are 582,000 and 458,000 barrels, respectively. Both breweries produce Labatt's 'Blue,' Labatt's 50 Ale and Labatt's Schooner Beer, while Halifax brews

Keith's India Pale Ale and St John brews Labatt's Light and license-brewed Guinness. Both breweries brew Oland Export, and Halifax also produces two other Oland name brands, Oland Lite and Oland Stout.

Pacific Western Brewing Company Ltd of Prince George, British Columbia is North America's northernmost brewery. It was originally established on a freshwater spring in 1957 under the name Caribou Brewing Company. Five years later it was bought by Carling-O'Keefe and promptly auctioned off. It was purchased by Ben Ginter and rechristened Tartan Breweries. Ginter's popular products, Uncle Ben's Beer and Uncle Ben's Malt Liquor, carried the company successfully until he attempted to expand. He ran out of cash building a second brewery at Richmond, British Columbia, and Tartan Breweries went into receivership. The brewery was purchased in 1978 by Nelson Skalbania who renamed it Canadian Gold Brewing. It was sold again in 1981 to W R Sharpe (formerly of Canada Dry) and his associates who operated it as the Old Fort Brewing Company until 1984 when the name was changed to Pacific Western Brewing.

By 1984, Pacific Western had a seven percent share of the British Columbia market and an aggressive marketing campaign aimed at the American West Coast. The brewery's annual capacity stands at 50,000 barrels, but the brewhouse could handle five times that capacity if more fermenting and storage tanks were installed. Early products of the present owners included Old Fort Premium Beer, Pacific Gold Lager and Yukon Hold Premium Lager, which are no longer in production. Pacific Western does, however, continue to produce Pacific Pilsner Beer, Iron Horse Malt Liquor and American Brand Lager Beer.

Above left: **Molson is Canada's oldest brewer. Moosehead's brands *(left)* are better known in the US than Canada. Products from Pacific Western Brewing *(above)* and Rocky Mountain Brewing.**

Rocky Mountain Brewing of Red Deer, Alberta (a subsidiary of Steeplejack Services in Calgary) operates the only independent brewery in the fast-growing oil-rich province on the eastern side of the Canadian Rockies.

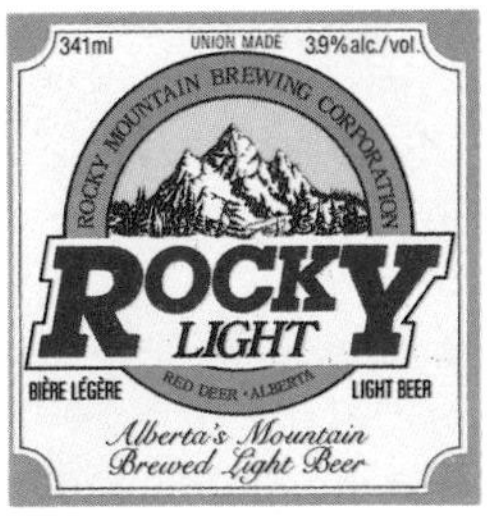

Products of this 204,000-barrel-capacity brewery include Gold Peak Premium Lager, 88 Pilsner, Steeplejack Pilsner, Steeplejack Special and Trapper Malt Liquor.

Sick's Lethbridge Brewery of Lethridge, Alberta was established by Emil Sick in 1980. Though his son Emil built a Sick's brewery empire in the 1940s that crossed the border into the United States, dominated Seattle and ran from Montana to Oregon, the original Lethbridge brewery is the only remaining Sick's brewery. The Sick's chain was sold to Molson in 1958, but the Lethbridge plant continues to carry its original name.

Sick's Lethbridge with its 624,000-barrel capacity is the largest brewery in Alberta. Products include Lethbridge Lager and Lethbridge Pilsner as well as Molson Canadian, Molson Light and Molson Malt Liquor.

MEXICO

Though brewing in Mexico did not develop as quickly as it did in the United States and Canada, it has made great strides since the 1970s, when it surpassed Canada as the continent's second largest brewing nation. Like Canada, Mexico's current brewing scene is overwhelmingly dominated by a big three. All three, Cuauhtemoc, Moctezuma and Modelo, developed from breweries established in the late nineteenth century by German or Swiss immigrants. By the 1970s the majority of Mexico's brands were available as imports in the United States.

Cervecería Cruz Blanca of Juarez, Chihuahua is the only existing Mexican brewing company founded since 1900. Located across the Rio Grande from El Paso, Texas (which hasn't had a commercial brewery since 1967 when Falstaff closed), the 400,000-barrel Cruz Blanca brewery brews Cerveza Austriaca, Cerveza Chihuahua, and Cerveza Liston Azul in addition to the flagship Cerveza Cruz Blanca.

Cervecería Cuauhtemoc, headquartered in Monterrey, Nuevo Leon is Mexico's second largest brewer and the one with the largest number of breweries (seven). These breweries are located in Tecate, Baja, California (1-million-barrel capacity); Mexico City (1.1-million-barrel capacity); Toluca, DF (3.1-million-barrel capacity); Guadalajara, Jalisco (350,000-barrel capacity); Monterrey, Nuevo Leon (4-million-barrel capacity); Culiacán, Sinaloa (310,000-barrel capacity) and Nogales, Veracruz (560,000-barrel capacity). The company's flagship brand is Carta Blanca, but another important brand is Tecate, a lager beer frequently served, both in Mexico and the United States, with salt and raw lemon. Other cervezas from Cuauhtemoc are Bohemia, Brisa, Colosal, India, Kloster and Monterrey. Cuauhtemoc also brews Cruz Blanca at its Culiacan brewery.

Cervecería del Pacífico of Mazatlán, Sinaloa was established in 1900 by Jacob Schuehle, who built the original Moctezuma brewery. The 700,000-barrel brewery is today owned by Cervecería Modelo, but retains its original brand names, Pacifico Clara and Ballena. The former is also brewed by Modelo in Guadalajara and Ciudad Obregón.

Cervecería Moctezuma, headquartered in Mexico City, was established in 1894 at Orizaba, Veracruz by Adolph Borkhardt, Henry Manthey, Wilhelm Haase and C von Alten. Today Moctezuma is Mexico's third largest brewer although its Orizaba brewery with a 5.3-million-barrel annual capacity is the second largest individual brewery in Mexico. The company's other breweries are a small 300,000-barrel brewery in Monterey, Nuevo Leon and a 2.2-

Beers of Cervecería Cuauhtemoc product line *(far left)* and of Cervecería Moctezuma. Moctezuma's Dos Equis brand sells very well in the United States.

million-barrel brewery at Guadalajara. Moctezuma's flagship brands are Dos Equis (XX) which is extremely popular in the United States and Superior. Other brands include Tres Equis (XXX), Sol Clara, Sol Obscura, Noche Buena and Bavaria, as well as two draft beers, Barril Claro and Barril Oscuro. In 1985, thanks, in part, to the marketing expertise of people like Robert Peyton at the company's American public relations firm Basso and Associates, Moctezuma began a unique and successful private label venture. Ensenada in Baja, California had been a popular destination for American tourists for over half a century and no Ensenada watering hole had developed quite as widely known a reputation as Hussong's Cantina. In 1985 Moctezuma teamed up with Hussong's to produce a private label clara (lager) under the Hussong's name that would be available not only at the Cantina, but at the retail outlets in the United States and Mexico.

Cervecería Modelo, headquartered in Mexico City, DF, is Mexico's largest brewing company. Modelo's annual production of 13.1 million barrels (1984) is greater than that of all but four American brewers and greater than any of Canada's brewers. Modelo operates a brewery in Mexico's Federal District at Toluca (3-million-barrel capacity) and one in Mexico City (6.5-million-barrel capacity) which is Mexico's largest brewery. The output for 1984 of the two breweries was 6.4 million barrels, which was 3.1 million barrels under capacity. Other Modelo breweries are located at Torreón, Coahuila (500,000-barrel capacity); and Ciudad Obregón, Sonora (450,000-barrel capacity). Modelo's flagship brand is Corona, a distinctive clara (lager) sold in a clear rather than tinted bottle. Other brands include Modelo Especial, a popular dark beer known as Negra Modelo, and a draft beer appropriately dubbed Corona de Barril.

Cervecería Yucateca in Mérida, Yucatán was started before the turn of the century by José María Ponce y Cia and is today owned by the Modelo Group, though members of the Ponce family still manage the brewery. The brewery has a 6-million-barrel capacity but in 1984 brewed just 270,538 barrels. This production is divided between Yucateca's house brands and the parent company's Corona. The Yucateca brands include Carta Clara, Leon Negra and Montejo.

Corona is Modelo's chief brand and Negra Modelo its popular dark beer.

CENTRAL AMERICA

The total beer production of Central America is less than 6 million barrels, but the area has a long brewing tradition and one that has shown more direct influence of German-trained brewers in the latter twentieth century than any of the nations to the north. The Central American brewers are listed below in alphabetical order.

Cerveceria Centro Americana in Guatemala City, Guatemala is one of Central America's oldest breweries, dating from the nineteenth century. With a 2-million-barrel annual capacity, it is also the largest brewery in the region. The brewery's brands include Cabro, Gallo, Marzen, Monte Carlo and Moza.

Cerveceria Costa Rica in San Juan, Costa Rica has a 900,000-barrel annual capacity and produces beer under the Bavaria, Imperial, Malta and Pilsner brands.

Cerveceria del Baru of Panama City, Panama has a 360,000-barrel annual capacity and brews the Cristal, Malta Del Baru, Panama, Soberana and Malta Super brands.

Cerveceria Hondurena in San Pedro Sula, Honduras is owned by Castle and Cooke, the North American food processing company. The products of the 600,000-barrel brewery include Imperial, Nacional and Salva Vida as well as Port Royal Export, which is available in limited markets within the United States.

Cerveceria Nacional, also of Panama City, is Panama's largest brewer. The company's brands include Atlas, Balboa, Malta and Vigor. Nacional is also the Central American brewer of Lowenbrau, the famous Munich brand.

Cerveceria Nacional in Quezaltenango is the last brewery in a town that at the turn of the century had three breweries, more than any other city in Central America. The 250,000-barrel-capacity brewery produces the brands Cabro and Pilsen.

La Constancia of San Salvador, El Salvador has a million-barrel annual capacity for production of its Malta, Pilsner, Regia and Suprema brands.

Cervecería Hondurena produces a total of four brands of beer. One of these, Port Royal Export, is a gold-medal winner and is obtainable in the US.

THE CARIBBEAN

The brewing tradition of the little golden flecks which are the islands of Caribe is long and varied. In the beginning it was the aboriginal people and their *tesguino* beer and then the English with their imported beers. By the seventeenth century, when brewing was really taking hold in the mainland to the north, the isles of the West Indies had already gone over en masse to the warm embrace of rum.

By the nineteenth century there was the enigmatic Guinness West Indies Porter that may have been brewed there, perhaps in Barbados or perhaps in Jamaica. It may even have been brewed in the British Isles and brought to the Keys at high tide by wily traders who just pretended that it was the local brew. There could be no lager brewed there because there was no ice; but then English tastes tended to give lager a wide berth in any event, and it was English tastes that formed the tastes of West Indian beer drinkers.

By 1898, there were just seven breweries in the entire region; one each in Barbados, Trinidad and Cuba and four in Jamaica. When the United States beat Spain in the Spanish-American War, Obermeyer and Liebmann came south from Brooklyn to open a second brewery in Cuba's capital and then there were eight altogether, the same number as today, but the faces of the players have changed.

By the mid-1980s, Cuban tastes included more Vodka than beer and Obermeyer and Liebmann were as much a distant memory in Havana as they were in Brooklyn. In Jamaica, Desnoes & Geddes had been brewing Red Stripe (which had originally been ale but was reformulated as a lager in 1934) for 60 years. Red Stripe was the Caribbean's best known brand elsewhere in the continent. Holland's giant brewer, Heineken, the largest in Europe, has licensed its products to Desnoes & Geddes and it owns breweries in the Antilles and Trinidad. From Denmark Carlsberg is licensed in the Dominican Republic and Tuborg is licensed in Puerto Rico. The eight breweries of the Caribbean are listed alphabetically.

Antilliaanse Brouwerij (Antillian Brewery) of Willemstad, Curacao in the Netherlands Antilles is owned by Amstel in Holland, which is now owned by Heineken. The brewery was officially opened in January 1960 as Prince Bernhard of the Netherlands ceremoniously tapped the first foaming keg, although it had actually been producing beer for three months. In addition to Amstel, the 140,000-barrel-capacity brewery brews Green Sands beer, which is also brewed at Heineken-owned National Brewing in Trinidad. Antilliaanse Brouwerij has won several gold medals for its Antillian Amstel beer, including one awarded in Paris in 1960.

Banks Barbados Breweries of St Michael, Barbados has a 180,000-barrel annual capacity and an interesting roster of brands including Banks Lager, Banks Strong Ale, Tiger Malt and the sugary non-alcoholic beer called Action Drink.

Brasserie Lorraine in Fort-de-France, Martinique with its 96,000-barrel annual capacity is the only French brewery in North America. Its only brand, Lorraine, is a lager reminiscent of the region of the same name in the mother country.

Cerveceria Corona in Santurce, a suburb of San Juan, Puerto Rico is the second largest brewer in the West Indies. The brewery's million-barrel annual output is divided between the Cerveza Corona brand and license-brewed Tuborg.

Cerveceria India in Mayaguez, Puerto Rico is the second largest brewery in Puerto Rico with an 800,000-barrel annual capacity. The company's brands include Cerveza India, Malta India and Cerveza Medalla.

Cerveceria Nacional Dominicana in Santo Domingo, Dominican Republic has an annual capacity of

1.8-million barrels and as such is the largest brewery in the Caribbean. Its brands include Cerveza Presidente, Coral, Morena and license-brewed Carlsberg.

Desnoes & Geddes of Kingston, Jamaica was founded in 1918 as a soft drink business by Eugene Desnoes and Thomas Geddes. It is today managed by their heirs, with Peter Desnoes as chairman and Paul Geddes as vice-chairman. Red Stripe Lager and Dragon Stout are the flagship brands for the 600,000-barrel brewery, which also produces Heineken under license.

National Brewing in Port of Spain, Trinidad is a 180,000-barrel subsidiary of Heineken producing, in addition to the Heineken brand, National brews Green Sands (Shandy), Stag Beer and Mackeson Milk Stout.

***Left:* The product line of Cerveceria India brewery of Puerto Rico. Red Stripe Lager *(above)* is the prime brew of Desnoes & Geddes. The Heineken-owned Antillian Brewery in Curacao makes Amstel Beer, for which it has won several gold medals.**

GLOSSARY

Ale: A top-fermented beer that originated in England as early as the seventh century and made with hops after the sixteenth century. It is fermented at temperatures ranging between 55°F and 70°F, somewhat warmer than those used to ferment lager. Ale is darker (a translucent copper color) and more highly hopped than lager, but usually less so than porter and stout. Like all beers of the English tradition, it is served at room temperature. Ale is much more popular in England and eastern Canada than in most of North America, though its popularity saw an increase in the United States during the 1980s.

Altbier: A top-fermented beer very similar to ale, except that it originated in northern Germany while ale originated in England. Virtually unknown in the United States after Prohibition, it was reintroduced by several microbreweries in Oregon and California during the 1980s.

Barrel: A container for beer, at one time made of reinforced oak, now made solely of stainless steel. Also a unit of measuring beer which equals 31 gallons, or 1.2 hectolitres.

Beer: A fermented beverage with an alcohol content of between two and six percent by volume. Ingredients include malted cereal grains (especially, but not limited to, barley), hops, yeast and water, although early English beers were unhopped. Subtypes are classified by whether they are made with top-fermenting yeast (ale, porter, stout, wheat beer) or bottom-fermenting yeast (lager, bock beer, malt liquor). Generally, top-fermented beers are darker, ranging from a translucent copper to opaque brown, while bottom-fermented beers range from amber to pale yellow. Because of their English heritage top-fermented beers are usually drunk at room temperature, while bottom-fermented beers are served cold.

Bitter: A full-bodied highly hopped ale (hence the name) that is extremely popular in England but much less so elsewhere. Bitter (or bitter ale) is similar in color to other ales, but it lacks carbonation and has a slightly higher alcohol content.

Bock Beer: A bottom-fermented beer which is darker than lager and which has a relatively higher alcohol content, usually in the six percent range. A seasonal beer, it is traditionally associated with spring festivals. Prior to World War II, many American brewers produced a bock beer each spring, but the advent of national marketing after the war largely eliminated the practice of brewing seasonal beers. In the 1980s several breweries began to reintroduce bock beer. The male goat (*bock* in German) is the traditional symbol of bock beer.

Brewing: Generically, the entire beer-making process, but technically only that part of the process during which the beer wort is cooked in a brew kettle and during which time the hops are added.

Cervecería: The Spanish word for *brewery*.

Cerveza: The Spanish word for *beer*.

Draft (Draught) Beer: A term which literally means beer that is drawn from a keg rather than packaged in bottles or cans. Designed for immediate use, draft beer is not pasteurized and hence must be kept cold to prevent the loss of its fresh taste. Draft beer is generally better than packaged beer when fresh but not so as it ages. Some brewers sell unpasteurized draft-style beer, which must be shipped in refrigerated containers.

Fermentation: The process by which yeast turns the sugars present in malted grains into alcohol and carbon dioxide. Chemically the process is written as:

$$\underset{\text{(glucose)}}{C_6H_{12}O_6} \longrightarrow \underset{\text{(alcohol)}}{2\,C_2H_5OH} + \underset{\text{(carbon dioxide)}}{2\,CO_2}$$

Hops: The dried blossom of the female hop plant which is a climbing herb *(Humulus lupulus)* native to temperate regions of the Northern Hemisphere and cultivated in Europe, the United Kingdom and the United States. Belonging to the mulberry family, the hop's leaves and flowers are characterized by a bitter taste and aroma. It has been used since the ninth century as the principal flavoring and seasoning agent in brewing, although it had been prized before that for its medicinal properties. In addition to its aromatic resins, the hop also contains tannin which helps to clarify beer.

Different strains of hops have different properties and much of the brewmaster's art is in knowing how to use these properties. For example, one strain may be particularly bitter to the taste without being very aromatic, while another strain might be just the opposite. The brewmaster will blend the two in various combinations just as a chef will experiment with various seasonings before settling on just the right combination for a particular recipe. Hops also serve as a natural preservative.

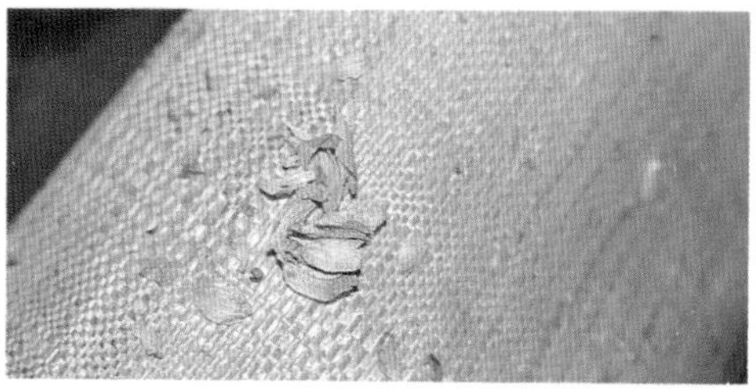

A female hop blossom, used in brewing beer to impart aroma and bitterness.

Early North American brewers used indigenous wild hops, but European strains were later introduced and imported. Prior to World War II, many regions in North America grew hops. For example, California's fertile San Joaquin Valley once produced hops. Today, however, most of the hops produced in North America are the Cascade hops grown in the Yakima Valley of Washington State. Most major North American brewers use a mixture of Cascade and imported European hops.

Krausening (Kraeusening): The process of instigating a secondary fermentation to produce additional carbon dioxide in a beer. Some brewers will first ferment their beer in open containers where alcohol is produced and retained, but the carbon dioxide escapes. The second fermentation, or krausening, then takes place in closed containers after a first fermentation (whether that first fermentation took place in open or closed containers) and is used to produce natural carbonation or sparkle in the beer.

Lager: A pale bottom-fermented beer of moderate strength that originated in Central Europe, roughly in the area bounded by Munich, Germany; Vienna, Austria and Pilsen, Bohemia (now Czechoslovakia). Lager is the most popular beer type in all of North America, especially in the United States where it accounts for well over 90 percent of production. Lager is fermented at much colder temperatures than top-fermented beers (between 32°F and 50°F depending on the brand), and it is also served much colder. In order to conform to local laws concerning alcohol content, lager in the United States usually varies between 2.7 and 3.2 percent.

Lagering: The process of cold fermenting at temperatures close to freezing to produce lager beer.

The Beer-making Process:

The steps in the beer-making, or brewing, process can be briefly summarized as follows:

1. **Malting** to produce **malt.**
2. **Mashing** the Malt to produce **mash.** (Other cereal grains may be added to the Malt at this stage.)
3. **Lautering** the **mash** to produce sweet **wort.**
4. Straining the wort through **grant** prior to **brewing.**
5. **Brewing** the sweet **wort** (during which time the **hops** are added), to produce bitter or hopped **wort.**
6. **Straining** the **hops.**
7. **Cooling** the **wort.**

Lautering: The process of straining in a lauter tun.

Lauter tun: The vessel used in brewing between the mash tun and the brew kettle. It separates the barley husks from the clear liquid wort. The barley husks themselves help provide a natural filter bed through which the wort is strained.

Light Beer: Introduced in the mid-1970s by nearly every major brewer in the United States and Canada, light beers are by definition reduced-calorie lagers or ales. They also have a slightly lower alcohol content than comparable lagers or ales.

Malt: The substance produced by malting (also known as malted barley).

Malt Liquor: A bottom-fermented beer, it has a malty taste more closely related to top-fermented ale than to lager which is bottom-fermented. Malt liquor has a much higher alcohol content (5.6 to 6.5 percent) than lager.

Malting: The process by which barley kernels are moistened and germinated, producing a 'green malt' which is then dried. This renders the starches present in the kernel soluble. If pale beers are to be produced, the malt is simply dried. If dark beers are to be produced, the malt is roasted until it is dark brown. The malt is then subjected to mashing.

Mash: The substance that is produced by mashing.

Mashing: The process by which barley malt is mixed with water and cooked to turn soluble starch into fermentable sugar. Other cereal grains, such as corn and rice may also be added (rice contributes to a paler end-product beer). After mashing, the mash is filtered through a lauter tun, whereupon it becomes known as wort.

Near Beer: Nonalcoholic beer which originated during the Prohibition era in the United States and which is still in production.

Pasteurization: Though this term has come to mean the heating of a substance to kill harmful bacteria, the process was originally proposed by Louis Pasteur as a means of killing yeast to end fermentation and hence end the creation of alcohol and carbon dioxide (carbonation). Nonpasteurized beers are no less sanitary than pasteurized beers.

Pilsner (Pilsener): A pale bottom-fermented lager beer originally associated with the city of Pilsen, Bohemia (now Czechoslovakia) where it was first brewed. The term is often used interchangeably with the term lager although pilsners are technically the palest of lagers.

Porter: A traditionally top-fermented beer which originated in eighteenth-century London. It took its name from the city's porters who had taken an immediate fancy to it. Similar to but sweeter than stout, it is a dark beer of moderate strength (alcohol, five to seven percent by volume), made with roasted unmalted barley.

Prohibition: The process by which a government prohibits its citizens from buying or possessing alcoholic beverages. Specifically, *the* Prohibition refers to the period between the effective date of the 18th Amendment to the US Constitution (16 January 1920) and its repeal by the 21st Amendment. Repeal took effect on 5 December 1933, although it passed Congress in February and the sale of beer was permitted after 7 April 1933.

Reinheitsgebott: A German purity law that permits only malted barley, hops, yeast and water to be used in the brewing of beer. Though it has no jurisdiction outside Germany, many North American brewers follow it, and some use the fact that they meet its guidelines as part of their advertising.

Sake: A fermented beverage that is a cousin to the family of fermented beverages we call beer. Sake originated in Japan where it is an important national drink. Several sake breweries have existed in both California and Hawaii over the years, but the only remaining American commercial sake brewery is in Hawaii. Sake is brewed from unmalted rice and is not hopped. The resulting substance is clear and has a 14 to 16 percent alcohol content. In contrast to beer, which is drunk either chilled or at room temperature, sake is warmed before drinking.

Steam Beer: A term that originated in San Francisco during the gold rush era to refer to beer that was produced with bottom-fermenting yeast but fermented at 60° to 70° rather than the temperatures required for true lager fermentation. Fermentation was allowed to continue in the kegs and the escaping carbon dioxide that resulted from the tapping of the kegs is the possible source of the term 'steam' beer. In any event, the term steam beer is now a registered trademark of The Anchor Brewing Company of San Francisco, brewers of Anchor Steam Beer.

Stout: A dark, heavy, top-fermented beer popular in the British Isles, especially Ireland (where Guinness stout is more popular than Budweiser lager is in the United States). It is similar to porter, though less sweet. Its alcohol content ranges from four to seven percent.

Tesguino: A type of corn beer produced by the Indians of Mexico and the American Southwest prior to their contact with Europeans.

Wheat Beer: A type of top-fermented beer in which malted wheat is substituted for malted barley. Originally brewed in Germany, it was produced by several small North American brewers in the 1980s.

Wort: An oatmeal-like substance consisting of water and mashed barley in which soluble starch has been turned into fermentable sugar during the mashing process. The wort is cooked, or brewed, in the brew kettle for more than an hour and for as much as a day, during which time hops are added to season the wort. After brewing, the hopped wort is filtered and fermented to produce beer.

Yeast: The enzyme that is added to wort before the fermentation process and which turns sugar into alcohol and carbon dioxide. Yeast can be either top fermenting as in ale and stout, or bottom fermenting as in lager.

Raw materials of the brewing process: hops, dark malt, malt and unmalted barley.

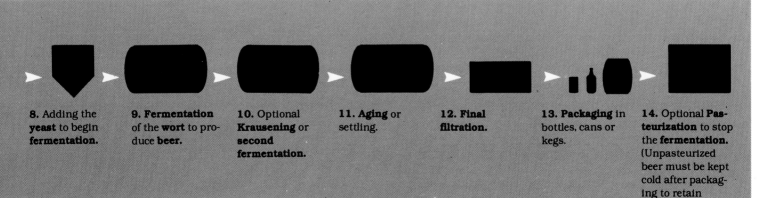

8. Adding the **yeast** to begin **fermentation.**

9. **Fermentation** of the **wort** to produce **beer.**

10. Optional **Krausening** or **second fermentation.**

11. **Aging** or settling.

12. **Final filtration.**

13. **Packaging** in bottles, cans or kegs.

14. Optional **Pasteurization** to stop the **fermentation.** (Unpasteurized beer must be kept cold after packaging to retain freshness.)

INDEX

Picture Credits

Adolph Coors Brewing 48 right, 50-51, 51, 54-55, 164, 165 bottom
Anchor Brewing 166 left, 189
Anheuser-Busch Creative Services 30, 31, 32 bottom, 33 both, 34, 35 both, 89, 103 both, 138 top, 140 bottom, 141 middle left, 143 bottom, 145, 158 bottom 3, 159
Antillian Brewery 87, 187 right
Basso & Associates, Inc. 85 top
Blitz-Weinhard 44-45, 46-47, 48 center
Louis Bolis via Coors 49
Boulder Brewing 152-53, 166 middle
Carling-O'Keefe 128 top, 176 bottom, 177 top left
Cerveceria Cuauhtemoc 182 left
Cerveceria Hondurena 88, 185 both
Cerveceria India 186 bottom
Cerveceria Moctezuma 182 right, 183 both
Cerveceria Modelo 184 both
Champale Inc 166 right
Cold Spring Brewing 167 top
Desnoes & Geddes 86
Dixie Brewing 167 bottom
F X Matt Brewing 168 left
General Brewing 113, 168 right
G Heileman Brewing 42-43, 162, 163 both
Gary Gold via William S Newman Brewing 151 top and bottom left
T Gras via F X Matt Brewing 150
Jim Harter Dover Publications 9 right, 26
Hibernia Brewing 169 left
Hudepohl 6-7, 76, 77, 169 right
Jacob Leinenkugel Brewing 170 left
Kathleen Jaeger 72 bottom, 74 top left, 75 top right and bottom left, 94 top center, 138 bottom, 141 top right, 188
John Labatt Ltd 129, 133 inset, 135, 136 top, 156, 177 right both, 178 both, 179 both
Jones Brewing 170 center
Joseph Huber Brewing 170 right
Latrobe Brewing 171 left
The Lion, Inc 171 middle
Manhattan Brewing 153 top, 171 top right
Lou Manna via Manhattan Brewery 153 bottom
Fritz Maytag Collection 17, 36, 37, 38 top, 78 top 2, 81 top, 82-83 all 6, 93 right, 101 bottom
Mendocino Brewing 171 bottom right
Miller Brewing 2-3, 143
Milwaukee County Historical Society 18-19, 20 bottom, 21 bottom, 24 left, 25, 79, 80, 106-107 both, 192
Minnesota Historical Society 39, 40-41, 90 top
Molson 124 all 4, 125 all 3, 126 both, 127 all 6, 128 bottom, 130-31, 136-37, 142, 154-55, 157 top, 180 top
Molson Collection/Public Archives of Canada 15, 110-11, 132 top, 133 top, 134 both
Montana Beverage 147 both, 172 left
Montana Historical Society 52-53, 53, 56-57, 58-59, 60-61
Moosehead Breweries 180 bottom
National Gallery of Art, Washington 11
Old New York Beer Co 172 top right
Pabst 41 bottom, 165 top
Pacific Western Brewing 181 left
Pearl Brewing 172 bottom right
Red Hook Ale Brewery 173 left
Rocky Mountain Brewing 181 right
San Francisco Archives 1, 4-5, 62-63, 64, 66-67, 68-69, 70-71, 78 bottom, 91 top, 93 left, 96-97, 104-105, 112
Sierra Nevada Brewing 146 both, 172 middle
Spoetzl Brewery 108-09, 173 top right
Stanislaus Brewing 173 bottom right
State Historical Society of Wisconsin 24 right both, 92
Stevens Point 144 top left, 174 both
Straub Brewery 175 top left
Stroh Brewery 22-23, 27 both, 28-29, 38 bottom, 98, 99, 100-101, 148-49, 161 left
Thousands Oaks Brewing 175 bottom left
Washington State Historical Society 114-15
William S Newman Brewing 151 bottom right, 175 top middle
Yakima Brewing & Malting 175 top right
© **Bill Yenne** 8, 9 left, 10 both, 12 both, 13 both, 14, 16 all 3, 20 top 3, 21 top 3, 28 left both, 32 top, 41 top, 48 left, 56, 65 all 3, 67, 69, 71, 72 top 2, 73, 74 top right and bottom, 75 top left and bottom right, 81 bottom, 84 both, 85 bottom, 90 bottom, 91 bottom, 94 right and left and bottom both, 95 all 8, 101 top, 102, 104, 105, 116 both, 117 both, 118 both, 119 both, 120, 121 all 5, 122-23, 132 bottom, 133 bottom, 138-39 all 3, 140 top 2, 141 top left and middle right and bottom, 144 top right and bottom, 157 bottom, 158 top, 161 right, 176 top, 182 top, 185 top, 186 top, 187 left
Yuengling & Son 175 bottom right

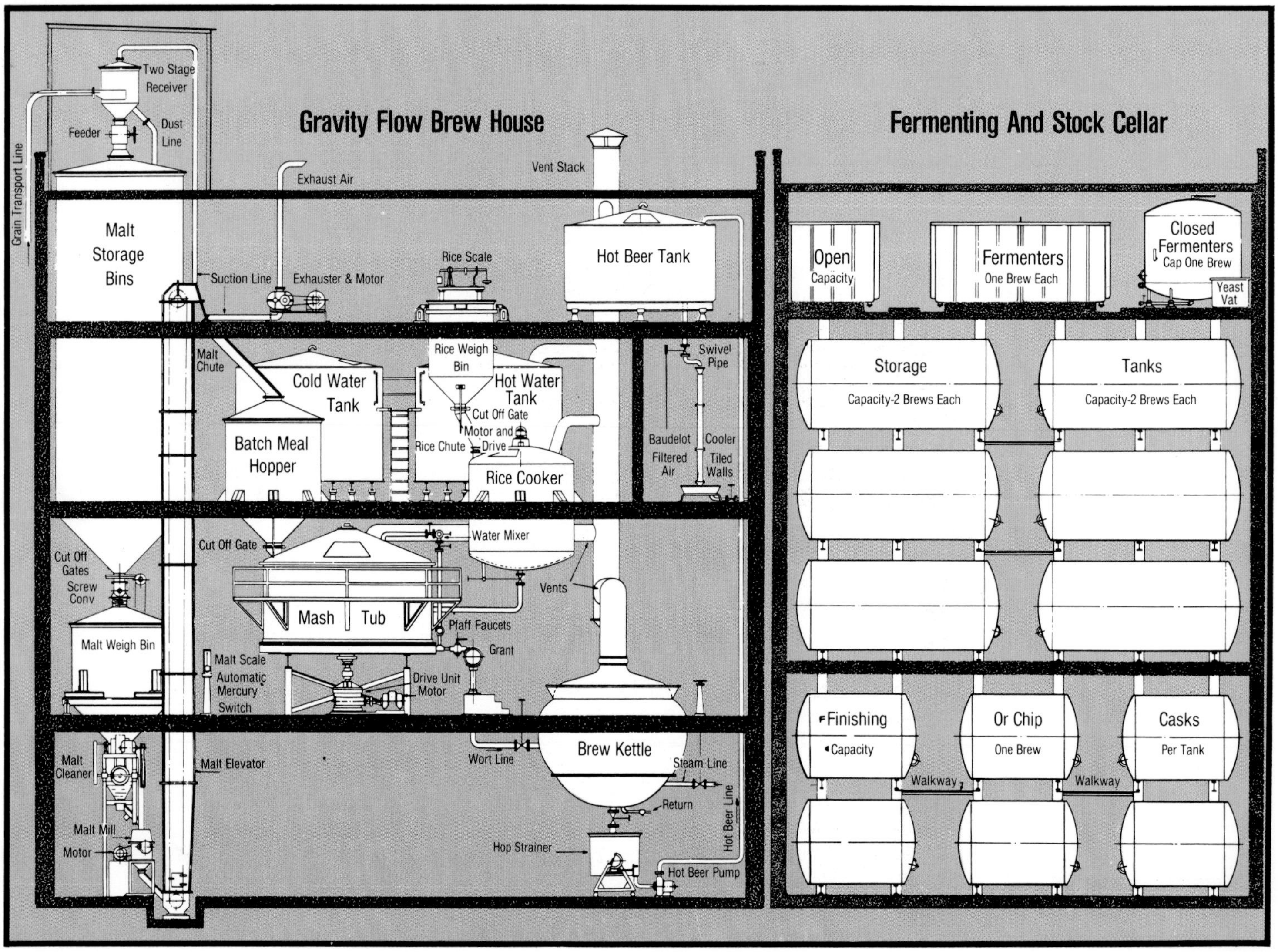